PERCEPTION
AND
COGNITION

PERCEPTION AND COGNITION

JOHN HEIL

UNIVERSITY OF CALIFORNIA PRESS

Berkeley   Los Angeles   London

University of California Press
Berkeley and Los Angeles, California

University of California Press, Ltd.
London, England

Copyright © 1983 by The Regents of the University of California

Library of Congress Cataloging in Publication Data

Heil, John.
    Perception and cognition.

    Bibliography: p. 230
    Includes index.
    1. Perception. 2. Cognition. I. Title.
BF311.H415   1983   153.7'01   82-20233
ISBN 0-502-04833-4

Printed in the United States of America

1 2 3 4 5 6 7 8 9

In memory of James Jerome Gibson

What is mathematically complex may be biologically simple.
J. J. Gibson

Contents

Preface

When I set out to write the present essay, my aim was to launch an attack on certain widely held cognitive psychological theories. It seemed to me that the theories in question incorporated serious *philosophical* flaws and that, in consequence, I was as equipped as anyone to examine them critically. The very fact that a self-proclaimed empirical science owed so many debts to philosophical speculation seemed bad enough. That the speculation was, in most ways, ill-conceived simply made matters worse. My plan was not merely to show that certain of the philosophical undercurrents of what we now call "cognitive science" were objectionable conceptually, but to advance the broader point that an empirical discipline founded on such things was an aberration that we should perhaps be better off without.

Arguments on these points survive here and there in what follows, but they are not treated in any detail except in a brief postscript. This is not because I have come at last to appreciate the somewhat Gothic splendors of the cognitive domain. Rather, I began to feel that whatever interests might be served by the launching of a critical assault would be better served by the construction of an account of one central constituent of that domain: perception. The upshot, then, is intended to be a contribution to that portion of the philosophy of perception that seems to influence the manner in which psychologists think about perceiving. I have sought, in this way, to harmonize certain traditional philosophical concerns with a variety of empirical matters of interest to psychologists. My hope is that half-baked philosophizing in combination with warmed-over empirical psychological speculation will result in a measure of palatable, if unspectacular, food for thought.

Psychologists, understandably, are apt to become testy when reproached in this way by philosophers. The notion that philosophy provides a special technique for the setting of a priori limits to the scope and character of empirical theory, never much appreciated outside the profession, is now out of fashion even among philosophers. In light of this development, it is somewhat surprising to discover, among the ranks of those representing themselves as cognitive scientists, theorists who seem ready to assume the role of conceptual referees and rule in advance on the permissibility of various theoretical moves. This trend is nowhere better exhibited than in recent discussion of the character of *mental representations*.

Psychology, as an explanatory discipline, is most readily distinguished from biology and physiology by the fact that psychological explanation seems essentially to involve reference to mental states the individuation of which is determined by some particular representational or intentional *content*. If the beliefs and desires of two persons differ in this regard, we should expect them to behave differently even when they are confronted by what is, from our point of view, the very same "stimulus." You and I react differently to the wiggly thing on the floor if I take it to be a snake and you take it to be merely a prankster's rubber imitation.

The difficulty is in understanding how representational states might be realized in purely biological (or perhaps non-biological, mechanical) systems. The prevailing view has it that mental contents are explicable by reference to certain purely formal "computational" properties of agents. The governing metaphor is that of the computing machine. Such devices, we are told, may be regarded as representing various states of affairs in virtue of the ways in which they are programmed. To know the program is to know the contents of the machine's intentional states.

Such an account of mental representation strikes me as ill-conceived. This is not because I doubt that computing machines might one day come to have thoughts, but because I suspect that the having of thoughts depends on more than certain computational properties of the creatures (or devices) that possess them.

I wish, then, to endorse the view that the primary subject-matter of cognitive psychology—or, more generally, cognitive science—is indeed comprised of representational states and episodes, but at the same time to reject the prevailing orthodoxy that these are best regarded as internal, computational features of intelligent agents.

Such matters are important to me because I wish to defend a "cognitive" account of perception without, at the same time, incurring a commitment to certain of the excesses of (what has been called) "computationalism." The view of perception advanced is intended to comport with that developed by the psychologist, J. J. Gibson. I share Gibson's distrust of theories that take perception to be essentially a matter of mental synthesis and construction, theories founded on the conviction that, in perceiving, one is obliged to assemble inside one's head a coherent and unified structure from an inchoate sensory "input." At the same time, I wish to call into question the Gibsonian notion that perception does not involve a cognitive component essentially. My suggestion is that Gibson's fundamental insight—that perception is largely a matter of information-pickup—is perfectly compatible with the notion that perception cannot usefully be divorced from cognition. In this regard I differ (or at least I *think* I differ) from those theorists who ought perhaps to be described as *neo*-Gibsonian.

Portions of this essay have appeared in one form or another in papers published in various places. Much of chapter III was first published as "Seeing is Believing," *American Philosophical Quarterly 19*: 229-239. The first half of chapter IV is based on "What Gibson's Missing," *Journal for the Theory of Social Behavior 9*: 265-269 (Basil Blackwell); and the second half of that chapter incorporates "On Saying What There Is," *Philosophy 56*: 242-247 (Cambridge University Press). The first portion of chapter VIII appeared as "Cognition and Representation," *Australasian Journal of Philosphy 58*: 158-168. I should like to thank the editors and publishers of these journals for allowing me the use of that material here.

I wish to thank as well the American Council of Learned Societies, the National Endowment for the Humanities, the National Institute of Mental Health, and the Virginia Commonwealth University Faculty Grant-in-Aid Program for much generous support, and the departments of psychology at Cornell University and the University of California, Berkeley, for their hospitality. I managed to see through many of my worst mistakes as a result of prodding from F. Bat, Kenneth Bower, Fred Dretske, Hubert Dreyfus, William Friedman, Burton Hurdle, Richard Konrad, Gary Monnard, Neale Mucklow, Ulric Neisser, Mark Overvold, and Eleanor Rosch and John Searle. I am particularly grateful to Robert Audi, Edward Averill, Arthur Collins, D. W. Hamlyn, and Patrick Heelan for detailed comments on earlier drafts of the manuscript, and to David Reid for invaluable editorial advice. I alone am responsible for the blunders that remain. I wish also to thank Norman Malcolm who, though not likely to approve of much of what follows, first led me to see whatever light I may have seen and Donald Davidson, who inspired me to rethink virtually everything touched on here. I owe, as well, an enormous debt to the person to whom this essay is dedicated. Finally, I wish to thank Harrison—for everything.

Berkeley
January, 1983

PART ONE
Perception

In the chapters that follow I shall develop and explore a certain picture of perception. The picture I have in mind combines what I take to be our ordinary, preanalytical thoughts about seeing, hearing, and the rest with certain low-level empirical concerns associated with the psychology and physiology of the senses.

It is sometimes felt that science and common sense are at odds here. Thus, common sense seems to have it that in perceiving, one becomes aware—in some obvious sense *directly*—of things and goings-on adjacent to or, more often, at a distance from one's body. In contrast, the scientific investigation of perceptual processes has regularly been taken to support the view that such awareness is inevitably mediated by interior representational states, cognitive or sensory proxies that stand *between* us and our world. The conception I shall recommend offers a means of accounting for the intuitions underlying each of these perspectives.

Very broadly, I shall contend that in perceiving, a creature is caused to be in a certain state, one that is, at least in part *cognitive*. Such states need not be conscious ones, although it is characteristic of them that they are available to consciousness in a way that digestive states, for instance, seem not to be. More importantly, perceptual states incorporate a significant component of a creature's *information* about its surroundings.

The issue of whether or not perception is cognitive or "epistemic," whether or not perceiving is inevitably a matter of belief-acquisition, hinges in part on two related issues. First, ought one to say that perceiving *is* the production of some cognitive state or states in a sentient creature, or only that it *leads* (often? usually? always?) to the production of such states? Second, even if perception is in some sense a form of cognition, are the cognitive states involved properly regarded as *beliefs?*

If one supposes, as I do, that perceptual states are the result of a certain causal process, one must be prepared to indicate where the process begins and where it ends, to specify its "boundaries." Determining its starting point is largely a matter of settling on what one takes to be the proper class of perceptual *objects.* Do we, that is to say, hear thunderclaps, or pressure waves, or vibrations in the inner ear—or perhaps cell-firings in the cochlear nerve? Pinning down the other end of the sequence requires some view about the distinction between perception and the *consequences* of perception. Thus, practically no one doubts that our perceptual commerce with the world is an important *source* of beliefs about the world. One may, however, doubt that the connection between perceiving something and forming beliefs about it is anything more than a contingent one: believings, one may feel, follow on the heels of perceivings.

I shall present considerations favoring the view that perception is best regarded as a linkage connecting beliefs to ordinary physical objects and events. Perceptual states are, on this view, cognitive states of a certain sort brought about in certain ways. Differences among the various ways in which these states are brought about determine the several *senses.* The latter are, I suggest, best regarded as systems enabling creatures to extract information about the world from different sorts or ranges of information-bearing physical stimuli. The capacity to extract information in this way is, I shall contend, affected by a creature's cognitive endowment and by its transitory needs and interests as well as by its biological constitution. This feature of perception, however, need not be taken, as it sometimes is, to support one or another form of representationalism. Perceptual states are indeed representational, but this is only to say that they are constitutive of a creature's awareness of familiar "external" objects and events.

I

THE SENSES

Preliminaries

"Perceiving" is a general term, a technical—or, at any rate, quasi-technical—expression covering what one does with one's senses. To perceive something is, at the very least, to *sense* it in one way or another: to see it, hear it, feel it, taste it, or smell it.[1] In putting the matter this way, I do not mean to suggest that these are the only "sensory modalities." They are simply the most familiar. An explication of the senses, a determination of what constitutes a sensory mode must, it seems, occupy a position of central importance in any theory of perception. It might turn out, for example, that differences among various senses are so great as to frustrate any attempt to erect a simple, unified account of perception that is, at the same time, interesting. What holds for sight may not hold for hearing or touch. What is true of taste and smell may not be true of vision.

Regrettably, philosophers have had little to say about what distinguishes the senses from one another. It is generally acknowledged that hearing, for instance, is not at all similar to sight, or smell, or to any of the other sensory modes, but the significance of these differences for theories of perception is not well appreciated. This fact, I think, places in jeopardy the long-standing philosophical dependence on vision as the primary source of data for perceptual theories. In the absence of an account of how the senses are to be distinguished, an account of

1. To do one of these or in some other way "sensorily to apprehend it." If this is so, then the expression "extrasensory perception" is, strictly, a misnomer. There may well be perceptual modes other than those familiarly discussed, but if they are perceptual, they must, perforce, be sensory.

3

what *constitutes* a sense, it is by no means clear that conclusions reached about visual perception can be taken to show very much at all about perceptions of other sorts.

This difficulty is, in the present context, particularly acute. First, I shall want to avail myself of the fruits of philosophical tradition in what follows and concentrate on vision. It cannot be merely accidental that we find it most natural to discuss perception largely in terms of sight. My hope, however, is that I shall be able to show that I am entitled to do this by showing that differences among the senses, although genuine and important, cannot materially affect the conclusions I wish to draw. Second, the view of perception that I shall recommend ties perceiving to the acquiring of beliefs. Not every instance of belief-acquisition, however, is an instance of perception. Roughly, my suggestion is that in perception we gain beliefs by way of the senses. And this way of putting the matter obliges me to offer some independent account of the senses. This is the goal of the present chapter.

Sensory Modalities

What is it, then, that distinguishes the several senses? How many senses are there? Might there be creatures with senses other than those with which we are familiar? What constitutes a "sensory modality?"

Grice (1962, pp. 135 ff.) has provided an inventory of ways in which these and similar questions might be answered. There are, he contends, at least four distinct criteria to which one might appeal.

(i) The senses might perhaps be distinguished by reference to the "features that we become aware of by means of them." Thus one becomes aware of colors, for instance, by means of sight, of sounds by means of hearing, of odors by way of one's sense of smell. (Such a view may be traced back at least to Aristotle; see *De Anima*, bk. ii.)

(ii) It might be the case that each sense has a characteristic

experience associated with it: certainly the experience of seeing something differs enormously from the experience of feeling or hearing it. And it seems possible that such differences afford a means of identifying and distinguishing sensory modes.

(iii) One could, instead, focus on the "differing general features of the external physical conditions on which the various modes of perceiving depend, to differences in 'stimuli' connected with different senses: the sense of touch is activated by contact, sight by light rays, hearing by sound waves, and so on" (Grice, 1962, p. 135).

(iv) Finally, one might wish to identify senses by reference to the organs involved. Seeing is what is done with eyes, hearing is accomplished by means of ears, smelling requires a nose.

I shall not here attempt to elucidate the view that emerges in Grice's discussion. I wish instead to offer an alternative account, one that avoids both the pitfalls and the inevitable complexities of views that attempt (as Grice's ultimately does) to distinguish among the senses by reference to some set of *internal* features of perceptual experiences or qualia.

The notion that the senses are to be defined and distinguished by reference to the phenomenal characteristics of sensory experiences—sensations—has a long and honorable history (one rehearsed admirably in Boring, 1942). Implicit in such views has been the belief that the senses comprise *pathways* (or "channels") that culminate in the production of sensations. The latter are, according to some theorists, specific to pathways: sensations arising from stimulation of the visual pathway differ phenomenally from those produced when the auditory pathway is activated (see Müller, 1838).[2] Awareness of sensations has been thought in this way to mediate perception of things and events outside the body. Perception, as distinguished from sensation, turns out on such a view to be always indirect, inferential.

---

2. If such a view were correct, it would be possible, perhaps, to conflate Grice's methods (ii) and (iv): commonalities and differences among sensory qualia would be accounted for by reference to biological features of perceivers.

Theories of this sort, however, theories that peg differences in sensory modes to characteristics of sensations or experiences (one may call them *internal feature* theories), are burdened with two major, and a host of minor, liabilities. In the first place, they are obliged to produce some *non-circular* account of those components of perceptual experiences or qualia that mark them off as experiences or qualia of one particular sense rather than another. This task (as Grice's paper attests) is by no means a simple one.

Second, an internal feature theory must provide a characterization of perceptual experiences that is suitably *universal*. Preanalytically it seems not unreasonable to suppose, for example, that both honeybees and human beings may correctly be said to *see* various features of the world. It is far from obvious, however, that we should want to say that a honeybee's visual experiences are very much like our own, or that the qualia encountered by a honeybee resemble the visual qualia with which we are familiar. More dramatically, there is nothing obviously wrong with the supposition that another person (or, if that seems implausible, a Martian) might, in seeing something, have the sorts of experience we have when we hear something. In any case, it would be disturbing to *begin* theorizing about the senses on the assumption that such things are impossible. The question seems largely (though perhaps not exclusively) an empirical one.

Further, the Aristotelian notion—embodied in Grice's first suggestion—that the senses are to be distinguished by differences in (as he says) "features that we become aware of by means of them," runs afoul of the evident fact that one may become aware of some one property in utterly different ways. Thus one may tell by feeling an object or by looking at it that it is warm or smooth. Difficulties here lead one back to the notion of distinctive internal features of sensory experiences.[3]

---

3. In fact the route back to perceptual experiences is more tortuous than this way of putting it suggests. Roxbee Cox (1970) has attempted to construct a theory in which the

It might, at first glance, appear more promising to pursue the notion that the senses are to be distinguished by reference to their respective "organs." Seeing, on this view, is what one does with one's eyes, hearing requires the use of ears. This is, of course, indisputably correct, though for the purposes at hand it is largely unhelpful. It is a matter of contingent empirical fact that most of the creatures with which we are familiar have eyes and ears with certain definite anatomical features. Even here, however, there are difficulties. The compound eye of a honey-bee, to take but one example, is in most ways unlike the eye of a human being.

It is surely imaginable, in any case, that there are creatures elsewhere in the universe who (we should wish to say) see and hear perfectly well, yet who lack anything physiologically similar to the eyes and ears of terrestrial species. Confronted with a race of such creatures, the most natural course for a scientific investigator to take would be to decide which anatomical bits are to be counted as eyes, which might be called ears, by determining, first, which portions of the creatures' anatomy enabled them to see and which enabled them to hear. And this requires that an investigator begin with some independent idea of what seeing and hearing are and how they are different.

Characteristics of "Stimuli"

There is reason, then, to regard with suspicion Grice's options (i), (ii), and (iv), that is, to resist theories that attempt to identify senses by reference to properties of objects perceived, to internal features of sensory experiences, or to anatomical characteristics of perceptual organs. What of option (iii)? Might the senses be identified and distinguished by reference to "the differing general features of the external physical conditions on

senses are distinguished by reference to certain "directly" apprehended "key features" of perceived states of affairs. I shall not discuss this possibility here (though see below). The view I shall offer appears to account for the facts cited in support of the notion of key features and to do so in a much simpler, less ad hoc way.

which the various modes of perceiving depend," might they, that is, be distinguished by tracing out their connections to certain sorts of "proximal" stimulus? Curiously, Grice spends little time exploring this possibility. It seems to me, however, at least if I understand rightly what Grice means by "stimuli" here, that this option affords a key to the solution of the problem. Very roughly, what I should like to suggest is that sensory modalities are to be identified and distinguished (insofar as this is possible) by reference to the kinds of "physical stimulation" from which a sentient creature extracts information about its surroundings.

On this account, seeing involves the activity of extracting information from light radiation; hearing occurs when a creature gains information from pressure waves of certain sorts; smell and taste involve the extraction of information from chemical features of the environment (the former from features borne through the creature's medium—the air or water through which it moves—the latter from chemical features of things ingested); touch incorporates the capacity to obtain information about things via mechanical contact of some sort.

I do not, I hasten to add, wish to defend the view that the senses can, in all cases, be distinguished *sharply* from one another. I want rather to suggest that to the extent that the senses can be distinguished at all, they are best distinguished by reference to characteristics of the physical stimuli that affect them, their respective sources of information.

Before taking things further, there are a number of features of the suggested taxonomy that are worth mentioning. First, it is a relatively simple matter to move from this way of talking about the senses to a classification of sensory "organs" or "receptors." An eye, for example, is a collection of receptors sensitive to light, an ear, one sensitive to vibration in the medium.

Second, it is clear that there may be a variety of ways to "build" receptors sensitive to the sorts of stimulation mentioned. What creatures that see have in common is the capacity to respond to and make intelligent use of a particular source of stimulation—light. What they need not have in common is a particular anatomical doodad nor, it seems, a particular sort of experience.

Third, I do not mean to imply that it is a necessary truth that seeing involves a creature's sorting through electromagnetic radiation. It may be that present-day theories of light propagation are false. I do, however, want to advance the notion that seeing, whatever else it is, is a matter of information-extraction from available light. It is the task of the physicist to determine what light is. I do not know whether the claim that seeing involves the picking up of information in the light, if true, is a necessary truth. It is, at least, a promising conceptual hypothesis.

These same points are meant to apply, of course, to the other senses. That hearing, for example, is the extracting of information from pressure waves transmitted through the medium, that smell is the picking up of information borne by chemicals dispersing through the same medium; these are partly empirical claims, partly something more. The empirical part concerns one's characterization of the physical stimuli and one's account of the receptors (and deeper-lying mechanisms) that make information contained in the stimuli available to the perceiver. The remaining part concerns the less straightforwardly empirical notion that the senses are a creature's means of finding out about its world. Information about that world transmitted in the light is picked up by way of devices we call eyes; information transmitted by pressure waves rippling through the medium is extracted by means of ears; and so on.

This approach provides an answer to a question sometimes posed by philosophical skeptics (and others) with certain theoretical axes to grind: "Couldn't one imagine a being able to see with its ears, hear with its eyes?" If one characterizes an eye as a bank of receptors used to extract information from light radiation, then any organ that allows for this *is* an eye. And, of course, there are (presumably) very good physiological reasons why one cannot do this with one's ears (or perform the opposite feat with one's eyes). If, in contrast, the questioner is in doubt about the sorts of experience perceivers might conceivably have when they look about themselves or listen, then, if I am right, his question is badly put. Seeing need not be distinguished from hearing by reference to features of the respective experiences. I suspect that there are solid empirical reasons for adopting the view of common sense here. Thus it seems somehow *likely* that the particular character of a creature's perceptual experience is a function of the character of its sensory receptors and their associated mechanisms. It seems correspondingly unlikely that two creatures, physiologically very similar, might experience the world in thoroughly different ways.

I cannot prove this, of course, but I do not need to. On the view endorsed here, the peculiar flavor of the experiences had by perceivers is just irrelevant to the question at hand. We are entitled to say that *S* and *T* see the same thing without committing ourselves to any theory at all about the internal character of their respective experiences. We may say that a visual experience is one arising from the process of extracting information from available light; an auditory experience is one brought about when information is obtained from the oscillating medium. I shall say more about the nature of perceptual experience in chapters IV and VI, below.

Gibson's Account

The view I have begun sketching here owes much to the work of J. J. Gibson (see e.g., Gibson, 1966, 1979; Schiffman, 1976). Gibson's fundamental notion is that perceiving is the picking up of information about the world made available to the perceiver by various sorts of physical stimulation. Such an approach is, I am convinced, essentially correct. I wish for the moment, however, to align myself with Gibson in just two respects. First, although Gibson does not directly appeal to characteristics of perceptual stimuli in constructing a taxonomy of the senses, such an account seems implicit in much of what he says (see for example, Gibson, 1966, chap. 3). Second, Gibson's characterization of perceiving as the picking up of information seems sound. I have tried already to make a case for the first point; now I should like to say a word about the second.

I have spoken repeatedly of the senses as devices (or, to use Gibson's term, "systems") enabling creatures to "extract information" about the world from various sorts of stimulation. This way of talking may offend some, but I think it need not. The information that a creature picks up may, in general, be characterized propositionally: that a certain object is green or rectangular, that it is loud or coarse, that it is sweet or warm. To say that a creature has picked up information describable in this way comes very close to saying that it has acquired a belief similarly describable.

I am not, I should say, suggesting that Gibson means by "information" what one ordinarily means by "belief." Information in the present context is a feature of a mode of stimulation; it may be picked up, or overlooked or ignored altogether. Information, in this sense, is "in the world," not (as a belief surely is) "in the perceiver." Nevertheless it seems right to say that the *picking up* of information is so close as to be indistinguishable from what I should prefer to call the acquiring of belief. Very crudely: we are able to acquire the beliefs we do about the world because the world is the way it is and because we are the way we are.

This way of putting the point is apt to seem spectacularly uninformative, but for all that it may be right. If light, for example, behaved differently from the way it does, it would *not* provide us with reliable information about such things as colors and shapes. Our visual apparatus, not surprisingly, evolved to take advantage of the information-providing characteristics of light: that light reflected from a smooth surface has different properties from light reflected from a rough surface; that light reflected by a tomato differs in systematic ways from that reflected by a cucumber. (The concept of information, what it might mean to say, for example, that light *carries* information, will be discussed in greater detail in chapter III.)

It is not, of course, that one perceives light radiation or pressure waves rather than tomatoes and thunderclaps. When one looks about the world, for instance, *what* one sees are objects and events illuminated by (or, in some cases, emitting) light. The notion that one might see *light* (a notion once fostered by impressionist painters) is, I am inclined to think, something very close to a category mistake.

Gibson's suggestion is that "ambient light" is structured by the objects and events it illuminates in such a way that it affords a creature, suitably equipped, with information about its surroundings. Light so structured at a "point of observation" (a point that may or may not be occupied) is labeled by Gibson the "optic array" (see Gibson, 1979, chap. 5). The latter may be thought of as embodying information about the objects and events that determine its structure. My suggestion is that the extraction of such information may usefully be regarded as a matter of belief-acquisition. The idea is that a creature's senses enable it to discover properties of its surroundings by way of such information-bearing stimuli as light radiation and pressure waves.

It is perhaps worth emphasizing that, for Gibson, it is not simply a range of stimulation (light radiation, pressure waves, and the like) that conveys information, but *structured* stimulation. Unstructured light results in a luminous fog or *Ganzfeld* (Metzger, 1930) that is visually impenetrable, unstructured sound in so-called white noise.

Concentrating for the moment on vision, it may noted that the structure of the "optic array"

> . . . can be described in terms of visual solid angles with a common apex at the point of observation. They are angles of intercept, that is, they are determined by the persisting environment. And they are nested, like the components of the environment itself. (Gibson, 1979, p. 92)

As a perceiver explores his environment, the point of observation changes and the visual solid angles comprising the optic array are transformed. The systematic character of the resulting transformations "specifies" an underlying pattern of permanence. The details of all this may be found in Gibson's writings (in e.g., Gibson, 1966, 1979), and I shall not take the time to rehearse them here. For our purposes the point to be emphasized is that it is structured stimulation, over time, that produces in us reliable perceptual beliefs about our surroundings. Earlier, I volunteered somewhat unhelpfully that we discover properties of our environment "by way of" structured stimuli. I am now suggesting that one take "by way of" in a causal sense: structured stimuli *produce* certain beliefs in (suitably equipped) perceivers.

Experimental Support: "Tactile Vision"

Perhaps all this can be brought into focus by considering a recent development in the applied psychology of perception. It is a virtue, I think, of the sort of view I have been advancing that it allows one to take account of the phenomenon I shall describe, and to do so in a way that seems perfectly natural.

In a paper entitled (in my view, perspicuously) "Seeing with the skin" (White, et al, 1970; see also Guarniero, 1974; Morgan, 1977; Reed and Jones, 1978), a group of researchers discusses a device characterized as a "tactile visual substitution system" (TVSS). The device consists of a television camera (its "eye") coupled to a mechanism that converts the visual image produced by the camera into an "isomorphic cutaneous display" in the form of a pattern of vibration produced by a collection of tiny vibrating pins arranged in a grid and brought into contact with the skin (usually on the back or the stomach) of experimental subjects. Practice in the use of this device enables persons who are blind to detect reasonably fine differences among objects and events that appear in front of the camera.

The details of this experimental work are fascinating, but this is not the place to go into them (see above for references). I wish only to raise the question of how we are to describe such cases. My suggestion is that a person making intelligent use of a TVSS may be said to be *seeing* (though perhaps only dimly) features of his environment. This, surely, is what we should say were we to discover a creature whose "visual system" turned out to be a biological analogue of the mechanism described.

Let us call a person armed with a TVSS (or a creature biologically equipped with such a system) a *T-perceiver*. On my view it would be proper to say that a T-perceiver *sees* his surroundings because the T-perceiver makes use of information contained in reflected light.

There are two matters worth noting here. First, T-perceivers will enjoy a range of capacities and limitations thoroughly analogous to the capacities and limitations attributable to ordinary sighted creatures. Thus, for example, both ordinary sighted observers and T-perceivers will be able to describe the shapes and orientation of things without having to touch them, both will find it difficult to make out objects and events that are dimly illuminated.

Second, although T-perceivers and persons with ordinary eyesight may well describe what they see (or "T-perceive") in the same way, it is unlikely that we should want to attribute to them the same sorts of experience. If a T-perceiver were sufficiently practiced and well equipped, the fact (if indeed it is a fact) that his perceptual experiences were different from those of an ordinary perceiver would not necessarily be detectable from the ways in which he described his perceptions. Indeed a T-perceiver might well be at a loss to describe the character of his "visual experiences" without simply describing what he T-perceived.

In this regard at least, a T-perceiver would be no different from an ordinary (sighted) perceiver. As Grice puts it,

> . . . such experiences (if experiences they be) as seeing and feeling seem to be, as it were, diaphanous: if we were asked to pay close at-

tention, on a given occasion, to our seeing or feeling as distinct from what was being seen or felt, we should not know how to proceed; and the attempt to describe the differences between seeing and feeling seems to dissolve into a description of what we see and what we feel. (Grice, 1962, p. 144)

The view I have set out here appears to provide one with a way of accounting for this difficulty; more, it leads one precisely to *expect* it. The point of perceptual talk is to describe things perceived, not to describe experiences of things perceived. It makes clear, in addition, just why the character of perceptual experiences—sensations—seems so often beside the point.

It is interesting to compare these musings with the testimony of one who has himself employed a TVSS, a living, breathing T-perceiver. G. Guarniero, a graduate student (in philosophy!) who had been blind from birth, was given a three-week training session in the use of the device. He recounts his impressions in a paper entitled "Experience of tactile vision" (Guarniero, 1974).

It is perhaps significant that Guarniero himself elects to describe what he has learned to do as *seeing,* rather than as feeling things. "Only when I first used the system did the sensations seem as if they were on my back" (p. 101). Later he came to be aware, as it were, not of vibrations, but of objects existing apart from himself.

Very soon after I had learned how to scan, the sensations no longer felt as if they were located on my back, and I became less and less aware that vibrating pins were making contact with my skin. By this time objects had come to have a top and a bottom; a right side and a left. . . . (p. 104)

These observations again make clear a difficulty inherent in attempts to describe perceptual experiences without simply describing characteristics of objects perceived. They provide, as well, a certain amount of support for the "information pickup" view of perception advocated by Gibson. The function of sensory systems is to extract information from some particular stimulatory source (in the case of vision, from ambient light radiation), not to create distinct experiences, sensations or internal models of what is perceived. Given suitable equipment and proper training, evidently one can learn to extract visual information by way of the skin.[4]

I concede that it is, to an extent, misleading to describe a TVSS-user as *seeing* in an unqualified sense. Such a person, one might say, is employing a device that *enhances* or *extends* his senses. But *which* sense is thereby enhanced or extended? That will be determined, on the view defended here, by the character of the "intervening stimulation" sampled.

In putting it this way, it may appear that I have missed a crucial point. After all, one deploying a TVSS seems to be making use of *two* sorts of physical stimulation—the light radiation that reaches the lens of the apparatus and the vibration of pins against his skin. One might thus suppose that, given the tenets of my view, I ought to describe the case as one comprised of both touch and vision.[5]

This, I think, is partly correct, but, insofar as it *is* correct, it is perfectly unobjectionable. To the extent that one wishes to describe a TVSS-user as availing himself of his sense of touch, the *objects* felt are not those in front of the television camera, but the vibrating pins put in contact with his skin. If, in contrast, one takes the objects of his sensing to be those scanned by the camera, it is more plausible, surely, to describe them as (in some sense) seen, the beliefs thus acquired as (in some sense) visual.

It should be noted that a device such as a TVSS is workable chiefly because it establishes a partial isomorphism between an "optic array" and a gridwork of vibrating pins, *not* one between the scanned items and the gridwork.[6] It is the optic array as

---

4. Further, cases such as these suggest difficulties for theories that tie modes of sensing to particular psychological or physiological "channels" (see below).

5. I owe this observation to Gary Monnard.

6. Properties of the optic array are determined by, but are not identical to, properties of illuminated objects and events. An object in motion relative to an observer, for example, may systematically transform the array without itself changing. Thus, an approaching object will "loom large," an object moving away will eventually "vanish." According to Gibson, visual information is conveyed largely by means of these and

sampled by the television camera that determines the character
of the vibrations. This is why the former may be taken as, in a
certain sense, primary, and *this* is why it seems not altogether
unnatural to describe a person employing a TVSS as *seeing*.

If I am right about this, then another interesting conclusion
appears to follow. As was earlier noted, the notion that
particular senses depend on particular neural pathways or
mechanisms is a longstanding one (see Müller, 1838). Thus
vision has been associated not only with retinal occurrences, but
in addition with goings-on in the optic nerve and the visual
cortex. This seems, however, unnecessarily restrictive. Not only
does it appear to rule out—unreasonably—the possibility that
creatures built in ways different from us might properly be said
to see (or hear, or taste, or smell) their environment, it confuses
as well questions about the ways in which sensory mechanisms
are in fact realized with questions about how they might be
realized—what is essential to a certain mode of sensing.

This confusion is associated by Gibson with the doctrine of
"specific nerve energies" formulated in the nineteenth century
by Johannes Müller (see Müller, 1838; Gibson, 1979, pp. 33
ff.). If the function of perception is, as I have suggested, to
produce in the perceiver certain cognitive or doxastic states, and
if the senses are distinguished chiefly by features of the world
that produce these states, then particular characteristics of the
internal mechanisms that mediate this process are strictly
inessential. Perception may depend upon a causal process, but it
is important to be clear about what is and what is not intrinsic
to that process. This requires, among other things, a specification of its beginning and end states. My suggestion is that the
process begins with physical stimulation structured by objects
and events in the environment, and ends with the production of
a belief (or belief-like cognitive state). Different senses are
distinguished by differences in one of these boundary states, not

similar *transformations* of the optic array that occur as the perceiver observes, moves
about in, and manipulates his environment.

by differences in neural pathways or by differences in the sorts of sensation generated by the activation of these.

The Possibility of Different Senses

Before going on to discuss particular sensory modalities, it will be useful to ask how many senses there might be. I have spoken of vision, hearing, smell, taste, and touch. In the section that follows, I shall discuss "proprioception," the awareness of one's own bodily disposition and movements. But what of the feats of bats, dolphins, and other creatures that seem able, through the use of sonarlike devices, to discover features of the world that we detect, if at all, in other ways? On the view I am recommending, the question of whether a creature is endowed with an entirely *different* sense will hinge on the extent to which the creature is equipped to pick up information of a sort that we are "blind" to. Creatures sensitive in certain ways to X-rays or to radio waves might be thus describable.

It is useful in this regard to distinguish creatures equipped with what I should call *extended* senses from those employing new or entirely *different* senses. (I am well aware that this distinction may turn out to be more a matter of degree than kind. My claim, however, is not that it is *sharp*, merely that it is *useful*.) Thus, many terrestrial creatures are equipped to detect light radiation or sounds that human beings are insensitive to. Given that, for such creatures, the sort of information picked up is *continuous* with that which we human beings extract from our surroundings, it is perhaps best to regard them as employing senses merely extended relative to our own. Spot responds to a whistle that we cannot hear. It is not that Spot has a special sense that we lack, but that he can hear more (or better) than we can.

What of bats, dolphins, and other creatures said to be capable of using sounds to discover things about their environments in ways analogous to our use of sight? Do we want to say that such creatures possess a sense different from any of ours? Perhaps not. A human being may be taught to use a sonar device that will enable him to probe his surroundings in ways comparable to the methods employed by bats and dolphins. Here it seems better to say that such creatures, in common with blind persons capable of detecting large obstacles "echoically," have developed more sophisticated and discriminatory ways of picking up information from sound waves that reach them through their respective media.[7] Other creatures have come to possess more highly developed chemical detection systems. Spot's nose enables him to make use of information that we are ill-equipped to detect, but which is not different in kind from what we encounter when we stroll past the bakery.

To make a case for an entirely different sense, one would want to show that its possessor is able to respond to information of a sort for which we have no receptors, hence *cannot* pick up. I have suggested that a creature able to detect radio waves, or one capable of responding to X-rays, might be said to enjoy a novel sense. If pigeons are equipped, as has been claimed, to discriminate features of the earth's magnetic field (or rather to use information in that field to discover something—heaven knows what—about their location), then this capacity, too, might begin to look like a genuinely novel sense.

Such cases are, at any rate, importantly different from a fanciful one discussed by Grice (pp. 146 ff.). Grice imagines that we are visited by friendly, intelligent Martians who teach us their language. At length we discover that there is no simple translation into Martian of the English verb "to see":

> Instead we find two verbs which we decide to render as "x" and "y": we find that (in their tongue) they speak of themselves as x-ing and also as y-ing, things to be of this and that color, size and shape.

7. Such creatures, of course, exhibit a capacity to *enrich* the auditory information available to them, as well, by emitting certain noises. This activity on their part is analogous to our carrying a flashlight to help us see our way about at night and in dark places where there is little natural light. Sensory enrichment of this sort is often relied upon by the blind in employing so-called "facial vision" (a misnomer—see e.g., Gibson, 1966, p. 2). An interesting first-person account of this phenomenon may be found in Mehta, 1982.

Further, in physical appearance they are more or less like ourselves, except that in their heads they have, one above the other, two
pairs of organs, not perhaps exactly like one another, but each pair
more or less like our eyes: each pair of organs is found to be
sensitive to light waves. (p. 146)

As it happens, "x-ing" is accomplished by means of the upper
organs, "y-ing" by means of the lower set.

Now should we say that "x-ing" and "y-ing" are both cases
of seeing? Or is it that one or both of these constitutes "a new
sense other than sight"? Grice's contention is that, before we
can settle this question, we should have to determine whether
the experiences of "x-ing" and "y-ing" were alike.

Would we not in fact want to ask whether x-ing something to be
round was like y-ing it to be round, or whether when something x-
ed blue to them it was like or unlike its y-ing blue to them? If in answer to such questions as these they said, "Oh no, there's all the
difference in the world!" then I think we should be inclined to say
that either x-ing or y-ing (if not both) must be something other than
seeing: we might of course be quite unable to decide *which* (if
either) was seeing. (p. 146)

This, I have wanted to suggest, is not so. If both "x-ing" and
"y-ing" involve the extraction of information from the available
light, then it seems best to regard them both as forms of seeing.
If the organs are different, perhaps they are sensitive to different
wavelengths of light. If that were so (the question would have to
be settled experimentally), it would scarcely be surprising that
"there's all the difference in the world" between "x-ing" and
"y-ing." But if we insist on that account that both "x-ing" and
"y-ing" could not be cases of seeing, then we should have to say
that honeybees and houseflies do not see either. Such a view has,
for me anyway, little intuitive appeal.

Surely it is both useful and correct to mark off what it is that
honeybees and human beings do when they make use of their
eyes, despite obvious and important differences, as the exercise
of the sense of sight, and to distinguish this from what goes on

when we listen to, taste, touch, or sniff about our respective habitats. Such distinctions can be made, and made in an altogether natural way, I have suggested, if one considers the character of the "information source," the physical stimuli probed by the creature in the process of getting about in the world.

It is now possible to see why attempts to distinguish the senses by reference to properties of objects *simpliciter* seem bound to fail. In the first place, not just any property will do. Smoothness, for example, or roundness may be both seen and felt. Roxbee Cox (1970) has attempted to overcome this difficulty by arguing that there are certain "key features" of objects that can be detected "directly" only by a single sense. Color, for example, might be such a feature. Colors may, it seems, be apprehended "directly" only by means of sight. If this were so, one might be able to construct a taxonomy of the senses by reference to commonsense properties of things perceived, and not have to bother with light radiation and similar exotica.

A fundamental obstacle faced by any such account is that it seems possible to imagine importantly different ways in which creatures could become aware of *any* feature of ordinary objects and events. Thus, even if it could be shown that the "direct" detection of color is, for a human being, limited to our sense of sight, it is anything but obvious that colors could not be "directly" sensed in radically different ways—via sonar devices, for example. A creature equipped in this way might, I am suggesting, best be described as *hearing* the colors of objects. Such creatures might be able to report on colors even in total darkness, but experience difficulty in doing so in a noisy room. Similar cases could be multiplied indefinitely. Admittedly, it may be possible to amend one's account of key features so as to cover each new possibility, but such a move appears suspiciously ad hoc.

If, in contrast, one adopts a taxonomy of the senses founded on kinds of stimulation sampled, difficulties of this sort are neatly avoided. It will, in addition, be possible to find a place for the intuition (appealed to earlier) that distinct senses possess distinctive liabilities and advantages: these are a function of particular characteristics of various sorts of stimuli. If touch, for example, requires mechanical contact, then objects touched must be contiguous—or, at any rate, mechanically connected—to a perceiver. If sight depends on light radiation, then factors affecting light—opaque barriers, for instance, or mirrors or lenses—will result in familiar deficits or enhancements of visual capacities.

Finally, the view I am recommending provides a relatively simple explanation of the data to which Roxbee Cox appeals. One can understand why it is that, for a human being, the apprehension of color, for instance, depends on sight: the stimulation that produces in us ("directly") beliefs about colors is structured light radiation. It is not that colors can only be seen, but that colors can only be seen by *us*. That colors are detectable "directly" only by sight is—at best—a contingent fact, not a necessary truth about vision.

To establish the presence of a sensory modality, of course, one must do more than simply locate receptors with appropriate ranges of sensitivity. The latter must be coupled, as well, to the production of the right sorts of cognitive state. Thus receptors must enable their possessor to extract information about the environment that is carried in the stimulatory source, not merely be sensitive to it.[8] A sensory mode requires not only the presence of receptive faculties, but the capacity as well to employ these in such a way that they provide their possessor with a source of information about how things stand in the world. In this regard, cameras and photocells—and eyeballs—are blind.

I conclude that a taxonomy of the senses must be founded on distinctions among physical stimuli. To the extent that these are

8. The latter, to be sure, is part of the environment, hence one may, it seems, imagine creatures equipped to pick up information about it, about light radiation, for example, as distinct from information *borne* by it about separate objects and events. I shall discuss this distinction in chapter II, below.

vague, to the extent that they run together, to that extent our taxonomy of sensory modes must be vague and indeterminant. This, however, can hardly be reckoned a flaw unless one has some argument to show that the boundaries between the several senses are, despite appearances to the contrary, sharp and firm. I am skeptical that such an argument can be produced.

A Preliminary Taxonomy of the Senses

The classification that follows is meant to be illustrative only. Its purpose is merely to draw together the various strands of the present chapter.

• Vision

The sensory capacity of sight allows its possessor to extract information about objects and events from ambient light radiation. If one prefers, a clause may be added specifying that the radiation must be of a certain sort or fall into a certain range, roughly that comprising those wavelengths and intensities to which human beings are sensitive "and adjacent wavelengths and intensities" (to allow for the vision of honeybees and similar creatures).

• Audition

An auditory system is one enabling a creature to extract information from pressure waves rippling through its particular medium (in the case of terrestrial animals, air, in the case of aquatic species, water). Again, one may attach a proviso restricting the range of such stimulation to those frequencies roughly continuous with frequencies to which human beings are auditorily sensitive.

- *Touch*

A creature's "haptic" system enables it to acquire information about objects and events via mechanical contact with those objects and events. This contact may be "direct" (as when one explores an object with one's hands) or "indirect" (as when one probes with a stick). There are, as always, borderline cases. Does a child who has learned to detect an approaching train by putting his ear to the rail hear or feel the train? This will depend on details of the case. (For some relevant considerations, see below.)

Both hearing and touch are *mechanical* senses, although the information afforded by sound is exclusively vibratory. Certain vibrations, of course, may be detected haptically, as when one feels a distant explosion "through the soles of one's feet." When the volume on a phonograph is excessive, the result can be both heard and felt.[9]

- *Smell and Taste*

A sense of smell incorporates a capacity to extract chemical information about objects and events that is dispersed through the medium, information pertaining to *volatile* sources. Like smell, taste is a chemical sense, though one associates it with things ingested rather than with things sniffed. Because the character of the physical stimuli are so similar, one may be inclined to lump the two senses together under the rubric "chemical senses." There is no objection to one's holding to the traditional distinction, provided that in doing so one realizes that the line between tasting and smelling seems impossible to draw with any precision. This, of course, is not a special problem for my account of the senses, it simply reflects a commonly recognized fact about taste and smell.

9. These somewhat cavalier remarks about touch conceal a great many interesting and important distinctions. See e. g., Gibson, 1966, chaps. 6 and 7 for a more detailed and informative discussion.

• *"Kinesthesis"*

It is not obvious what one should say about the knowledge one evidently has concerning motions and dispositions of one's body and its parts. It is far from clear, for example, that one is obliged to regard such knowledge as *perceptual*. One knows without, as it were, having to look, that one's hand is resting in one's lap. Is this something one perceives?

In common parlance, the notion of perception seems restricted to the detection of goings-on "in the world," things and events *outside* one's body. There are no special perceptual verbs for the activity of detecting bodily states and occurrences. One does, it is true, speak of *feeling* one's hand to be in one's lap, but this seems only a way of indicating that one can tell this without having to look at or touch anything, in particular without having to look at or touch one's hand.

It is doubtful, in any case, that there is a special perceptual mode of "feeling" that is brought into play here. Feeling one's hand in one's lap is not like feeling the edge of a table or feeling a spider scuttle across one's arm; feeling one's body to be upright is not like feeling a doorknob in the dark. Further, there seem to be no special receptors designed exclusively for the picking up of kinesthetic or, as I shall designate it (following Gibson, 1966), *proprioceptive* information. In fact, such information apparently comes from a variety of distinct sources including occurrences in the inner ear, happenings in the muscles and joints, and from ordinary visual perception (as when one suffers the illusion of motion in a stationary railway carriage when another carriage passes on an adjacent track). Such considerations suggest that it would be a mistake to regard proprioception as a distinctive sensory mode (see Gibson, 1966, pp. 33 ff.).

One consideration that, historically, has had considerable influence on this matter strikes me as wrongheaded. It has occasionally been pointed out that there are no distinctive proprioceptive *sensations*. This was hinted at above when it was noted that the proprioceptive use of "feeling" differs from its use in haptic contexts. I have suggested, however, that it is wise to distinguish sensation and perception. It is not altogether clear, for example, that there are distinctive visual or auditory *sensations,* yet vision and audition are paradigmatically perceptual modes (see Gibson, 1966). The fact, then, if it is a fact, that there are no simply identifiable proprioceptive sensations (or, if there are such, their seeming not to form a natural class) is neither here nor there so far as the matter at hand is concerned.

A further source of confusion springs from the circumstance that the notion of perception has a technical employment that does not, in every case, sit comfortably with our ordinary ways of talking about the senses. This technical or specialized application is traceable, perhaps, to certain vaguely epistemo-logical concerns of philosophers and psychologists. There is a professional interest in our knowledge of the world, that is, *empirical* knowledge, its sources and its warranting conditions. From this point of view, beliefs about one's own body are on all fours epistemologically with beliefs about spatially discontinu-ous states of affairs.

This is not to say that the notion of proprioception is exclusively a technical one, that concern with proprioception is entirely absent from ordinary discourse. On the contrary, it seems rather to be taken for granted. Beliefs about one's own bodily dispositions and movements seem so often to be true, that questions concerning their evidence or warrant may tend to be regarded as out of place, superfluous. Because my aim here is not to chronicle ordinary usage but to elucidate the quasi-technical notion of perception, I shall not want to exclude proprioception from the list of perceptual modalities solely because it differs in many ways (physiologically and phenome-nologically) from other perceptual categories.

There is, however, a residual problem. I have recommended that the senses be distinguished by reference to features of physical stimuli. In the present case, unfortunately, the stimuli in question appear to be extremely diverse, ranging from occurrences in muscles, joints, and inner ears, to optic arrays undergoing certain sorts of global transformation. How, then, can one speak sensibly of a single proprioceptive modality?

I concede that this way of speaking is improper, indeed that it is, in some respects, positively misleading, but I shall argue that this fact is, for present purposes, beside the point. It is not my intention to produce here an exhaustive taxonomy of the senses—that, after all, is, on my view, an empirical task—but to indicate, first, a logic for such a classification and, second, to show how this logic fits even our ordinary commonsensical classifications reasonably well.

It may be, then, that what is called proprioceptive information is in fact determined by a variety of disparate physical stimuli. If this is so, then proprioception may be reducible to some combination of sensory modes. The use of a single expression here comes, I suspect, mainly from an implicit theory of sensory classification, one that encourages us, roughly, to lump together information-sources because they all provide information about a single subject matter, in this case one's bodily dispositions and movements. Proprioceptive information (as distinct from, say, visual or auditory information) is typically classified by reference to its *content,* rather than by reference to its source.

I doubt, then, that it can be very useful to regard proprioception as *a* sensory mode. Rather, there seem to be several proprioceptive modalities. I shall use this term merely to stand for whichever of these modalities remain (if any) when one subtracts those discussed already (vision, touch, and the like). Thus, if some proprioceptive information is gleaned from goings-on in the muscles and joints, then such goings-on may form the basis of *a* proprioceptive mode. To the extent that these goings-on differ from vistibular occurrences in the inner ear, we may wish to regard the latter as a second proprioceptive mode. Again, such matters cannot be decided in advance; they are, in the broadest sense, empirical. It is, for that reason, pointless for me to speculate on them here.

I shall use the term "proprioception," then, as a cover for my empirical ignorance. In fact, of course, this point can be extended to what I have said about *all* the senses. I have not sought an exhaustive listing. Indeed, I could not set out to do that given my suggested classificatory technique. The number of possible sensory modes depends upon the number of possible information sources, and there is no obvious way to specify these in advance. My goal, however, is not to legislate for the physiologist, but merely to pave the way for a general account of perception. Such an account must, I have insisted, be defined over all the senses, all *possible* senses.

Intuitively, the conditions that must be satisfied in order for it to be the case that S sees something may not be very much like the conditions that must be satisfied in order for it to be true that S feels or hears something. My hope is that I can provide a characterization of perception that can be completed for any sensory modality by "plugging in" the special conditions associated with that modality. This seems to me the proper route to take even though it may be impossible to say in advance much about those special conditions. Certainly it is preferable to the elaboration of an extremely general characterization of perception applicable without modification to any sensory mode. Even if such a broad account were feasible, something one may easily doubt, its very generality would serve to obscure more than it would illuminate.

My strategy will be to follow tradition and focus in most of what follows on visual perception. It is hoped, however, that the present chapter provides at least an inkling of how claims founded on characteristics of one modality may (or, in some cases, may not) be extended to others. I begin with vision, not because I regard visual perception as in any epistemological sense privileged. Rather it is just that vision seems, for whatever reason, both more interesting and simpler to talk about. A discussion of perception that takes off in this way from features of a single modality would, in most cases, merit suspicion. In providing a principled way of distinguishing the senses, however, one provides (in principle, anyway) a technique for generalizing across modalities. This, perhaps, is as close as one can reasonably expect to come to a thoroughly general or neutral characterization of perception.[10]

10. I have deliberately left aside discussion of our awareness of "bodily sensations," such things as pains, tickles, itches, and (perhaps) afterimages. These are, it seems, *had* rather than perceived. Later (chiefly in chapter IV) I shall argue that perception is best regarded as "epistemic," that in perceiving a thing we come to have beliefs about it. In contrast to this, one's having a bodily sensation, *B,* seems not to depend on one's having any beliefs at all about *B,* in particular, not on one's having the belief about *B* that it is a *B*-type sensation.

II

PERCEPTUAL OBJECTS AND "DIRECT" PERCEPTION

Determining the Objects of Perception

The method of characterizing and distinguishing the senses set forth in chapter I provides, I wish now to suggest, a way of distinguishing the *objects* of perception, hence a means of "anchoring" one end of the causal chain of which perceiving is comprised. This, surely, is significant—although an appreciation of its significance requires that one first recognize the problem for which it is offered as a solution.

In a typical instance of visual perception, for example, there is a source of illumination, the sun, perhaps, or a light bulb. This source emits a stream of more or less unstructured light radiation. When the latter interacts with the surfaces of objects constituting the environment (tables, trees, clouds), it is structured in certain ways. Our visual system reacts to this structured, ambient light (not simply to the lower-level properties of light, wavelength, intensity, and the like) and, if all goes well, we see tables, trees, and clouds.

Here one finds a causal chain running from a light-emitting source to the surfaces of objects in the vicinity. These objects, in turn, impart a particular structure to the light they reflect, and this structured light is transmitted (perhaps directly, perhaps via intermediate links—mirrors, spectacle lenses, and such) to our retinas where it is transformed into nerve impulses that make their way inwards to the brain. The question is, why should we pick out one stage in this more or less continuous process and say that it is items at *this* stage that are perceived? Thus, we commonly say that we see tables and trees, rather than light radiation, or retinal stimulation or occurrences in the visual cortex. Is this merely a *façon de parler,* or is there some deeper reason to suppose that such objects deserve a special status?

My suggestion is that in cases in which one visually encounters ordinary illuminated objects and events, we may say that these objects and events have a privileged role because it is these that impart structure to the ambient light from which one may, by means of one's visual system, extract information.[1] In the case of hearing, it is again the oscillatory motions of ordinary objects that structure the vibratory medium. It is significant that both ambient light and pressure waves carry information *primarily* about the objects and events that have structured them and only secondarily or indirectly about occurrences earlier or later in the causal chain (see chapter III, below). Such information is, or may be, detected by perceivers furnished with eyes and ears. These circumstances may, however, seem insufficient motivation for the claim that it is proper (or, at any rate, *more* proper) to hold that one sees, for example, tables and trees rather than light waves, that one hears bells and voices rather than pressure waves.

At least part of what is missing, perhaps, is some accounting of the role of perception in the lives of sentient creatures. In order to make one's way about one's habitat, one is obliged to keep abreast of those features of the environment that in various ways affect one's livelihood. Some of these represent danger, some serve as sources of nourishment or shelter. As it happens, information about the presence or absence of such things is carried by ambient light, pressure waves, chemical dispersal, and the like. A creature engineered so as to take advantage of this fact will have a somewhat better chance of coping with the rigors and vicissitudes of day-to-day survival than one not so constructed. Not *everything* about light radiation, or pressure

---

1. A slightly different case is that in which one observes a radiant source. To simplify the discussion, I shall focus on illuminated rather than illuminating things. An account of the former, one may suppose, includes the latter as a special case.

waves, or dispersing chemicals is in this way useful, however, only those structural features that bear on determinate and *relevant* aspects of the environment. Sentient creatures are equipped with mechanisms sensitive to *these* information-bearing features of physical stimuli; they are detected, not because they are particularly important features of those stimuli (indeed, from the point of view of physics, they may seem utterly accidental), but because of their lawful relations with the objects and events that inform them.

One might imagine a creature (a Jovian, perhaps) that feeds on light radiation of certain intensities and wavelengths. In describing the foraging behavior of such creatures, one might well wish to say that they *see* light radiation, not illuminated or luminous objects. In such cases, it would be information about certain properties of *light* that the creature would detect, not information about luminous sources or reflecting surfaces.

Consider a case in which *S* employs a stick to feel about in his environment. With a little practice, *S* may come to "feel things at the end of the stick," the stick may come to function as a natural extension of *S*'s body. When this happens, information about the world is transmitted *through* the stick to *S*, and we should cease to describe this as a case in which *S* feels the stick; he feels, rather, things touched with or by the stick. Such examples illustrate the extent to which the notion of a perceptual object is connected to the needs, interests, and capacities of perceivers. Once these have been ascertained, one may begin to decide which segment of the perceptual sequence might reasonably be regarded as the *perceived* segment.[2]

"Direct" and "Indirect" Perception

It is sometimes argued that this picture of what is perceived is inaccurately drawn. Thus, "strictly speaking," *S* does not

2. These points are, I think, related to Gibson's notion of *affordances*, features of the world that are significant in virtue of relations they bear to the needs, interests, and capacities of perceivers. See below; also Gibson, 1979, chaps. 3 and 8.

perceive the items touched by his stick, but only sensations in his hands and fingertips. These are "perceived directly," everything else is "inferred." Similarly for the other sensory modes: what is "really" perceived is an occurrence or set of occurrences in one's body. These one somehow learns to attribute to external causes. The "external world" is never apprehended immediately, rather it is a construct, an edifice built from elementary sensory bricks and beams and held together with the mortar of inference.

What, one would like to know, *can* be perceived? *How much* of the world does one actually see, hear, and feel, and how much does one in fact *infer* from what one perceives? Does one, for example, *see* rocks and trees, or does one see only points of light, or perhaps patches of color, and infer that these in some sense *belong* to rocks and trees?

It is important to separate these questions from the question of what psychological processes might be required for perception. Thus, I do not wish to argue from the fact that one is not ordinarily *aware* of any such inferential processes to the claim that no such processes occur. As theorists are fond of pointing out, such things may occur "automatically," or "unconsciously," or so rapidly that they are not readily detectable by means of introspection. My interest for the moment is in the *logic* of perceptual inference: in what sense and to what extent must perceptual beliefs rest on *inferences?* Must, that is, inferential processes of some sort be postulated to account for even the simplest perceptions of "external" objects and events? Holmes infers the identity of the criminal the moment he sees footprints in the garden. Does Holmes also infer the footprints from some simpler perceptual clue or clues?

Such questions can arise, one may feel, only if one takes perception to be in some measure *cognitive.* If perception were connected only indirectly with the having of beliefs or other cognitive states, then perceiving would never be inferential—although subsequent cognitive and doxastic states might be thought to be inferentially generated from basic, non-cognitive states or processes. Even on such views, however, it is possible to ask whether the cognitive states most closely *associated* with perception are necessarily inferential. If my perception of x that it is F produces in me the belief about x that it is F, must that belief be inferred from something else, or might it rather be a direct, albeit contingent, consequence of my perceptual state?

It appears, then, that questions about the role of inference in perception are, in this sense anyway, perfectly general: they may be raised in one way or another for cognitive and non-cognitive theories alike. In either case, the question will pertain to the status of whatever cognitive states are taken to arise *in* or *from* one's perceptual encounter with the world. Are these cognitive states produced "directly," at a stroke, or are they always mediated by higher-level inferences that bridge the chasm between the particularity of perceptual experience and the generality of thought and language?

I shall follow the practice adopted earlier of describing perceptually induced cognitive states as beliefs. The argument, however, does not depend on the states in question being doxastic. Should the reader hesitate over this feature of the account, he is invited to substitute some less objectionable expression for "belief."

A mistake commonly made in discussions of perceptual inference is to suppose that if the forming of beliefs (or at any rate ordinary empirical beliefs) requires the application of concepts, such beliefs must, by that very fact, be inferential. Thus, if I believe (truly *or* falsely) of x that it is F, I must know, at the very least, what it is for something to be (an) F, I must recognize that x satisfies these conditions, and I must draw from these cognitive tidbits the conclusion that this particular, x, instantiates F.

This way of describing the application of concepts, however, seems infelicitous in at least two respects. First, it vastly "over-intellectualizes" the process of conceptualization. Second, it raises the specter of an endless inferential regress: if I recognize x to be apt for the application of F, I must, it seems, do so in virtue of my (further) recognition of b's being G (where G is whatever it is about x that licenses the application of F). But now one is obliged to account for the aptness of G's application to x. We seem embarked on a regress that can only be terminated when one allows for some sort of "direct" conceptualization.

To forestall the threat of conceptual regress, I shall adopt the view that at least some instances of "bringing things under concepts" are *basic* in the sense that they do not require any additional act of conceptualization. What counts as basic conceptualization and what counts as non-basic or derivative conceptualization depends both on the cognitive and perceptual capacities of the agent *(S* can tell straight off that this is an elm, *T* must *take steps* before he can tell the same), and on the conditions confronting the agent *(S* can tell just by looking that this is an elm, but not that the tree in the distance is an elm).

It is possible, of course, to grant that some states of affairs are "directly" detectable, but severely limit the scope of such direct perception. As the preceding paragraph makes clear, I wish to resist this move. What can be seen (or heard, or felt) "directly" is largely a matter of one's perceptual capacities. Such capacities are, in part, purely sensory—those, for instance, that enable Spot to hear what I cannot hear, a honeybee to see what I cannot see. To lack a capacity of this sort is to lack a piece of sensory equipment, or perhaps to lack a characteristic refinement of such equipment. Such deficits may, on occasion, be compensated for through the use of various instruments. When the employment of the latter becomes a routine practice, those who make use of them may come to speak and behave as though they were nothing more than extensions of ordinary sensory capacities. The sonar operator in this way *hears* an approaching submarine, the meteorologist *sees* with the eye of his weather satellite.

Perceptual capacities may be limited as well by what I have called (somewhat vaguely) *conceptual* factors. For me to see what the botanist or the bird-watcher sees, I must have more than simply good eyesight or a pair of binoculars. I must have, as well, an *appreciation* for what it is I am gazing at. One may glamorize this sort of appreciation by calling it a theory, or a conceptual scheme or, as is now fashionable in some quarters, a schema or frame. I prefer the slightly less pretentious expression, *belief-complex*. In any case, the crucial point is a simple one. A creature's ability to perceive, to pick up information about its environment, may be limited by cognitive as well as by purely physiological factors. (It may be limited, in addition, by obvious external occurrences, as when the lights are extinguished, or the room is filled with noise.)

Given this picture, however, one may be driven to wonder whether there are any states of affairs (that is, state of affairs *types*) that are in principle incapable of being perceptually detectable under *any* circumstances. I want to allow the use of specialized instruments (to detect, for example, items too small or too far away to be seen by the naked eye) to count as a *form* of perceptual detection.[3] Thus, when I pose the question as to whether certain things might be in principle unperceivable, I do not have in mind such things as white blood cells, water molecules or remote galaxies. If such things are unperceivable, they are so contingently. I have in mind such Humean chestnuts as *causality*, *force*, and *velocity*, items that seem intimately connected with, but not quite identical to, things we perceptually encounter.

The "Perception of Causality"

Long ago, Hume adduced arguments intended to buttress the view that causality and force were in principle unobservable. Although we *seem* to feel and see such things, although we often

---

3. Even if one feels that the use of a specialized instrument to detect the presence of otherwise undetectable items (that is, items undetectable *by us*) ought not be described as a case of perception (even "extended" or "enhanced" perception), one may feel less inclined to say this about a creature equipped with a biological analogue of such a device. My concern here is with the question of whether there are (actual, physical) states of affairs that are "in principle" unperceivable, incapable of being perceived by any sentient being at all.

speak as though this were a simple matter, Hume argued that we in fact perceive only distinct events and, through "association" or force of habit, supply the mechanism of causality ourselves.

Hume regarded it as obvious that causality could not be perceived, not *strictly* anyway, and concluded that "perception of cause" so-called was simply a *way* of perceiving events of a sort that are regularly conjoined (or at least of perceiving events sufficiently *similar* to ones regularly conjoined). Others, relying on many of the same "data" as those to which Hume appealed, have argued, in contrast, that it is clear that causality *is* perceived. Michotte, for example, set out to prove this contention by showing that observers will produce judgments about causality in some, but by no means all, cases in which events are repeatedly conjoined (Michotte, 1946/1963).[4]

There is something decidedly unsettling about a dispute in which observational data of the same sort are marshaled to support conflicting claims about what is observed. In at least some cases where this occurs, one wants to say that the disputing parties have different things in mind, and that this fact is masked by a superficial similarity in terminology. Thus, while both Hume and Michotte may speak of "perception," it seems unlikely that they would agree about what it is to perceive something. If this is so, it is no wonder that they must differ in their views of what can and cannot be perceived.

I wish to suggest that disagreements about such matters as the perceivability of causality may be settled in a more or less

---

4. It seems to me enormously doubtful that Hume would have been much impressed with Michotte's experimental work. The latter's technique amounts chiefly to showing both that it is a relatively easy matter to induce in observers an impression of causality, and that not just *any* combination of events is sufficient to bring about this effect. In response, Hume might only point out that (i) not all (or perhaps not even very many) instances of causal relations resemble Michotte's simple paradigms, and that (ii) the fact that the latter produce an impression of causality, although an interesting psychological discovery, is neither here nor there so far as the question "Are causal relations perceived?" is concerned. Michotte's work shows neither that an impression of causality is necessary nor that it is sufficient in instances of genuine causal interaction, a result that Hume could easily have applauded.

empirical fashion once one comes up with a satisfactory understanding of what it is to perceive things and events. If I am
right, for instance, in regarding perception as the extraction of
information from available physical stimuli, then the question
will center on what features of the world can or cannot be
"specified" by such stimuli. Whether a causal relation can be
seen, then, will depend on whether information concerning such
relations could be borne by light radiation. Similarly, the
question of whether causality might be perceived other than
visually will depend on the extent to which information about
causal relations could be carried by physical stimuli of other
sorts.

At first glance, this reformulation of the question may seem
to offer no improvement over other, more familiar, formulations.
It does, nevertheless, afford certain significant advantages. I
shall try to illustrate these by discussing, briefly and somewhat
superficially, the relations between (certain) events connected
causally and the physical stimuli that seem to carry information
for the occurrence of such events. I shall simplify matters
further by restricting discussion to visual perception. The
question to be addressed concerns whether or not causal
relations could in certain circumstances be *seen*.

I take it that only things *visible* are things that can be seen.
Does it make sense, then, to regard causal relations as visible?
This, I have suggested, will depend largely on whether the
presence of a causal relation can be indicated via properties of
light radiation (perhaps complicated, "higher order," structural
properties of such radiation, over time).

The catch is that light seems capable of carrying only
kinematic information, that is, information only about the
geometrical features of objects and events (such things as
distance, direction, movement, and location fall under this
rubric).[5] Causal relations, in contrast, are fundamentally *dy-*

5. In saying that light radiation is capable of carrying "only kinematic" information,
I mean kinematic as opposed to *dynamic* information. I am not denying, certainly, that
light may carry information of other sorts, for example, information concerning the
colors of things.

namic. They involve, essentially, such things as mass, force, friction, momentum, and energy. Ordinary observable sequences of events manifest both kinematic and dynamic properties. This is an important matter for, should a particular sequence lack the requisite dynamic characteristics, it would not be an instance of causality at all but, at best, a case of *apparent* causality. Examples of such apparent causality are not difficult to find: animated films in which objects appear to collide, blips on the screen of a "video game"; perhaps even the moves of actors simulating a fist-fight are all familiar and perfectly unexceptional phenomena. Michotte's own experimental apparatus, consisting of patterned discs rotating behind a slotted screen, was designed so as to produce apparent causal sequences. In general, it appears that one can concoct such sequences by assembling the right combinations of kinematic properties and relations.

The fact, uncovered by Michotte, that only certain highly constrained combinations of kinematic properties will produce the illusion or appearance of causality is crucial. Kinematic properties are, as it were, *apt* for visual detection. Information for such properties may, it seems, be straightforwardly carried by structured light radiation (over time). This seems not the case, however, for dynamic properties. The latter appear to be detachable from their kinematic counterparts (as indeed the examples above illustrate). In order visually to apprehend a causal sequence, then, as opposed to apprehending a sequence that happened to be causal, one would be obliged somehow to detect the presence of *both* kinematic and dynamic properties given only kinematic information. It is no wonder that such a task has been regarded by many as hopeless.[6]

Consider, however, the evident fact, mentioned already, that not just *any* kinematic sequence will produce the appearance of causality. The sequence must be of a certain sort. What, one may wonder, is responsible for this set of constraints? Mi-

---

6. There are, of course, many other reasons for doubting that causal sequences are in any sense directly observable (see e.g., Mackie, 1980). I am not addressing those here.

chotte's work, as well as more recent work by Runeson and others suggests the following answer (Runeson, 1977*b*).

Kinematic sequences that are *consistent with* dynamic sequences of events related causally will engender in most observers the impression of causality. To the extent that such sequences depart from these constraints, the appearance of a genuine causal relation will diminish. The physical laws governing dynamic interactions limit the range of permissible dynamic relations. By extension, these laws restrict as well the range of kinematic relations possible in dynamically related bodies and events. If the dynamic constraints on kinematic properties of ordinary physical occurrences were *unique,* if the relation between dynamic and kinematic goings-on were a *simple* one, then it would be possible to "read off" an event's dynamic characteristics from its kinematic features, and the notion that causal relations are ("directly") visually detectable would receive some measure of vindication.

In fact, however, the relation between dynamic and kinematic properties is not so straightforward. One may put this by saying that, at best, *proportional* information about dynamic properties is kinematically determinable. Roughly, two dynamic sequences that differ with respect to their absolute properties will nevertheless exhibit (more or less) identical kinematic characteristics (hence *look* the same) so long as certain proportional relations are maintained. Thus, one may be able to tell just by watching a collision between *A* and *B* that *A* is roughly twice as heavy as *B,* but not that *A* and *B* have some *particular* weight. Kinematic simulations of causal sequences will preserve the appearance of causality only so long as they are, in this sense, compatible with lawful dynamic sequences, sequences in which certain proportional relations are maintained.

In ordinary life, of course, kinematic properties are very much richer in information about dynamic characteristics of objects and events. Friction, elasticity, viscosity, and the like place additional constraints on the kinematic features of genuinely causal sequences. Further, observers typically know a fair amount about the dynamic characteristics of familiar objects in advance. Such factors enable a sufficiently practiced observer to tell much about the "hidden" dynamic features of ordinary goings-on just by looking, just by picking up kinematic information.

What should we say, then, about the visibility of causal relationships? If one means only to ask whether one can, in some cases, tell just by looking that events *A* and *B* are related causally, then it seems clear that a case can be made for the view that causality is indeed observable, that it can be *seen*. If, in contrast, one means to ask about the extent to which dynamic properties are *visible*, that is, the extent to which information for dynamic properties of such sequences is carried in the "optic array" (or rather in transformations of this array over time), then one may wish to insist that the observation of causal sequences is at any rate more *complex* than observation of colors and shapes, properties more immediately related to visual stimuli.

This response will be felt by some to be unsatisfying. I think, however, that we would do well to be suspicious of simple answers to questions of this sort. Such answers may fail to do justice to the underlying issues that puzzle us when we pose the questions in the first place.

It is perhaps worth pointing out that the conclusions reached here may be generalized to non-visual perceptual modes. In all cases the question will be: to what extent can information for the dynamic properties and relations presumably constitutive of causality be carried by the physical stimuli appropriate to a particular sensory mode? And the answer to this question will be, I have argued, largely an empirical matter.

Perceiving and Inferring

I have focused on the perception of causality for two reasons. First, the topic is one with both a philosophical and a psychological history. Second, it provides for a reasonably clear application of the view of perception that I am recommending to a familiar problem. I am not, I hasten to add, endorsing talk about "the perception of causality." It seems likely that this locution is one that invites confusion. One must, in any event, distinguish cases of billiard ball-like interactions from cases of other sorts, ones involving, for example, biological or chemical processes. It goes without saying that my discussion of the relation between dynamic and kinematic properties is of little help in occurrences of the latter sort. It was never meant to be. My purpose has not been to provide an exhaustive account of our apprehension of instances of causality, but merely to show how certain—fairly narrow—traditional concerns fit into a particular theoretical orientation.

A more serious difficulty stems from the fact that the account I have provided thus far fails to address satisfactorily the matter of distinguishing "direct" from "indirect" perception. This distinction, as I should wish to make it, is not intended to mark off cases in which mirrors, Geiger counters, or light meters are employed from those in which only the naked eye comes into play. Cases of the former sort may turn out to be indirect in my sense, but this will not be in virtue of the fact that they add links to the causal chain running from object to eye. Indirect perception, as I shall speak of it, is perception that relies essentially upon inference. To take an example mentioned earlier, Holmes *infers* the identity of the burglar from his observation of the culprit's footprint, but he does not, or at any rate need not, infer the footprint.[7]

It is central to the view I should ultimately wish to defend that perception is cognitive, that perceiving involves more than a simple, unstructured reaction to perceptual stimuli. It must include what I have elected to call (again, following tradition) the application of concepts. It may well be the presence (or

---

7. I should maintain this even if Holmes's detection of the footprint required him to don a pair of "infra-red spectacles."

absence) of this conceptual dimension that distinguishes the categories of perception and sensation. That, however, is a topic I shall for the present leave aside. In any case, I earlier contended that it is at the very least misleading to regard concept application per se as a species of inference. This feature of concepts illustrates what I should like to think of as their *innocuous* character. In attributing concepts to perceivers, I mean only to be attributing to them the possession of certain abilities or capacities. To have the concept of X is simply to have the capacity to distinguish X's from *non-X*'s (under favorable conditions) and to "entertain thoughts in which X's figure" (Armstrong, 1973, chap. 5). To have the concept (of) X is not, in general, to have the ability to *say* what X's are, although the latter ability may entail the former.

There is, so far as I can tell, no particular reason to withhold ascription of concepts to mute creatures (that is, creatures lacking a language), despite its being the case that the attribution of concepts to such creatures can be an enormously tricky matter (see below, chapter VIII). By speaking, then, of "thoughts in which X's figure," I mean only to speak of such things as desires for X's, fears of X's, beliefs about X's, and the like.

In one sense, then, the claim that the perception of X's requires that the perceiver possess the concept (of) X is trivial. If perceiving an X is to be in a certain cognitive state, one presumably in which X figures, and to have a concept of X is just to have the capacity to be in such cognitive states, then "having the concept" is simply part of the more general "ability to perceive." The appearance of triviality may be diminished, however, if one thinks of the having of a concept not merely as the having of certain *perceptual* capacities. This is one facet of one's possession of a concept, but not the only one. The abilities in question are complex and intertwined; they range over a variety of "propositional attitudes." (These and related matters will be taken up again in chapters V and VIII.)

What, then, are we to conclude about the "directness" of ordinary perception? First, I have suggested that if some perception is indirect, that is, inferentially mediated, then some perception must be direct. To deny this is to invite a seemingly bottomless inferential regress.

Second, the application of concepts is not (or need not be in all cases) a species of inference. Thus to argue, as a cognitive theorist would argue, that perception always involves the application of concepts is not to deny that perception might sometimes be direct.

Third, there is no general way of specifying in advance what can or cannot be directly perceived. That will depend upon the cognitive and sensory equipment of particular creatures. What one creature can apprehend directly may require, for another, a lengthy chain of inferences.

Fourth, there may nevertheless be certain things that are perceptually detectable *only* indirectly. A specification of these is largely an empirical matter, one hinging on the relation between properties of (perceived) objects and events and properties of perceptual stimuli potentially available to observers.

To say that our perception of the world is (often) direct, then, is not to say that it is unconceptualized. More importantly, to say that it is conceptualized is not to say that it is indirect. The sense in which concepts "mediate" perception has nothing to do with the notion that the world we encounter as we look about ourselves is a construct, or that it is a phenomenal (or cognitive) artifact. It would be a mistake to suppose that honeybees and human beings "inhabit different worlds" simply because their respective visual systems are sensitive to different ranges of light radiation. In just the same way, it would be rash to suppose that Eskimos, for instance, and nuclear physicists inhabit different worlds because their *conceptual* systems are importantly different. There may be solid philosophical reasons for embracing the Kantian notion that the perceived world is something constructed by the mind. This conclusion, however, manifestly does not follow from the fact that, in order to perceive something, one must possess certain cognitive as well as sensory capacities. (I shall return to this issue in chapter V.)

Perceptual Objects and Perceptual Content

I have said that these points are largely moot for non-cognitive perceptual theories. I suspect, as well, that the issue of what one ought to count as a proper perceptual object is similarly moot for such theories. The notion of a perceptual object has work to do only in relation to a perceiver's cognitive states. Questions about the contents of perception—as these pertain to things perceived—apparently make sense only if one supposes these contents to have a propositional or cognitive character. A non-cognitive theorist, of course, can get to a notion of perceptual objects by tying these to cognitive states that presumably follow in the wake of perceptual states.

This brings to mind another central feature of the determination of the class of perceptual objects. Earlier I mentioned the importance in such matters of one's taking account of the needs and interests of perceivers. Thus, a medium-sized terrestrial creature must know about stones, trees, and ponds in navigating through its environment, not about light radiation or retinal stimulation. This makes it sound as though the specification of objects of perception were exclusively a pragmatic matter. I think, however, that the issue is more complicated than this.

I have spoken of the determination of perceptual objects as a determination of one of the "boundaries" of the causal chain of which perception is a part. At one end of the visual sequence, for example, are things seen, perceptual objects; at the other end are the perceptual states of the perceiver. What needs now to be recognized is that the specification of these boundaries cannot be achieved *independently:* what should count as a perceived object will depend largely, if not exclusively, on the character, the *content,* of a perceiver's perceptual state. If one's perceptual state, for example, has a content consisting of ordinary medium-sized bodies and their properties, then it is difficult to see why anyone should be tempted to regard anything other than these bodies and their properties as objects of one's perception. Crudely: if S (correctly) takes something on the plate in front of him to be a hamburger, medium-rare, why should one suppose that what S sees is something other than a hamburger—light radiation, perhaps, or retinal stimulation? The appropriate link in the causal chain, the link that constitutes the *object* of S's perception on some occasion (as well as the appropriate "level" on which this link ought to be described) is determined (at least in part) by the character of S's "percept" on that occasion.

This meshes nicely with earlier suggestions concerning the relevance of the needs and interests of perceivers. If a creature requires information about trees, stones, and ponds for its survival, and if information for such things is available in the ambient optic array, then the creature's percepts, although mediated by the array, will be most plausibly connected to the trees, stones, and ponds that structure the array. These will be the objects of perception for creatures of this sort, what they can directly perceive.

Concluding Remarks

In general, I have wished to advance the view that the class, P, of perceptual objects for a perceiving creature, S, is determined by two distinct though related features of S.

First, S's sensory equipment must be considered. S will be sensitive to (that is, sensorily equipped to detect) certain sorts or ranges of ambient physical stimulation and not others. More importantly, S will be equipped to detect only certain "higher order" *features* of this stimulation. Human beings, for instance, appear capable of responding to or registering particular structural properties of light, properties that are themselves determined by certain features of illuminated objects and events. Ambient light radiation has, as well, a variety of special characteristics to which we are (normally) insensitive. By setting out an inventory of those aspects of light radiation to which a perceiver, S, is sensitive (and capable of making intelligent use of), and by determining what is responsible for those aspects, we may uncover a *natural* link between S and the world.

Thus, suppose that S is sensitive to a collection of features, F, of a stimulatory source, L. Suppose, further, that F is determined by certain characteristics of S's environment, F', that is, the relation between F and F' is a nomic one. When this condition obtains (as, arguably, it does in the case of visual perception), one has prima facie grounds for concluding that F' characterizes a class of potential perceptual objects for S. F' is a link in a complex and continuous causal chain, but it is, in one important sense, a *privileged* link.

Notice that one oughtn't say without qualification that S perceives the constituents of F' (that $F' = P$). This is because S may be sensorily equipped to perceive such things, yet fail, for other reasons, to do so. I am equipped in this way to see all that a botanist sees, yet may not succeed in doing so because of my relative ignorance of an assortment of botanical facts.

This brings us to a second determinant of P, the class of perceptual objects: the collection of concepts employed by the perceiver. Again, it is not that there is a simple connection between the concepts one possesses and the states of affairs one can be said to perceive. The set of concepts attributable to most perceivers is presumably much broader than this. It will include concepts of things that are either unperceivable (for example, numbers and thoughts) or only "indirectly" perceivable (measles, tensile strength). Nevertheless, if one examines what might roughly be described as the intersection of the set of concepts attributable to a perceiver and the set, F', of features of the world sensorily available to him, one comes away with a crude but serviceable means of specifying P, the class of perceptual objects for that perceiver. P, then, is determined for S by the content of S's percepts, the content, I should prefer to say, of S's perceptual beliefs.

There are certain advantages of this way of approaching the topic of perceptual objects. First, it provides something like a principled way of specifying, for any perceiver, S, the class of perceptual objects, P, for S. Further, it does so in a way that fits comfortably with what one seems obliged on independent grounds to say about perception.[8] Second, the class of objects picked out in this way conforms rather well to one's pre-theoretical expectations about such things: the objects of perception turn out to be, in the main, what one had all along thought they might be.

If these remarks are on the right track, then one upshot (again, I gather, a welcome one) is that classes of perceptual objects are invariably perceiver-relative. It goes without saying that this does (or need) not entail any very interesting form of epistemological relativism. To say that S and T perceive different things when they gaze across their habitat is not to say that what they perceive is in any sense unreal, or that it is a private, phenomenal construct.

An important consequence of such a view is that psychological accounts of perception must, it seems, begin with some specification of the "perceptual world," those features of the environment to which a creature responds and about which it comes to have beliefs. Such a specification cannot be made once and for all. It cannot be made without taking into account the sensory and conceptual endowment of particular creatures. More significantly, it cannot be framed solely in terms of fundamental physical and chemical properties of the world. If a psychological theory of perception is a function from the world to perceptual states of perceivers, then it is a function from a world comprised of perceptual objects, not one consisting of "punctate physical stimuli." This, I should say, is my way of expressing at least a portion of what is contained in Gibson's much-maligned doctrine of "affordances" (see Gibson, 1979, especially chaps. 3 and 8).

This is not the place to set out an ontology of physical objects

---

8. A somewhat different way of characterizing perceptual objects may be found in Goldman, 1977.

and properties. It seems, at any rate, reasonable to suppose that any such ontology must account for (as distinct from explain away) familiar "molar" features of middle-sized physical objects, the items with which our world is cluttered. In any case, the view endorsed here is meant to be consistent with the ("objective," "physical") reality of these no less than the reality of their "underlying" molecular determinants. (On this, see below, chapter VII; also Kim, 1978, and Peacock, 1979, chap. 3.) This, I surmise, is a further point in its favor.

III

THE CONCEPT OF INFORMATION

Three Senses of "Information"

In discussing perception I have repeatedly availed myself of the notion of information. My suggestion has been that perception consists largely in the picking up of information—as distinct, say, from the having of sensations. In light of my reliance on this notion, I feel obliged to pause briefly and say a word or two about it. My concern is not to set out a full-scale theory of information, but to say enough to establish that my use of the term is felicitous and not, as one might otherwise suspect, ill-advised.[1]

What, then, *is* information? More to the point, what is it that psychologists (and nowadays philosophers) mean to be saying when they speak of perceivers *picking up* information or of brains (or computing machines) *processing* information? What is it that is picked up and processed? How, if at all, is the notion of information connected to the notion of *meaning?* How is the *possessing* of information by an intelligent creature related to that creature's holding *beliefs?* Does information exist independently of creatures for whom it is informative? Or is something only information *for* some intelligent creature or other?

It might be supposed that these questions are idle. On the one hand, the character of information is something that must, it

---

1. A detailed and sophisticated theory of information may be found in Dretske, 1981. Although the account of perception endorsed by Dretske is in many ways at odds with that presented here, a substantial portion of what Dretske says about the concept of information seems both correct and consistent with my view. The discussion below owes much to the first two chapters of Dretske's book.

seems, be ascertained *empirically*. On the other hand, we possess already a perfectly straightforward theory of information, a branch of applied mathematics (see e.g., Shannon and Weaver, 1949). What is to be gained by muddying the water with further conceptual speculations?

First, I am concerned for the moment with the notion, the *concept*, of information as I wish to employ it in discussing perception, and as I believe it to be employed in familiar psychological accounts of intelligent behavior. To discuss such matters is to engage in what may, without stretching the point, be regarded as conceptual inquiry. It may be that such investigations are distinguishable from empirical inquiry only pragmatically. So be it. My concern is to illuminate what it is that theorists seem to have in mind when they talk about information and to connect this to my use of the term. In doing this, one does not say all that can be said on the topic; one leaves out much that is of interest. But one does not, on that account, say nothing at all.

Second, I am well aware that there exists a mathematical theory of communication, a theory that incorporates a specification of the notion of information. Further, it is obvious that there are connections between what communication theorists say about information and what psychologists, for example, say about it. Nevertheless, the mathematical theory is concerned for the most part with quantitative matters: *how much* information may be contained in a given signal, the *average amount* of information conveyed via a given "channel," *signal-to-noise ratios*, and the like. One can say a great deal about such things without doing much to clarify the *concept* of information, just as one can learn in detail how to *measure* a particular substance without coming to know anything very interesting about what it is one is measuring.

In what follows I shall focus on the notion of informational *content*, as distinct from the more technical matter of information quantity. This is not because I regard these concerns as unrelated. I do, nonetheless, regard them as *different* concerns.

My aim is to make the notion of information as I wish to use it conceptually respectable.

I shall focus here on three ways in which information may be regarded. There is, in the first place, the notion of something's *being* information that something is the case, that b is F, for example. Second, there is the (related) notion of something's being information *for* some sentient creature, that b is F *for* S. These two ways of speaking about information are related in roughly the following way: something can be information *for* some sentient creature that such and such is the case only if it is (quite independently) information that such and such is the case. If X is information for S that b is F, it must be the case that X is information that b is F. This may be put by saying that information spoken of in the second manner, that is, information relativized to a perceiver, *incorporates* the conception of information spoken of in the first way, non-relativized information.

This seems not to be the case for what I shall characterize as a third means of considering information. Here, something, X, may be information for S that b is F at a time, $\pm$, without its being the case that X (just by itself) is information that b is F. These distinctions will, it is hoped, emerge naturally in the course of the discussion. In any case, I want to insist on the desirability of keeping these three ways of regarding information distinct and, in particular, to discourage the tendency to conflate the second and third ways of talking about it.

Non-Relativized Information

Consider, then, what it is for X to be information that b is F. I have in mind cases in which the level of mercury in a thermometer, for instance, provides information that the liquid in a particular beaker is a certain temperature. This will be so, I submit, whether or not anyone has any beliefs about or interest in the temperature of the liquid. It will be so even when there is no one in the vicinity to appreciate this fact. The connection between the height of the mercury column and the temperature of the liquid is a *nomological* one. It is this connection that makes the behavior of the mercury column informative, and it is this connection that makes the notion of information perfectly objective. I propose the following characterization:

I. X is information that b is F = (roughly) $X \rightarrow$ *(b is F)*, (where "$\rightarrow$" represents a *nomic dependence* of X on b's being F).

In this sense light radiation structured in a certain way may be said to carry the information that a tomato illuminated on the table in front of me is red (or perhaps that it is either red or white and illuminated under a red light—see below). This will be so whether or not I know or care anything at all about redness, whether or not I am blindfolded or color-blind. Presumably light radiation carries much information to which human beings are insensitive, though other creatures may be better equipped to detect it.

It may be thought that cases of the sort alluded to here conceal a fatal difficulty inherent in this conception of information. Thus, it seems obvious that virtually any instance of information will be in many ways "ambiguous." Ambient light radiation will be structured in a particular, definite way under an endless variety of different (and incompatible) conditions. In the present case, a given optic array carries information for there being a reddish tomato illuminated under a white light, *or* for there being a reddish wax sphere illuminated under white light, *or* for the presence of a white tomato illuminated under a reddish light, *and so on*. The best we can ever do, it seems, is to say that X is information that b is F, or G, or H, or . . . .

I doubt, however, that this complication represents a genuine defect in the account I am setting out. First, it seems right to say that collections of disjuncts of the sort mentioned form a class of perceptual equivalents: a red tomato (in normal light) *looks* like an imitation tomato or a white tomato under special illumination. An appreciation of facts of this sort is required if one is ever to come to grips with the notion of perceptual error (a topic that will be taken up in more detail in the next chapter).

Second, ambiguities of the sort envisaged are, in practice, highly constrained, something one is likely to lose sight of so long as one focuses only on imaginary or highly artificial examples. In the ordinary case, not only is a tomato visible to a perceiver, but much else as well: the surface on which the tomato is resting, its surroundings, the perceiver's own body, and often even the source of illumination. The ambient optic array, then, taken as a whole (and especially if one considers it over time), is very much more specific than one's contrived examples are likely to suggest. Perhaps such arrays are never *utterly* specific, but this is only to admit what we have all along recognized, that things are not always as they seem to be.

It should, in any event, be obvious that information in the sense just described has no direct connection with the notion of *meaning*, insofar as one takes meaning to pertain to *semantic content*. We do of course say that smoke "means" fire, that dark clouds "mean" rain. Information as I have characterized it above has, of course, *everything* to do with the category of non-semantic, *natural* meaning. Smoke, in this sense, means fire just in virtue of the fact that it is connected to fire nomologically, in virtue, that is, of the fact that it provides information for the presence of fire. If one reserves talk about meaning, however, for what has been called non-natural meaning, instances of genuine semantic content, then information as I have thus far characterized it is an independent notion.

Relativized Information

Now consider what it is for information to be information *for* some sentient creature.

II. X is information that b is F for $S =$ (roughly)
   (a) X is information that b is F;
   (b) X causes S to believe of b that it is F.

I shall want to modify this characterization slightly, but before doing so it will be useful to illustrate what I have in mind.

Imagine that structured light radiation of the sort mentioned above (that is, radiation bearing information that a certain thing is red) impinges on S's retina and in this way causes S to believe that something he sees is red. Here we may say that the information borne by the light radiation is information *for S* that a certain thing is red. This may not be true of T who, let us suppose, is color-blind, hence insensitive to radiation of *this* sort. Information may exist and be available, yet fail to be information *for* a particular creature because the latter lacks the requisite detectors. Thus, something may be information for a honeybee or a pigeon and not for a human being, even a normal human being. I have suggested already, and shall discuss in more detail below, the apparent fact that there are, as well, other ways of being "blind" to information, ways that seem to involve *cognitive* as distinct from biological deficiencies.

All of us, at any one time, are immersed in an apparently limitless sea of information. Some of this we fail to detect because we lack the requisite sensitivity. Even if we were suitably equipped, however, there is far more available to us than we could reasonably hope to pick up. On any particular occasion we ignore, "filter out," or neglect much that on other occasions we might focus on or in some way register. I tread on your cat not because I am blind to it, but because I did not *notice* it; I fail to spot an assailant, not because he is invisible, but because I am looking in the opposite direction. Consider the case, however, in which you and I look at the very same thing yet, apparently, pick up different information about it. You and I watch the antics of a bird in the garden. My impression is of a smallish brown bird flying about distractedly. You, in contrast, see a crested warbler stalking worms. It is tempting to say in such cases that although you and I are in possession of the same information, you are able to *make more of it* than I. This way of putting it is, I wish to suggest, in an important respect, misleading. It blurs a useful distinction, namely that between observation and inference.

Consider the information, more particularly the visual information available to both of us as we gaze at the bird. Imagine that at least a portion of this is information that a crested warbler is at a certain place in the garden. Embedded in this information, however, is information that there is a brown bird in the garden, that there is a bird in the garden, that something brown is in the garden. All this and much more besides may be included in the information that there is a crested warbler in the garden in virtue of the fact that the former, as we should say, *less specific* information is definitionally incorporated in or entailed by the latter. Anything that is information that something is a crested warbler is *thereby* information that it is a bird, that it is brown, and that it is many other things as well. We may put this by saying that information is *transitive:* if X is information that b is F, and if b's being F entails that b is G, then X is information that b is G.[2]

Further, given the fact that the connection between information and the states of affairs for which it is information is a nomic one, we may suppose that this transitivity will hold as well for nomic relations. If streaks of a certain sort in a cloud chamber are caused by (and only by) alpha particles passing through the chamber, then whatever is information for the presence of such a streak is thereby information for the passage of an alpha particle through the chamber: if X is information that b is F, and if b's being F nomically requires that c is G, then X is information that c is G.

It should perhaps be mentioned that this sort of transitivity does not hold for simple, non-nomic generalizations. Even if everything that is F is also G, it does not follow that if X is information that b is F, it is, on that account, information that b is G. If every crested warbler in the garden has eaten exactly one

---

2. It is crucial to note that if X is information that b is F for S, and if b's being G is "embedded in" b's being F (so that X is information that b is G), it does not follow that X is information that b is G for S. Information is, in this sense, "intensional."

grub, it does not follow that if X is information that b is a crested warbler, X is (thereby) information that b has eaten exactly one grub.[3]

Returning now to the case in which you and I are presented with the very same bit of visual information, namely information that there is a crested warbler in the garden, what are we to make of the differences in what I have loosely described as our respective *impressions?* Evidently, the same information is available to both of us, yet we register it differently, acquire different beliefs about the scene in the garden. Let us call the information that b is a crested warbler, W. We have noted that W is, as well, information that b is brown, that b is a bird, and so on.

There is, it appears, some feature with respect to which you and I differ, a feature that enables you to be caused by W to believe that b is a crested warbler, whereas W causes me to believe only that b is a brown bird. If we suppose that you and I are both visually normal, we shall, it seems, have to say that the distinction between us is, in some sense or other, *cognitive.* We may say that you have a concept that I lack, namely the concept of crested-warbler-hood. Or, if one disdains talk about concepts, one may say that you and I differ with respect to our background beliefs: you have certain beliefs about crested warblers, for instance, that I evidently lack. In any case, it appears that for me to acquire the capacity to glean from W what you do, I shall have to acquire a capacity (roughly) to tell crested warblers from other sorts of bird. This capacity is, in some fairly obvious sense, an intellectual or cognitive one.

In the case I have been discussing, one may say that whereas W is information *for me* (only) that b is a brown bird, W is information *for you* that b is a crested warbler. That b is a crested warbler is "contained in" W. That b is a bird is contained in W as well—in virtue of the fact that crested warblers are brown birds. The information available to us is the same; we differ,

3. These points are discussed more elegantly and in more detail in Dretske, 1981; see esp. pp. 71 ff.

however, with respect to our *appreciation* of (or capacity to appreciate) that information. In general, then, X may be information for S that b is F, while, for T, X is information that b is G. X is the same for both S and T, but the beliefs caused in them (by X) will be different (owing, I have suggested, to cognitive differences in S and T).

It is important to recognize that nothing I have said here provides support for the sort of perceptual relativism favored by some theorists. I do not wish to say that S and T, for instance, "live in different worlds." On the contrary, they inhabit the same world, it is just that they have different beliefs about it. I believe that there is a brown bird in the garden, you believe that the garden contains a crested warbler. Here, as we shall see presently, one may say that we *see different things* (you, a crested warbler, I, merely a brown bird). This need not mean, however, that we are aware of distinct "perceptual objects" or that our perceptions are in any special way "incommensurable." It is just that you, because you know rather more than I do about birds, are able to see *more* than I can see.

Information Further Relativized

Thus far I have distinguished two rather different ways of speaking about information. In the first place, one may talk of information available to perceivers. Such information is a perfectly objective and independent feature of the world. It may be embodied in "optic arrays," wave-trains, or tree rings. One can, in addition, speak of what is or might be information *for* a perceiver. This involves a determination of the sorts of belief that can be caused in a perceiver as a result of his perceptual encounter with a particular informational array. These beliefs are constrained, on the one hand, by assorted biological characteristics of a creature's sensory endowment and by various attentional factors. On the other hand, they are constrained, as well, by intellectual, cognitive features of the perceiver.

There is, in any case, a third, perhaps derivative sense in which we may speak of something's being information for a creature. Imagine a hallway along which there are three doors, two of which open into empty rooms, while the third opens into a room containing a prize. *S* is given a chance to win the prize by selecting one of the doors and opening it. He chooses door *A*, opens it, and discovers an empty room. Suppose now that *T* is brought forward and given the same opportunity. He knows that there is a prize behind one of the doors, but he does not know that that *S* has already established that the prize is not behind door *A*. *T* chooses door *B* and opens it, but discovers no prize. Here *T*'s opening *B* provides *S* with more information than it provides *T*. On observing *T*'s choice, *S* learns that the prize lies behind door *C*; *T* learns only that the prize lies behind *either A* or *C*.

In this case something is information for *S* in a way that it is not for *T*. Further, the situation differs from that involving the crested warbler discussed earlier, for it seems not to be the case that the information that the prize lies behind door *C* is related either logically or nomically to the information available to both *S* and *T*, namely the information that the prize is not behind door *B*. The latter is related to the former only via an inferential link with information acquired earlier by *S*, the information that the prize is not behind *A* (see Dretske, 1981, pp. 78 ff.).

We may characterize this third manner of talking about information as follows:

III. *X* is information *at t* for *S* that *b* is *F* = (roughly) at *t*
(a) *S* knows (or at any rate believes truly and justifiably) that *c* is *G*;
(b) *X* is information that *d* is *H*;
(c) *X* causes *S* to believe that *d* is *H*;
(d) "*d* is *H*" and "*c* is *G*" entail (or perhaps "nomically warrant") "*b* is *F*";
(e) *X*, together with *S*'s belief that *c* is *G*, causes *S* to believe that *b* is *F*

The idea expressed in this characterization is rather less complicated than it sounds. The point is simply that the information that S acquires in watching T open the second door *taken with* information previously acquired by S (that the prize is not behind the first door) provides him with the information that the prize lies behind the third door.

It is not, I think, important in cases of this sort that S engage in any sort of reflection or conscious inference. He need not, for example, deduce anything (although *we* may wish to describe the relations holding among S's beliefs as deductive relations). The crucial point is that one person may be privy to information not available to another person. When additional information is made available, this, together with the previously acquired information, "adds up" to the information, for instance, that there is a prize behind door C. In such cases persons differ with respect to their access to information. Differences of this sort are neither biological nor cognitive: T cannot, in the case described, discover what S can, but this is not because T is in some way blind or because he lacks some concept possessed by S. It is simply that S has seen *more* than T.

It is tempting to regard what I have described as the second and third "senses" of information as, at bottom, the same. This would, I think, be a mistake. Cases in which information is passed over because of a cognitive deficit (not to mention those in which a biological limitation is involved) must be distinguished from those in which the deficit is itself purely informational. One may, of course, quibble with the labels I have used here. Thus one may feel that both sorts of deficit are in some measure cognitive. There is nothing wrong with saying this so long as one then distinguishes different sorts of *cognitive* deficit.

Before summarizing these somewhat sketchy remarks on the concept of information, I must add two caveats. First, the causal relation holding between information (in the world) and beliefs produced by that information (information "in the head") must be *appropriate*. Thus, for example, if light reflected from a tomato triggers a switch that releases a stone that falls on S's head and causes *S* to believe that there is a tomato on the table, we should deny that *S*'s belief was caused "in the right way." Considerations of this sort are important for accounts of perception that, like mine, characterize perceiving in terms of information pick-up. The difficulties associated with attempts to distinguish standard from non-standard, "wayward" causal chains are notorious, and I shall not attempt to cope with them here (though see chapter VI, below). This, however, seems not to be a special problem for the view I wish to defend, but one that is perfectly general, one that attaches to any epistemological theory that relies, as this account does, on the presence of causal connections.

Second, I have said that information may cause *beliefs*. One may wish to employ some expression other than "belief" here, and I have no objection so long as it is understood that the new expression does what I take beliefs to do. Thus, beliefs are *cognitive* states; they may be characterized *propositionally*. Further, beliefs play a certain epistemological role, namely that of bestowing *warrant* on other beliefs. One might argue that in picking up information, perceivers are caused to be in certain non-cognitive states, and that it is these states that produce beliefs. Again, I have no objection to such a doctrine, so long as it is stipulated that the picking-up of information includes *both* components: if the internal causal connection is broken and no belief (or belieflike cognitive state) is produced, then it would be incorrect to say that information has been picked up or that anything has been perceived.[4]

Now to summarize. I have suggested that there are (at least) three usefully distinct ways of talking about information. First, we may speak of information "in the world," that is to say, informational properties of physical stimuli. Second, we may speak about what may or may not be information *for* a particular observer. Something may be information in the first

---

4. Although it may be correct to describe such cases as ones in which information is *transmitted*, that is, transported (via light radiation, for instance) from one place to another.

sense but not in the second if the observer lacks a particular sort of sensitivity or if he lacks a particular concept or cognitive skill. One may be blind—physiologically or cognitively—to certain types, or varieties, or ranges of information. Note that if something is information in the second sense, if it is information for someone, it must be information in the first sense as well. It must be information, as it were, *simpliciter*. Third, on a given occasion, something may be information (that such and such) for one person and not for another because the one, but not the other, has access to additional, pertinent information. I have recommended that we avoid conflating the latter two senses of information.

Much more could be said about these matters, but perhaps enough has been said already to enable one to employ the notion of information with a reasonably clear conscience—without giving the impression that one is merely trading on the special aura of a modern-day buzz-word. This is not to say that a term like "information" cannot be put to illegitimate or unscrupulous use, that it is never employed to paper over a variety of sins. I wish only to establish that my use is innocent, straightforward, and even innocuous.

IV
SEEING AND BELIEVING

Sensation and Cognition

In the preceding chapters I have wanted to suggest a number of respects in which it seems appropriate to regard perception as fundamentally cognitive. In putting the matter this way, I do not wish to deny that perception may incorporate non-cognitive or sensational components as well. Rather I have wanted to indicate a sense in which such components are inessential, even if familiar, accompaniments of ordinary perceivings. That this may be so is one aspect of the view that perception is essentially cognitive: it is cognitive as distinct from sensational.

A second aspect of that view pertains to the logical character of perceptual states. In holding that the latter are cognitive, I have wished to suggest both that they possess a certain intentional *content* and that they comprise elements of a perceiver's overall *doxastic state*. A perceptual state (or "percept"), then, is representational, it is *directed on* some state of affairs. It, in addition, plays an epistemic role: it is relevant to the warrant of a perceiver's beliefs about states of affairs and empirical regularities. These two features of percepts provide comfort for the view that perception is epistemic, that percepts are not merely intimately connected with or related to beliefs, but that they *are* a sort of belief: seeing *is* believing (see Pitcher, 1971).

Such a view seems to me right, but I doubt that I can conclusively prove that it is right. At best I can attempt to show that much of what we know about perception nicely fits the cognitive, belief-based model, and that certain reservations one might have concerning the aptness of such a model are less serious than they at first glance appear to be.

Seeing as "Concept-Laden"

What is it for two observers to see the same thing?

> ... [C]onsider Johannes Kepler: imagine him on a hill watching the dawn. With him is Tycho Brahe. Kepler regarded the sun as fixed: it was the earth that moved. But Tycho followed Ptolemy and Aristotle in this much at least: the earth was fixed and all other celestial bodies moved around it. *Do Kepler and Tycho see the same thing in the east at dawn?* (Hanson, 1958, p. 5)

I shall call this question, in honor of its author, the Hanson question. Hanson and a host of like-minded theorists have argued at length that no, Kepler and Tycho do not see the same thing. This stems, they contend, from the fact that seeing is not pure but "theory-laden," that all perception is imbued with concepts, that all seeing is "seeing as," that there is no such thing as "uncolored" or "direct" observation.

One is, in this way, invited to embrace something like the following picture. What one sees is invariably *tinted,* filtered, and interpreted by one's "conceptual framework." Direct contact with the world is a myth, one fostered by epistemologists bent on evading relativism (and thus side-stepping skepticism— or worse, solipsism). The content of one's awareness of things in the world is, in reality, a conceptually structured *representation* of those things. What one sees is determined by (i) what there is to be seen, and (ii) the gridwork of concepts *through* which one glimpses what is there. If the conceptual frameworks of two persons differ dramatically, they will see different things. And if the world consists of what one sees (hears, feels, and so on), then they will inhabit different worlds as well.[1]

Proponents of this picture have sometimes suggested that its only alternatives are, on the one hand, naive realism, and, on the

---

1. This is at least *close* to the view often associated with Kuhn, 1962.

other hand, some strain of phenomenalism, views that construe perceiving as an act of bare, unconceptualized awareness. Against this it has been argued that direct, concept-free awareness is a fiction, a philosophical artifact. To be aware of anything at all is to be aware of it *as* something or other, and this involves being aware of it as exemplifying some concept or other.

I shall argue that this line of reasoning is off the mark, that it is in fact an *ignoratio elenchi*. I have contended already that the fact (if it is such) that perception incorporates a cognitive or conceptual element goes no way at all toward showing that we are not "directly" aware of what we perceive. I shall, in the next few pages, say more on this topic. I shall say more, as well, about my suggestion that perception is essentially cognitive, that seeing is, in an important sense, believing.

"Epistemic" and "Non-Epistemic" Seeing

There has been considerable discussion in recent years of the extent to which perception involves beliefs, the extent to which seeing, for example, is *epistemic*.[2] It has been argued by some that, although belief-acquisition is a regular and familiar concomitant of perception, it is not a necessary one: some perceiving is *non*-epistemic. I shall refer to those inclined to such a view as "non-epistemic theorists," and distinguish them from those who wish to say that perceiving is, inevitably, believing.

Non-epistemic theorists may hold different views about the relation between non-epistemic and epistemic perceivings. It is possible, for example, to regard each sort as independent of the other. In contrast, one may regard epistemic seeings, hearings, and the like as, in some sense, basic, and imagine non-epistemic awareness to be in one way or another derivative. The most

---

2. The following are representative: Armstrong, 1973; Close, 1976, 1980; Dretske, 1969, 1981; Hamlyn, 1978; Pappas, 1976; Pitcher, 1971; Sibley, 1971.

common account, however, has it that non-epistemic perceiving
is fundamental, that every case of epistemic seeing or hearing
includes a non-epistemic, purely sensational component. Those
who regard perception as two-tiered—at one one level is the
having of sensations, a primitive, non-epistemic form of awareness, and, on a second level, the cognitive parsing of these
sensations to yield a belief or judgment, an epistemic perception—would qualify as members of this camp.

I wish to contend that there are a variety of reasons to
suppose that perceiving is *always* a matter of belief-acquisition,
hence to throw my lot in with the epistemic theorists. The
reasons I shall adduce in support of this contention are, in some
respects, different from those ordinarily cited. My view is
motivated not merely by familiar epistemological concerns but
by an interest, as well, in what may be called the theory of
intelligent behavior. I shall assume without argument that such
a theory would provide explanations of intelligent behavior
framed largely in terms of beliefs, wants, intentions, and the
like. It will be supposed, further, that beliefs and wants are best
regarded as states of the creatures possessing them, that they are
causally tied at one end to goings-on in the world, and at the
other end to responses of creatures to those goings-on. I shall
return to these topics in chapters VII and VIII.

Seeing Without Believing

In keeping with my earlier decision to concentrate on vision, I
shall focus in what follows on cases in which seeing is alleged to
occur in the absence of belief. My hope is that the way has been
paved already for the extension of conclusions about one sensory
modality to other modalities.

As a preliminary, it ought to be noted that a non-epistemic
theorist need not be committed to the view that all cases of non-
epistemic perception occur without the accompaniment of beliefs. The idea, rather, is that any beliefs that do occur are
inessential to such perceivings (see Dretske, 1969, pp. 40 ff.).

Indeed, one of the usual aims of non-epistemic theories is to account for the derivation of beliefs from perceptual states and occurrences that are not themselves beliefs. Hence it is no criticism of such a view to point out that it is highly likely (indeed that it is certain) that *S*'s perceptually apprehending something will *lead S* to form certain beliefs.[3]

I shall not spend time going over individually the scores of examples that have been offered as instances of non-epistemic seeing. Others have done that already (see e.g., Close, 1976, 1980). I wish instead to take up briefly three *sorts* of case that seem to me to be representative.

Case 1. S looks at a shelf containing 143 books, sees them all, yet does not come to believe that the shelf holds this number of books.[4]

The phenomenon here is a familiar one. An observer sees a room full of people, a flower with many petals, or a lot full of parked automobiles. In each case there is some definite number of items—people, petals, automobiles—visible to the observer. The latter, however, does not (or, certainly, need not) form any beliefs at all about the number of things seen. If there are beliefs, these will typically be beliefs to the effect that *many* or *a large number* of things were seen. Thus, it seems true, in the example above, that *S* sees 143 books, not true that *S* believes that he sees (or has seen) this number of books, hence it must be that *S* sees this number of books *non-epistemically*.

The crucial feature of examples of this sort is not that they involve large numbers of objects, but that they show that there are cases in which a state of affairs seen may have properties— even ordinary, visible properties—that a perceiver does not detect or recognize the state of affairs to possess. I may see a Tasmanian devil and not know (or believe) that this is what I

3. In the same way, an epistemic theorist may not wish to deny that sensations invariably *accompany* the acquisition of perceptual beliefs, only that these sensational components are essential.

4. This example was supplied by Fred Dretske.

am seeing, although my companion, S, is perfectly aware that
this is what we have seen. Later, S may report that I have seen a
Tasmanian devil without my knowing that this is what I have
seen. My beliefs, should I care to air them, are only that I have
seen a woolly, badgerlike creature disappearing into a burrow.
Here it would be said that I have seen a Tasmanian devil non-
epistemically (though, presumably, I have seen—epistemically—a woolly, badgerlike creature).

In such cases it seems correct to say that (i) S sees an x that is
F; (ii) S does not believe that x is F (or that he sees an x that is
F). What is less obvious, however, is the claim that S's seeing is
non-epistemic. I shall argue presently that S sees *something*
epistemically and that this fact, together with the fact that what
S sees may be described in many different ways, accounts for
our willingness to accept (i) and (ii). It is not that there are two
sorts of seeing, an epistemic and a non-epistemic sort. Rather
there are two points of view from which one may characterize
what S sees. We may say if we like that perceptual verbs have
both epistemic and non-epistemic uses, but it is at the very least
misleading to put this in the form of a claim about kinds of perception.

It ought, perhaps, to be pointed out that the identification of
instances of putative non-epistemic perceivings may be, in a
certain way, parasitic on the prior identification of epistemic
perceivings. Thus, what will be allowed to count as a case in
which S sees (non-epistemically) 143 books? It is not enough
that S's eyes be open and that the books be in S's field of view. S
may be blind, or hallucinating, or distracted, or in some other
way cut off from the scene before him. So long as S sincerely denies having noticed the books, there is no obvious way to rule
out such possibilities and, in consequence, no guarantee that S
has seen the books in *any* sense.

What is required, apparently, is that S see *something*
epistemically, and that this something bear an appropriate
relation (one of identity, perhaps, or some mereological relation)
to the thing seen non-epistemically. S sees (epistemically) a

collection of books, for instance, and this collection consists of 143 members, hence S sees (non-epistemically) 143 books. S sees (epistemically) T, and T is, although S has no notion of it, a Nobel Prize nominee. S, then, presumably sees (non-epistemically) a Nobel Prize nominee.[5]

In general, then, it appears that in order for one to describe S as seeing x non-epistemically, one must suppose that S sees something, y, epistemically, and that y bears an appropriate relation, R, to x. I shall not attempt here to spell out the character of R that is a task befalling the non-epistemic theorist. In any event, we shall discover presently that there are rather better ways of dealing with cases of this sort.

Case 2. Some object, x, looks red to S, but S knows that it is not red, hence does not believe or come to believe that x is red.

It is not uncommon, certainly, for things to appear other than they are. Once we discover this fact and once we learn something about the circumstances that are likely to affect the appearance of things, we may come to "make allowances" for such circumstances. One learns that fluorescent lighting is not to be trusted when one is buying a new coat, that the shirt that appears white on one's television screen may in fact be blue.

Such examples show, I think, that "x looks F to S" does not entail "S believes that x is F." But this is rather a long way from establishing what the non-epistemic theorist wants to establish. In fact, if one examines such cases more carefully, they appear to cut the other way.

To see why this might be so, consider first a case in which S *is* taken in by the appearance of x; that is, x looks red to S, and S believes (wrongly) that x is red. Here, plainly, there is a belief (the belief, namely, that x is red) produced in S. One may

---

5. The situation here parallels one associated with the theory of action. When S *does* something non-intentionally, the non-intentional deed must, it seems, be related (in an appropriate way) to some intentional act performed by S. It is not that all things done are done intentionally. But if a thing is done (and not merely suffered) it must be linked in some fashion to something done intentionally.

wonder, of course, whether this belief is merely contingently associated with x's looking red to S. The fact that, on some occasions, x can look red to S without S's having the corresponding belief suggests that it must be, and thus that the having of beliefs is, in general, separable from the having of "visual experiences."

Such considerations, however, at best show only that the connection between *particular* beliefs and particular visual experiences is not a simple one. Beliefs are not acquired and maintained in isolation. The beliefs I harbor at any particular moment will affect (in a variety of ways) the beliefs I come by as I gaze about my surroundings. Thus, in the present case, if S believes the lighting to be in some way unusual, he may not come to believe that the item before him is red even though it "presents itself" to him in a way that would, in other circumstances, produce this belief.

These examples illustrate the evident fact that, given certain *background* beliefs, it is possible to take the looks of things in more than one way. But, of course, we knew this already. The beliefs one has about anything at all will play a role in determining the beliefs one will acquire when one is perceptually confronted by that thing. If I believe that a certain species of snake is poisonous and you do not, the appearance of a snake of the species in question on the path in front of us will produce in us widely different beliefs. It does not follow from this, however, that there must be a way of seeing the snake not connected with the acquisition of beliefs, let alone that this way of seeing is in some sense perceptually foundational. On the contrary, it seems evident that the capacity to take into account the *appearances* of things is anything but primitive (in either an epistemological or a genetic sense). Nor does it follow that cases in which a perceiver takes something to be other than it appears do not require beliefs essentially.

Case 3. S may see something without really "noticing" it, thus (apparently) without acquiring any beliefs whatever about it.

You and I converse all morning, yet I may fail to notice what color shirt you are wearing. I saw it, surely. Yet I find that I have no beliefs at all about its color.

Such cases in fact show not that in seeing your shirt I acquired no beliefs about it, but only that I now, at a later time, find that I have no beliefs about it. (Really this is not quite right. I may well believe that you had a shirt on, that it was not bright red, that it was not covered with sequins. Perhaps the example could be modified so as to rule out such beliefs. In any event we may simplify the discussion by considering just those cases in which I find in myself no beliefs at all about something I must surely have seen.)

One might wish to argue (as Dretske does, 1969, p. 21) that it is just implausible to suppose that one forms beliefs about all the countless things that pass before one's eyes in an ordinary day. But even if this were a consequence of the notion that seeing is believing (something that seems manifestly not the case), it is by no means obvious that such a conception *is* implausible. How we should go about counting beliefs is far from clear (see e.g., Goldman, 1970, p. 95; Vermazen, 1982). I shall, in any case, return to this matter in later chapters. For the present, one need only notice that the view being sketched here will seem implausible in this regard only if it is supposed that beliefs exist as separate, clearly individuated psychic bits. This is a supposition one need not endorse.

It would be useful at this juncture to appeal to some agreed-upon account of the phenomenon of "noticing" (or, in the parlance of psychologists, "attending"). Aside from the fact that there *are* no such agreed-upon accounts, the interests of clarity will be better served if we postpone an explicit examination of noticing until chapter V when it will be somewhat better motivated. In the absence of a worked-out theory, then, what are we to say about cases in which things apparently are seen but not (in the fullest sense) noticed? Is there room in these cases for some notion of beliefs acquired but unmarked?

First, as was suggested earlier, it is far from obvious that cases of the sort under discussion provide anything approaching clear-cut support for the non-epistemic theorist. One speaks routinely of things unnoticed as *unseen*. I doubt, however, that it is possible to dismiss the matter quite so simply (although this is a point to which I shall return presently).

Second, there may turn out to be independent grounds for supposing that in certain cases beliefs are indeed acquired, albeit "nonconsciously." In fact it appears that the most natural way of distinguishing cases of seeing-without-noticing from cases of outright failure to see requires an appeal to some account of nonconscious belief-acquisition.

Consider what happens when one drives down a busy street while, at the same time, conversing with a friend in the adjacent seat. One skillfully maneuvers one's automobile around various obstacles, slows down for pedestrians crossing in in the street ahead, signals for turns, and responds to the ebb and flow of traffic, all the while concentrating on one's conversation.

I do not know whether we should say in such cases that one does not *see* the automobiles one steers around or the pedestrians one avoids. Still, they engage one's attention, if at all, in only a minimal way: one does not notice *much* about them. Even so, one's actions quite plainly suggest that one is in some sense taking account of various complex features of the traffic through which one is driving. One's movements are not blind but intelligent, guided, appropriate. And perhaps it is not altogether misleading to regard belief as a central component of whatever it is that connects goings-on around one with actions appropriate to those goings-on. This would require that one have beliefs about which one has no obvious awareness, as well as beliefs about which one is aware—beliefs about which one has further, second-order beliefs. Whatever the difficulties with such a view, it would at least enable us to account for cases in which something is seen but not, in the most obvious sense, noticed, and to distinguish these from cases in which an encountered object is not marked at all.

Further, to return to an earlier point, cases of the sort under discussion seem not to provide the non-epistemic theorist with the sort of clear-cut paradigm he needs. Some instances, at least, of not noticing appear to be cases of not *seeing* as well. If I step on your cat and claim not to have seen (or noticed) the creature lurking in the corridor, what would be the point of insisting that I *must* have seen it, although it is possible that I simply failed to register this fact? My failure to take account of the cat's being where it was (together with my longstanding desire to avoid treading on largish sentient creatures) seems strong evidence in support of my claim not to have seen the beast. And this suggests that the distinction between seeing without really noticing and simple failure to see, should we care to make it, might best be made by describing the former case, but not the latter, as one in which a belief of some sort was acquired.

There is a final matter worth considering. It might be suggested that because one's seeing x to be F can be offered as evidence for the belief that x is F, one's seeing cannot itself be a form of belief-acquisition. If it were (so one might argue), citing what one sees in support of one's belief would have no force, certainly no *evidential* force. Evidence must, in such cases, be logically independent of that for which it provides warrant.

Here I think one must say that supporting one's belief that x is F by noting that one *saw* x to be F is, at least in some measure, a matter of making explicit the origin or cause of the belief. On the one hand, one indicates that one's belief is not based on a newspaper account, the testimony of a friend, or a hunch, but is derived from one's own perceptual commerce with the world. On the other hand, it seems in general true that beliefs brought about in this way (by looking or by listening, touching, smelling, tasting) are, more often than not, reliable. For this reason, one's claim to have seen x to be F provides others with (some) evidence that x *is* F. What seems not true in such cases is that one might first see x to be F, then, on the basis of this seeing, come to have the belief that x is F.[6]

6. I am not, of course, denying that some beliefs about what one sees are derivative. One may see that an apple is green and conclude from this that it will taste sour. I want only to suggest that it is not implausible to suppose that seeing the apple to be green is, whatever else it is, the acquisition of a belief, the belief, namely, that the apple is green.

Perceptual Experience

If one takes vision (or, more generally, perception) to be essentially the acquisition of beliefs, what is one to say about perceptual experiences? Is it merely a contingent fact that in seeing *x* to be *F* one has visual experiences of a certain sort? Might there be creatures who acquire beliefs that we should otherwise regard as perceptual, but who have no clearly identifiable perceptual *experiences* at all? What *are* perceptual experiences, anyway?

I wish to suggest in the first place that it is indeed nothing more than a contingent fact that in seeing something, for example, one has the *particular* visual experiences one does. The way in which a thing is apprehended, the character of one's perceptual experience of that thing, is surely determined to some extent by the character of one's sensory apparatus. Things may not look quite the same when one has received a blow on the head or had too much to drink. Both a honeybee and a human being may see a particular flower. We know enough about the visual system of a honeybee, however, to know that it is just enormously unlikely that the flower looks the same to the honeybee as it does to us (see von Frisch, 1971). Nor is it difficult, as we have observed already, to imagine creatures with altogether different sorts of visual receptor who are nevertheless able to make the same kinds of visual discrimination we make. In such cases the common element appears not to be a particular sort of experience but rather a particular sort of cognitive state, a belief brought about in a certain way.

In chapter I, I discussed the use of so-called "visual substitution systems," devices that apparently enable blind persons to "see with their skins." Such systems work by projecting images produced by a television camera onto the stomach or back of the person using them by means of a bank of tiny vibrating pins. It seems reasonably clear that a person equipped with such a device has a capacity to acquire what may best be described as visual beliefs about his surroundings. It can scarcely be claimed, however, that the experiences of persons making use of the device have very much in common with the visual experiences of an ordinary sighted person.

I have been speaking of perceptual experiences as though it were obvious what these were. In fact the whole notion of "experience" here is somewhat confusing (see Grice, 1962; also chapters I and VI of the present essay). When one is asked to describe one's experiences, one typically mentions features of whatever it is one has seen (heard, touched, or whatever). If by "characteristics of perceptual experiences," then, one means nothing more than "features of things perceived," it is trivially true that, whatever the nature of their visual equipment, two creatures seeing the same things must have the same (sorts of) experience.

If, in contrast, one takes "perceptual experience" to mean something like "sensation," then it is far from obvious—indeed it seems to me highly doubtful—that two creatures, differently equipped, who see (hear, feel) the same thing must have the same sorts of experience. The sensations encountered by a person armed with a visual substitution system are not at all like the sensations (if in fact it makes sense to speak of such) of an ordinary sighted person scanning the same scene. Things do not, in this sense, look the same to honeybees and people (see von Frisch, 1971).

One difficulty in using the notion of sensation to characterize whatever is meant by "perceptual experience" is that awareness of sensations seems peculiarly to exclude the perception of things external to the body (see e.g., Reid, 1764/1970; Gibson, 1966; Neisser, 1977). Perhaps one may be convinced of this by performing the experiment of pressing one's finger against the edge of a table and concentrating on "what is felt." One may, in so doing, feel the object—the table—or a sensation of pressure, but *not,* it seems, both at the same time. Awareness of the one excludes awareness of the other in something like the way in which one's awareness of one "aspect" of an ambiguous figure (a Necker cube, for instance) excludes the (simultaneous) awareness of another aspect. One's awareness can switch, certainly, but it cannot be directed both places at once.[7] In the case of a visual substitution system, as we saw, practiced subjects invariably report that at a certain point in their training they cease to be aware of vibrations on their backs and become aware instead of the objects that give rise to those vibrations (see Guarniero, 1974, for a firsthand account). This phenomenon, like the one just mentioned, is akin to the "Gestalt switch" that comes when one learns to regard an ambiguous figure in a new way. It is at least arguable that the switch *must* take place before perception can properly be said to occur. So long as one is aware only of sensations, one is aware solely of the effects of certain objects on one's receptors. The move from this to an awareness of the objects themselves involves (roughly) one's coming to appreciate these effects as information about the world, as distinct from, say, information about the state of one's receptors.

Where does all this leave the notion of perceptual experiences? It remains far from obvious what philosophers and psychologists have in mind when they appeal to such episodes, but for my part I should like to use the notion to mark the difference between the way things look to a honeybee, for example, and the way they look to me. Things, of course, may *not* look different to a honeybee. That they do is a broadly empirical hypothesis, although I think a reasonable one. We, at any rate, seem to *expect* things to appear very different to creatures that are very different from us (see Nagel, 1974; Natsoulas, 1978).

As a first approximation, then, one may characterize perceptual experiences as experiences that arise (if at all) in the process of our extracting information about our surroundings (that is, acquiring beliefs about those surroundings) by way of

7. In passing it might be noted that the Necker cube example provides some support for the notion that seeing is epistemic. Seeing the cube in one way, on the latter view, would involve taking one face of the cube as the front; seeing it differently would require taking the same face differently. If "taking" here is thought of as a form of believing, then attempting to see the cube in two ways at once would require that one set out to entertain incompatible beliefs simultaneously.

the senses.[8] To the extent that the sensory mechanisms of two creatures differ, one may suppose that their perceptual experiences differ correspondingly.

There are, admittedly, difficulties with this characterization, difficulties centering largely on what is meant in saying that experiences "arise" in the process of information-extraction, but it will serve for present purposes. It enables one to see why, for example, it is apparently a contingent fact that in seeing what we see we have the particular experiences we have: the latter are not merely a function of what is perceived but also (and crucially) of our sensory apparatus.

One can see as well why it cannot be quite right to contend that perception is nothing more than a certain sort of belief-acquisition. Perceptual beliefs must be acquired *somehow,* and it is evidently the operation of the mechanisms of acquisition that "results in" experiences (though see below). On the present view, what is essential to perception is the extraction of information about one's surroundings from available "physical stimuli" and this, although it may be accomplished by means of widely different sorts of mechanism, must be accomplished by means of some mechanism or other. The character of what one may if one likes call perceptual experiences hinges, in part, on the nature of the system employed.

Perception Without Perceptual Experience

Thus far I have argued that it is merely a contingent fact that the perceptual experiences one has in perceiving some state of affairs have the particular character they have. The suggestion was that perceptual experiences might reasonably be thought to be in some measure determined by the character of a perceiver's sensory apparatus. I doubt that such a view, even if utterly wrong, can be dismissed as idle metaphysical speculation, but I

8. I am tempted to say that perceptual experience just *is* the process of information-extraction or belief-acquisition, although I am not certain how I should go about defending such a view if pressed. These matters will be discussed further in chap. VI.

admit that it is not a simple matter to imagine a satisfactory philosophical or empirical confirmation of it. In any case, I should here like to raise briefly the question of whether perception might occur in the absence of any perceptual experiences at all.

Given the protean character of the notion of perceptual experience, of course, it is not easy to see how one might go about evaluating such a question. Further, the view under discussion—that perception is first and foremost cognitive, that it is best taken to be a matter of belief-acquisition—in no way depends on the envisaged possibility. Nevertheless, a case of perception that lacked anything obviously describable as perceptual experience would lend some comfort to this thesis—at least to the extent that many views would seem to predict that such things are impossible, whereas this one does not. It would be natural, for example, to regard such cases as ones in which the perceiver acquires the right beliefs without the usual sorts of "phenomenal" accompaniment.

At first blush this possibility seems ridiculous. What would it be *like,* one wonders, to see something and to have no experiences at all of what one is seeing? The case I shall discuss is far from conclusive. It does, nevertheless, lend itself to an interpretation under which one may be inclined to say that an agent *in some sense* sees something yet lacks any sort of relevant visual experience. The "sense" in which he sees, perhaps, is just that he acquires the right sorts of perceptual *belief.*[9]

It has long been supposed that lesions in a particular region of the visual cortex cause severe and permanent blindness in human beings. Surprisingly, monkeys with comparable lesions appear to be relatively unimpaired. L. Weiskrantz and his associates have speculated that these apparent functional disparities might be due less to genuine differences in brain operation than to the ways in which people and monkeys are tested for blindness. Typically, one *asks* a person whether he can see an

---

9. The case I shall examine is discussed in detail in L. Weiskrantz, 1977. Page numbers cited are to that paper.

object placed before him. A negative answer indicates that the object is not visible, that it is not seen. In the case of a monkey, however, one must determine visual capacities "indirectly," by designing tasks that depend in some way on the creature's acquiring the appropriate visual information. If these tasks can be executed, it is concluded that the monkey must have been able to see what it has been shown.

What is fascinating is that if similar tasks are given to human beings with cortical lesions, their performances are remarkably good, better even than those of the monkeys tested. Weiskrantz describes the performance of one such person:

> On routine clinical testing he appeared densely blind in his left field, even with intense lights, except for a small crescent of fuzzy vision in the upper peripheral part of the field. Accordingly all of our testing was in the lower quadrant. He is a very cooperative subject and we asked him to respond as we asked our monkeys to respond—by reaching out and touching a screen on which visual stimuli were projected in his blind fields. This, at first, was a very odd task—how can you reach out for something you cannot see? (p. 441)

Weiskrantz discovered that this subject's capacities were, in all respects, "remarkable." This, despite the fact that, when the results of the testing were revealed to him, he was "openly astonished."

> He thought he was just guessing. Later he described "feelings" that there might be something there, but he consistently refused to call this "seeing." We went on to require him to "guess" the orientation of lines—whether horizontal or vertical, or vertical or diagonal, and again his performance was remarkable. We also showed that he could carry out simple form discriminations, if required to guess between two alternatives such as "X" and "O," provided the stimuli were large enough. (p. 441)

The subject continued to express doubts about the task he was asked to perform, yet continued to perform remarkably well. In the end, the researchers were able even to "measure his visual

acuity in the blind field" (p. 441). Weiskrantz calls the capacity
exhibited by persons with such afflictions "blind-sight."

There are a number of things that could be said about such
performances, and I have no intention of suggesting that cases of
the sort described are unambiguous or clearly understood.
Nevertheless, the view of perception as the acquiring of beliefs
that I have been spelling out seems to provide one reasonably
straightforward interpretation. Persons with blind-sight appear
to possess a capacity to acquire perceptual beliefs while lacking
anything like the usual sorts of perceptual experience. The
absence of the latter, perhaps, accounts for the reluctance of
persons afflicted in this way to describe themselves as seeing
anything at all. (Later, in chapter V, I shall discuss the
possibility that such persons have a capacity only for first-order
perceptual beliefs; they lack the ability to acquire beliefs about
these beliefs in the usual way.)[10]

Whatever the eventual outcome of research on such phenomena, one seems obliged to distinguish cases in which "observers"
evidently pick up visual information—that is, acquire what
apparently are visual beliefs—without manifesting a normal
awareness that this is what they are doing, from cases in which
there is no information-pickup at all. One may insist that
neither case is a case of seeing on the grounds that neither
involves common sorts of visual experience. Such a move,
however, betrays a certain unwarranted confidence in the clarity
of the notion of "visual experience." Granted that a person
relying on blind-sight differs importantly from a normally
sighted person, what is there to recommend the claim that the
former cannot see at all? By distinguishing the beliefs acquired
in perception from the experiences attending their acquisition
one has a perfectly natural way of marking off these cases.

10. Earlier I remarked that perceptual processes seem "available" to consciousness in
ways that other processes, for example, digestion, are not so available. In this regard,
blind-sighters seem to lack access to their perceptions rather in the way that ordinary
people lack access to their digestive processes.

Indeed, given the present account, the phenomenon of blind-sight is almost predictable; certainly it is not entirely unexpected.[11]

Seeing and Believing

Up to this point I have spoken only about the causal properties of beliefs. My rather vague claim was that beliefs serve to establish a connection between one's surroundings and one's response to those surroundings, one's intelligent behavior. But beliefs have, in addition to causal properties, representational properties as well. Beliefs have some *content* or other, they are *about* this or that. (I leave aside for chapter VII the question of how, if at all, a belief's representational properties are related to its causal properties.) It will be instructive, in any case, to consider how the doctrine that seeing is believing is affected by this feature of beliefs. In doing so, it will, I think, be possible to see our way through the Hanson question with which we began: given that Kepler and Tycho have vastly different beliefs about what they see, do they see the same thing? It is my hunch that, even if much of what I have set out in support of the notion that seeing is believing, is in error, attention to the representational aspect of beliefs may serve both to buttress that view and to account for the intuitions underlying the idea of non-epistemic perception, most particularly those discussed earlier as instances of Case I.

Suppose, then, that for S to see x to be F is, *inter alia*, for S to acquire a belief about x.[12] In the simplest case, this would involve S's acquiring the belief that "this is an F" just by looking at x. More broadly, S's seeing x requires that S gain *some* belief about x (that it is a greenish object, perhaps, that it

11. Marcel (1982) has suggested that persons with blind-sight may well pick up *all* of the information picked up by ordinary sighted observers, despite being, in some sense, unaware of this fact. It is the "second-order" mechanism of awareness that seems impaired in such cases, rather than the first-order mechanisms of perception.
12. For a discussion of the causal role of x, see chapter VI below.

is a bush, that it is a boxwood). Now imagine some occasion in which one poses the Hanson question about *S: what* does *S* see? Does *S* see what his companion, *T,* sees? What if *S* and *T* are different in ways paralleling the differences between Kepler and Tycho?

There may be a temptation to say that there is a *sense* in which *S* and *T* see the same thing and a sense in which they do (or might) not. This suggests the view that there are (at least) two sorts of seeing, and that the question is, in consequence, ambiguous. But if there are two sorts of seeing, what are they? One (by now) familiar response is to suppose that on the one hand "seeing" denotes an experience, a bare, non-epistemic apprehension or awareness. On the other hand, "seeing" may stand for something more cognitive or judgmental (see e.g., Price, 1932; Ayer, 1940). The idea is that in the former sense, *S* and *T* do see the same thing, in the latter sense they do not. There are other, perhaps better, ways of getting at this distinction, but I have no wish to take those up at present. I should prefer to show that the distinction is quite unnecessary, that it is in fact misplaced.

Let us return to the question of what *S* sees, allowing for the moment that, in seeing something, *x, S* acquires a belief about *x.* It may be possible to concede that the phrase "what *S* sees" is indeed ambiguous, without conceding that it is ambiguous in the way suggested above, that is without supposing that there are two senses of "see" corresponding to two kinds of visual perception. When we ask what it is *S* sees, we may be asking for information about either (i) the *content* of the belief *S* has acquired in looking at *x,* or (ii) the *identity* of *x,* the object or state of affairs about which *S* has come to hold a certain belief. So long as our interest is in *S,* in deciding what he is likely to do or say, for example, we shall want to characterize the content of his belief. If, in contrast, our interest lies not in *S,* but in picking out the state of affairs at which *S* is gazing (and which presumably has given rise to his belief), there is no need to do this. It is the object, not the content, of *S*'s belief that we focus on. In such cases it would be perfectly fitting to say that S sees a boxwood or that Tycho sees a stationary sphere, even though S has no inkling that what he is looking at is a boxwood and Tycho believes that what he sees is in motion.

S, let us imagine, claims never to have seen Garbo. We point out to S that he has indeed seen Garbo, that she was the woman who, with S, took the elevator to the thirty-fifth floor of the Ritz. Here we should say that S saw Garbo but did not know it. Did S then see Garbo non-epistemically? There is no particular reason to say this. When one says that S saw Garbo but did not know it, one is characterizing not the content of S's perceptually acquired belief, his "percept," but its object. The case is in all respects parallel to the one in which we say that S believes Garbo is sad when S believes that the woman in the elevator is sad and that woman (as we know but S does not) happens to be Garbo. If we, standing with S in the elevator, come to believe that Garbo is sad, do we have the same belief as S? Our beliefs differ in their content but not in respect to the object on which they are directed. In both cases that object, as it happens, is Garbo.

In one sense, then, it is correct to say that Tycho and Kepler see the same thing when they gaze eastward at dawn, in another sense, not. In the sense in which they do, we are speaking about the object (or state of affairs) that they are perceptually confronting, and which presumably is causing them to have certain beliefs. In the sense in which they do not, we are speaking about the content of their perceptual beliefs.

If we allow that seeing always includes the acquisition of beliefs, then there is a straightforward way of explicating this ambiguity that does not embroil us in debates about different kinds of seeing. In asking about someone's belief, one may be in doubt about the object on which the belief is directed or about the internal character of the belief so directed. There are not two sorts of believing in such cases, but simply two ways of characterizing beliefs. The same may be said to hold for seeing: there are not two kinds of seeing, merely two ways of characterizing perceptually acquired beliefs. One may do so "opaquely" (that is, by reference to their representational content) or "transparently" (by reference to the states of affairs on which they are directed).

Perceptual Relativity

What follows from the fact that two people looking at the same thing may come to see it differently or, as I should prefer, come to acquire different beliefs about it? Not anything very remarkable, perhaps. Certainly it does not follow that seeing must be indirect or mediated, that what one sees has been parsed, tidied-up, filtered through a pair of "conceptual spectacles." It is true that observers will, on occasion, differ dramatically in the beliefs they acquire about things in looking at them. The beliefs one can acquire in this way will depend, as we saw in the last chapter, on many things. They will depend at the very least on one's further beliefs, in particular on one's further beliefs about the state of affairs at which one is looking. A specialist can see more than a layman, but this may just be to say that a specialist can see more of what is there to be seen.

Much of what may seem odd, or surprising, or controversial about the epistemic status of visual perception is due, I have suggested, not to special characteristics of vision, but instead to commonplace, unsurprising, uncontroversial features of beliefs. Once this point is appreciated, disagreements about the Kantian role in perception of "conceptual frameworks" and the like are bound to subside. It is not that there are no such frameworks, only that their role has been misconstrued. We have known all along that different people hold different beliefs about the world. Some of these are simply mistaken. This is common enough. It is also possible (and again unremarkable) for people to hold different *true* beliefs about one and the same state of affairs. The question "How many (true) beliefs about *x* could there be?" is unanswerable, not because correctness in such matters is agent-relative, but only because one has no idea how to go about counting such things. How many beliefs can one have about a telephone, for example, or a potato?

There is, then, no special threat of relativism here. Nor is there any particular reason to regard the question "Do *S* and *T* see the same thing when they look at a potato?" as anything more than an invitation to a state of philosophical befuddlement. If one is interested in characterizing the beliefs that *S* and *T* acquire in scanning the potato, then there is no mystery at all in supposing that they "see different things." This is a fact about their beliefs, however, not a fact about their respective visual experiences, or their sensations or their "perceptual world." (Much less is it evidence for the doctrine that their awareness of the potato is indirect, that the real potato is hidden from them behind a cognitively erected veil.)

If, in contrast, one is interested in characterizing the state of affairs that, as we should say, gives rise to *S*'s and *T*'s beliefs, one may do so without particular concern for the content of their respective psychological states. How we elect to characterize "what is seen" will depend, in general, on whether we are interested in the perceiver and what he is likely to do or say (in which case we shall want to pin down the content of his beliefs), or whether we are interested, as we often are, in some item that has attracted the perceiver's attention (in which case the belief he has acquired may be of no particular interest or concern).

It is now possible to make better sense of the question of whether seeing involves "conceptualization." Very briefly, it appears that to the extent that the having of beliefs requires the application of concepts, then this will be true of seeing as well. The following view of the relation of beliefs to concepts seems to me on the right track, although nothing I have said here depends in any way on its being true. (The role of concepts in perception is taken up in more detail in chapters V and VII, below.)

To have a belief about something (that this is an *F* or that this *x* is *F*) is, at least in part, to take something as falling under or "instancing" some concept or other (that this is an instance of

F, or that this *x* exemplifies *F).* Further, it seems perfectly natural to say that for an agent to possess a concept is for that agent to possess a capacity of some sort. To say that *S* has acquired the concept "boxwood," then, might be to say something about *S*'s capacity to distinguish boxwoods from other sorts of vegetation. I am not concerned, at present, however, to develop a theory of concepts (see below; also Armstrong, 1973; Hamlyn, 1978). I wish merely to point out that the role of concepts in perception, if indeed they have a role, may plausibly be connected to their role in the having of beliefs.

I mention these points not because they seem to me striking or remarkable, but because there has been a tendency in some quarters to move from platitudes about the "cognitive aspect of perception" to perceptual theories in which percepts are assembled, spruced up, and then inspected somewhere behind the eyes. Perhaps something like this occurs. Its occurrence does not, however, seem to be supported by the sorts of consideration advanced, say, by Hanson. These considerations, I have tried to show, are among the entirely unremarkable consequences of the fact that perceiving seems to be, whatever *else* it may be, the acquiring of beliefs.

Perceptual Error

From their vantage point in the armchair, it often seems to philosophers that perceptual errors are easily induced. Indeed, one may, in lapsing into skeptical reveries, begin to wonder how it is possible for perceivers *ever* to get things right. Once we stir ourselves and arise from the armchair, of course, as Hume drolly observed, we find it more difficult to maintain these fantasies. The perceptual errors we in fact make tend to be trivial and philosophically uninteresting. We are rarely fooled in the way it seems we ought to be.

Such points ought not, I think, to be dismissed by philosophers but, on the contrary, ought to be regarded as both significant and, in a certain way, remarkable. Theories of perception, one suspects, must be formulated so as to account for the possibility of perceptual error, but so as to account, as well, for the fact that such error is so very uncommon. I shall address this matter, although only briefly, here and again in chapter VI. Earlier I spoke of cases in which one comes to hold a false perceptual belief. This can happen for a variety of reasons. I may, for example, believe falsely that there is a crested warbler on the window sill because I am confused about what crested warblers look like. I have sought to explicate cases of this sort (which one might dub *cognitive* errors) by appealing to the notion that the beliefs one acquires in looking at, listening to, touching, or smelling features of one's environment will depend on other beliefs one happens to hold at the time. It is doubtful, however, that this maneuver will suffice to explain all instances of perceptual error. I shall, in the present section, attempt to patch up this deficiency.

Philosophers of perception have tended to focus on instances of perceptual error in which it looks (seems, appears) to a perceiver, S, that there is an F in front of him (or that the x in front of him is F) when in fact there is no F in front of S (or the x in front of him is not F). This is not the place to explore the conceptual intricacies of theories formulated to cope with such cases. I want rather to suggest that the task of accounting for such misperceivings is not obviously one belonging exclusively to the domain of philosophy.

Looked at in a certain way this pronouncement seems almost a platitude. It is a fact about perceivers that they can, and occasionally do, misperceive their surroundings. Anyone, it seems, may be taken in or tricked in a variety of ways. Similarly, perceivers can learn to "make allowances" for the looks or appearances of things and so to reduce the chance of error. One may be fooled by an oar partially immersed in water, but one need not be fooled. Surely the task of explaining such matters is largely one for the empirical investigator. Philosophical theories concerning illusion and error seem, for the most part, inappropriate here.[13]

Considered in a different light, however, these remarks may seem beside the point. Philosophical theories of perception have traditionally placed enormous emphasis on illusion and error. The fruits of these endeavors are an assortment of specialized philosophical entities (of which "sense-data" are merely the best known), items postulated to stand between ordinary physical states of affairs and our apprehension of these.

It is not clear, however, what one might hope to gain by such undertakings. The phenomena in question—various modes of perceptual illusion—are in many cases perfectly real and, significantly, perfectly familiar features of "external" states of affairs. As such, they are presumably amenable to straightforward empirical investigation and analysis. This, at any rate, is what I shall suppose. A philosophical theory of perception is in no position to dictate concerning such matters. On the contrary, I should think it a point in favor of such an account that it leave room for and accord with the requirements of empirical theory (see chapter VI, below).

In offering such an opinion, I am merely supposing what most of us, anyway, seem to believe, namely that we are, at bottom, biological (or, at any rate, physical) systems adapted to a particular natural environment. Our misperceivings are as much a function of our biological constitution and the physical environment as are our veridical perceivings. From this vaguely naturalistic point of view, theories that appeal to specialized non-physical sensa and the like are to be shunned. Entities may, from time to time, have to be postulated but not, I think, because they are required for the articulation of a *philosophical* theory.

I shall endeavor to support these claims by providing an illustration of how illusions and other sorts of error *might* be dealt with experimentally. My remarks will have, unavoidably,

---

13. I am not suggesting that there are no philosophical problems about error and illusion, only that empirical investigations of such matters may have some bearing on these problems.

an empirical cast, but they are meant only as examples, not as unlicensed armchair speculations. I wish only to demonstrate how a conception of perceiving as belief-acquisition may be harmonized with a naturalistic account of perceptual error.

First, then, I propose the following simpleminded taxonomy of perceptual error. Misperceivings may be due either to conditions attributable to the perceiver (these may be called *subjective* errors), or to conditions external to the perceiver *(objective* errors). (Cognitive stumblings of the mistaken-crested-warbler sort mentioned above may be classified as species of subjective error.)

Again, we should remind ourselves, that perceivers can, in general, learn to overcome or "allow for" the conditions that might otherwise produce errors of either sort. When this occurs, a perceiver may recognize that some perceived thing *appears* or seems to be other than it is. I shall suppose that my earlier remarks on the effects of background beliefs (in this case beliefs about the conditions under which certain objects or events are observed) on beliefs acquired in perception will at least partially account for such cases. Where there is a possibility of error, there is as well the possibility of compensatory belief. I shall, then, speak of perceptual error only, leaving it understood that most of the "errors" discussed are of a sort routinely overcome in ordinary life.

This may be regarded as excessively cavalier, as a naive dismissal of such entities or occurrences as *appearances* or *appearings*. I take it, however, that one task of a theory of perception is that of coping with such things in a reasonable way, and one way to do this is to develop a view in which they seem not to be *needed*.

I shall first say a word about *objective* perceptual error. I have in mind here cases involving mirrors, distorted rooms (as in the Ames experiments; see Ittleson, 1952), odd sorts of illumination, oars-in-water, and the like. "Illusions" belonging to this category—and we may include in their number, if we like, so-called illusions of perspective in which round coins (allegedly) appear elliptical, railroad tracks (supposedly) appear to converge at the horizon, and large buildings far away (purportedly) appear tiny—are objective in the sense of being publicly observable indeed they may be photographed or otherwise reproduced (see Austin, 1962, chap. 3). They may, it seems, be accounted for with reasonable simplicity by invoking Gibson's notion of the "optic array" introduced in chapter I. Roughly:

> ... [I]f an artificial source of stimulation conveys information equivalent to a natural source, the perceptions will be to that extent equivalent. For vision the same structure (or transformation) of an optic array, whatever its source, will always afford the same perception. The virtual object behind the mirror is also the result of this rule. (Gibson, 1966, pp. 310 ff.)

That perceivers can, on occasion, be taken in by such things, then, should hardly be thought surprising, indeed it is precisely what one should *expect*. If perception is a matter of extracting information from physical stimuli, to the extent that two stimulus arrays are indistinguishable, they may be expected to present equivalent appearances and give rise to equivalent beliefs. Nor is it any more remarkable that perceivers can learn to overcome errors produced in this way. One learns that some perceptual situations are not normal or standard, and one learns what to expect when this is so.

The matter of subjective error is only slightly more complicated. It is widely held that perception can be influenced by such things as blows to the head, fatigue, excessive alcohol consumption, and perhaps even by direct electrical stimulation of the nervous system. A variety of phenomena including double vision, the seeing of "stars," and outright hallucination can be produced by tampering in one way or another, purposefully or haphazardly, with the mechanisms of perception. In these instances it is the perceiver who is affected, not the external pattern of stimulation.

We do best, I have wished to suggest, to regard the perceiver as an agent equipped to pick up information about his surroundings by way of his senses. The various mechanisms that comprise the senses (and various *levels* of such mechanisms, from receptors to neural circuitry in the brain) have been designed to register stimulation and, ultimately, to produce reliable beliefs about the environment. Like any mechanical device, however, a perceptual mechanism is liable to failure, short-circuitry, and malfunction (see Gibson, 1966, chap. 14). When malfunction occurs, we may expect perceivers to err in the familiar ways mentioned. Thus S may "see stars" as the result of a blow on the head that causes S's perceptual system to misfire and operate in ways resembling, in some respects, the ways in which it would operate were S looking at the sky in the evening or watching an exhibition of fireworks. As in the case of objective perceptual error, it is possible to make allowances for sensory malfunctions of this sort and in this way to avoid being taken in by them. Again, this seems explicable largely by reference to the general principle of belief-acquisition cited already: the perceptual beliefs one acquires depend on beliefs already possessed.

I conclude that neither the possibility of perceptual error (whether objective or subjective), nor the possibility of perceivers overcoming such error tells against the account of perception endorsed here. Certainly it does not require that one embrace some version of sensationalism or representationalism at the expense of the realistic doctrine espoused, for example, by Gibson. I shall do more to flesh out this view in the two chapters that follow, though I recognize that my doing so will not satisfy readers who crave an exhaustive analysis of the concept of perception. My goal is not the production of such an analysis, however, but the more modest one of making sense of a variety of facts—some conceptual, some founded on ordinary observation and some derived from the empirical investigation of the senses.

V

SEEING AND CONCEIVING

Concepts and Relativism

I have argued that it is both possible and desirable to regard perception as "epistemic": to perceive is to be caused (in a certain way) to be in a certain cognitive state, one exhibiting many of the marks of belief. In chapter II, I sketched an account of the causal mechanisms involved in perception, and in chapter IV, I advanced a number of considerations favoring the doctrine that seeing is believing. I shall, in the present chapter, move on to a discussion of the character and role of "conceptualization" in perceiving.

It may be felt that by failing to provide some accounting of the sufficient conditions of perception, in speaking only of selected necessary conditions, I am leaving too many loose ends. I admit to the loose ends, but I am not convinced that their presence is harmful to the enterprise at hand. I should, in any case, prefer to leave unresolved certain points if their resolution would take us into the realm of exotic counterexamples and away from the central concerns of this essay which are rather more general. I shall, in chapter VI, attempt to draw together much of what has been said already, and set out with a certain degree of precision the resulting view of perception.

Earlier I opined that it was at least an open question as to whether perception involves, necessarily, the application of concepts. I provided a few hints on the matter, but claimed only that *if* perceiving incorporated the use of concepts, it did so because of its cognitive (belief) content. In this chapter I wish to carry the discussion further, and to suggest independent reasons for supposing that concepts might be required in the perception of anything. I shall then return to the issue of relativism and try to show that nothing I shall affirm here necessitates one's acceptance of the notion that the world one perceives is a mere construct, an artifact assembled inside one's head.

This topic has been broached already with reference to the beliefs we acquire in perceiving our surroundings. I concluded that, because perception seems to be, among other things, a matter of belief-acquisition, it is hardly surprising that different perceivers can come to see things differently, that is, come to hold different beliefs about the world. Many of these beliefs are neatly compatible, some are false. And this, surely, is unremarkable. One needs more than differences of this kind if one wishes to defend the sorts of relativistic theses that have become recently popular (theses one associates with views defended in Kuhn, 1962; and in Hanson, 1958). In any case, the latter doctrine has been advanced on slightly different grounds as well, namely, on the grounds that reality is "carved up" by our concepts, that we inhabit a shared world only to the extent that our thoughts are molded by a shared "conceptual scheme."

For philosophers, this issue is most often taken to be purely an epistemological one. In psychology, however, the epistemology that underlies conceptual relativism of this sort seems to lead naturally to the view that we all construct representations of the world inside our heads, and that it is these constructed internal representations that mediate our perception of our environment.

I protest such a move for three broad reasons. First, it seems perfectly clear that the fact that creatures' actions seem not to be determined directly by the objective character of goings-on in their vicinity, but by how these are "interpreted" by the creature, may be explained adequately on the supposition that actions are determined by the confluence of beliefs, wants, and intentions. No further story about interior world-copies needs to be told. Second, I suspect that there are serious logical difficulties with theories that postulate internal representations of the sort required. (My reservations on this point will be addressed in Part Two of this essay, below; see also Heil, 1981.) Finally, I am convinced that the sorts of consideration typically advanced in support of conceptual relativism are open to question. I shall return to this point later in the present chapter.

First, then, I shall try to show that the possession and application of concepts is indeed required in perception by discussing one attempt to get by without recourse to such things. Rather than beginning with an account of what I take concepts and "conceptual schemes" to be, then, I shall instead try to suggest something of their character by indicating what it is that theories that forgo them seem to be leaving out. My hope is that an appreciation of the nature and role of concepts will emerge naturally in the course of the discussion.

Gibson's "Non-Conceptual" Account of Perception

The theory I shall examine is one that in previous chapters was generally lauded, namely the account of perception defended by Gibson. I have discussed already various features of Gibson's doctrine, but I should now like to characterize it more systematically and generally. The exercise may prove useful not simply because it will enable one to appreciate the significance of concepts in perception but also because Gibson's theory seems, in the main, perfectly sound. Indeed, the approach to perception recommended in the preceding chapters was inspired through and through by Gibson's views. It will be part of my aim here, then, to suggest that although Gibson may be wrong about concepts, his error may be dealt with in a manner altogether consistent with the rest of his theory.

I shall continue to focus on visual perception, but I wish the conclusions drawn to be generalized, where this is possible, to the other senses. This emphasis is particularly appropriate in the present context. In recent years Gibson has concentrated more and more on vision while insisting that many of the most interesting conclusions reached about the conditions constraining the picking up of visual information are applicable as well to distinct modalities.

Gibson is, in any case, at pains to distinguish his "information pickup" account of visual perception from what he labels "sensation-based" theories. The latter (he contends) typically begin with a specification of certain properties of the "retinal image," and attempt to explain how these are transformed, processed, and converted to yield perceptions of stable, three-dimensional scenes, objects, and events (see e.g., Gregory, 1973). The picture here is of a world presented to us in momentary bits and pieces, then patched together or "synthesized" inside our heads.

Such a view of perception, Gibson argues, comes not from empirical studies of "perceptual processes," but from a batch of unexamined epistemological assumptions of the sort advanced by certain philosophers (Locke, Berkeley, and Kant, perhaps) who take it as obvious that our perceptual contact with our surroundings is indirect, mediated by discrete, atomistic sensa. The latter, when one attends to them carefully, seem to lack many of the properties evidently possessed by objects and events in the world (various sorts of "constancy," for example, unity, three-dimensionality), hence these must be *added* (imposed, inferred) by various mental operations. On such a view, the task befalling the perceptual psychologist is that of describing the features of these mental operations and, presumably, relating these to particular goings-on in the nervous system.[1]

It has been noted already that Gibson's account of vision embodies a rejection of sensation-based theories and their underlying epistemology. Visual perception begins, according to

1. I shall leave aside the question of whether such a view is in fact implied by the doctrines of Locke, Berkeley, and Kant. It is odd, certainly, to move from epistemological analysis directly to psychological theorizing about allegedly empirical processes. Whether such a move is legitimate (probably not), and whether it is envisioned by the philosophers in question (this is not altogether clear), it does seem to be the case that something like it has operated in the theorizing of psychologists of perception (see below, chapter X).

Gibson, not with retinal images or sensa, but with the pattern of ambient light reflected from the surfaces of objects—the "optic array":

> The complex structural properties of this *optic array* are determined by the actual nature and position of the objects. This structure *specifies* those objects; the information about them is in the light. When the observer or an object moves, certain higher-order characteristics of the optic array remain invariant while others change, and these invariants over time specify the layout of the environment still more precisely. The observer perceives simply by "picking up" these invariancies. He may have to search for information, but he need not process it because it is all in the light already. (Neisser, 1976, pp. 18 ff.; see also Neisser, 1977.)

Our perceptual systems have evolved to pick up and "resonate to" certain higher-order "invariants" in the array that "specify" sorts of object and event. What we *perceive*, however, are not "invariants," but the states of affairs specified by these. Perception is in this way characterized as the extraction of information, not the construction of an interior world. The information to be extracted, in the case of vision, is in the light reflected from things and occurrences in the world, not in one's retinal image or visual cortex.

Gibson describes the epistemological stance of his view as "direct realism," and perhaps he is right in this. On his account, the role of perceptual mechanisms (whatever these may, in the end, turn out to be) is to unearth information, not to translate punctate retinal occurrences into integrated representations.

In this sense, at least, perception is thought to be unmediated and direct. There is no epistemological chasm between the objects of our awareness and the world that we inhabit. That world *is* what we perceive, *is* the object of our awareness, though this awareness is, of course, dependent upon the proper functioning of our perceptual systems. When one reaches into a cookie jar and feels about with one's fingers, what one feels (if one is lucky) are cookies, not sensations or interior cookie-constructs. To be sure, one's capacity to feel the cookies is dependent on various complicated things going right in one's fingers and in one's nervous system. But this fact should not be taken as evidence for the view that *what* one perceives is the product of neural activity, its "end result."

Gibson has steadfastly refused to find any room in this account for concepts—or for any psychological concept-analogue. He regards such things as belonging to the sensation-based tradition in which it is imagined that perception requires the supplementation of momentary and impoverished sensory "inputs" by various cognitive mechanisms. For Gibson, in contrast, no such supplementation is required; the information is already present in the light and needs only to be collected, gathered up by the perceiver.

Concepts in Perception

This, however, seems not to be be the whole story. As Gibson himself points out, the information available to a perceiver on any particular occasion is virtually infinite, yet much of it is *not* picked up. Further, two observers (Kepler and Tycho, for instance) with access to the same "ambient optic array" may differ significantly in what they are *able* to pick up. Some of these differences may be due to attentional factors *(S* notices that the figure approaching is wearing a necktie, *T,* concentrating on the figure's gait, does not), but not all of them can be explained in this way.

You may see things that I cannot see, not because your eyes are better than mine, or because you are more favorably situated, or because I am distracted, but, to put it crudely, because you *know* things of which I am ignorant. You see a crested warbler hunting worms, I see only a brown bird. The meteorologist sees a front approaching from the west, I see only a bank of dark clouds. A botanist is able, in the same way, to see much that I altogether miss. In such cases it would not (or at any rate it need not) avail me to look more closely or to focus my attention in a certain way. To see all that the meteorologist or the botanist sees I must come to know what these people know: what an approaching front *looks* like, how elms and oaks differ with respect to their appearance. To possess such knowledge is, I should say, to possess a concept.

The same point may be put in a variety of ways. If one is willing to grant, for example, that seeing is a form of belief-acquisition, then we shall want to say that the beliefs one can acquire just by looking about the world will always depend in some measure on beliefs one already possesses, what may be called "background" beliefs. A meteorologist's beliefs about the weather are more sophisticated, richer, and more highly developed than mine. A botanist's beliefs about *flora* are similarly ramified. Such people are better equipped to pick up information (that is, to acquire beliefs) about certain things than I am.

Let us suppose, then, that to possess a concept is (in part, anyway) to possess a capacity to pick up information of a certain sort, to acquire beliefs about certain things just by looking (listening, feeling, tasting, sniffing).[2] D. W. Hamlyn puts the point in the following way:

> ... [W]hen an object in a given context affects a perceptual system in such a way that information is derived about it because of the structure of stimulation, the perceiver is enabled to see the object in a certain way, *as a such and such*. It is impossible for something to see something as X unless it has some idea of what it is for something to be an X. To say this is to say that it must have in some way, and to some extent, the concept of X. (Hamlyn, 1977, p. 14)

Ulric Neisser, too, has argued that perception, even if we suppose this to be a matter of information-pickup, involves the exercise of certain conceptual or cognitive skills:

---

2. This is not intended as a general characterization of concepts. Not all concepts are of this sort, not all concepts have a perceptual application. Mathematical and logical concepts, for example, involve skills that need not, so far as I can tell, be perceptual. (See below, chapter VIII.)

... [T]he difference between a skilled and unskilled perceiver is not that the former adds anything to the stimulus but that he is able to gain more information from it: he detects features and higher-order structure to which the naive viewer is not sensitive. A new-born infant ignores information that older children and adults acquire effortlessly. (Neisser, 1976, p. 20)

Gibson has perhaps confused the fact that, once a particular concept has been acquired, its employment may be unreflective and "effortless," with the notion that apparent lack of effort implies the absence of a skillful performance (see e.g., Gibson, 1966, chap. 13).

Perception Without Conception

Gibson's contention that conception has no place in perception has been defended recently by a pair of psychologists, E. S. Reed and R. K. Jones, on the grounds that the invocation of concepts in accounts of perception leads to insoluble *philosophical* difficulties:

[I]f we have to explain the normal case of perception in terms of knowledge already had, in terms of data to be processed, or in terms of inferential processes, we are lost—for any such knowledge presupposes perception on which to base itself. If we have to infer from data on our retinal images that there is a dangerous animal, the only way in which we can know that that inference is correct is by testing it against ... a perception that there is a dangerous animal. (Reed and Jones, 1978, p. 526)

Such an argument, however, appears to conflate a pair of distinct issues.

First, it seems to require that one adopt quite gratuitously and uncritically the empiricist notion that concepts must be got by generalizing over experiences, that is, concepts are always obtained via perception. If this were so, of course, then it would indeed be wrong to argue that perceiving incorporates the application of concepts. We should have to *have* concepts in order to acquire concepts but, since all concepts must be obtained perceptually (the empiricist thesis), we should never be able to get the process off the ground. From this, we are told, it follows that perception must precede, hence be logically independent of, the employment of concepts.

Second, the argument suggests that theories that invoke concepts are thereby committed to some form of representationalism. Concepts are depicted as mechanisms designed to license inferences from (awareness of) retinal images to perceptual beliefs. This, too, is worrisome, for if it were true, we should never be in a position to test our inferences against an independent external reality: our tests would, of necessity, simply appeal to further, inferentially sanctioned perceptual beliefs (see Wittgenstein, 1953, para. 265).

It seems clear, however, that each of these lines of reasoning is muddled. The error is compounded, perhaps, when one fails to keep the two strands of argument separate. It is not obvious, for example, why it should be supposed that all concepts are, of necessity, perceptually acquired. Surely it is imaginable—even likely—that creatures are brought into the world with certain rudimentary information-acquiring skills (see e.g., Neisser, 1976, pp. 63-70). To dismiss this possibility out of hand is merely to vent a particular prejudice.

One suspects that at least some of the Gibsonian distrust of concepts is founded on a special view of what the possession of a concept amounts to, a view that one need not endorse. On such a conception, it might well seem implausible to suppose that a creature could possess a concept of X prior to its perceptually encountering an instance of X. Putting the matter this way, however, appears to invoke a bogus dichotomy of the chicken-or-egg variety. The view might be caricatured as follows: it could not be the case that all chickens come from eggs, for that would require that there were eggs before chickens, an obvious impossibility.

Aside from the fact that it may be stretching matters to regard such occurrences as impossibilities, it seems clear that one response to anyone wishing to argue about chickens in this fashion involves pointing out that it is probable that *neither* chickens nor eggs arrived on the scene in some fully developed form. Chickens evidently evolved from more primitive, chicken-like creatures, and these from still more primitive ones. It seems not outrageous, anyway, to suppose that something analogous happens in the case of conception and perception. Creatures may be born with certain rudimentary perceptual skills or aptitudes. Whether we wish to designate such skills *conceptual* may be, at the lowest levels, a matter of preference. (Do we wish to call Pleistocene proto-chickens, *chickens*?) In any case, it is not difficult to imagine these simple capacities developing into more and more complex skills, skills enabling the creature possessing them to pick up more and more of the information available, to acquire more and more complex beliefs about the world. There is, in any case, no need to imagine beasts roaming about, their heads filled with elaborate, though idle, conceptual systems waiting to be put to use when the opportunity presents itself. Skills in the picking up of information are, in all likelihood (and in common with most skills) acquired piecemeal, gradually, not all at once. They may evolve from more primitive talents, bit by bit, in the course of a creature's development.

The second assumption embodied in the quoted passage, that theories incorporating the use of concepts are thereby committed to some form of representationalism, seems equally off-target. To hold that perception involves the formation of beliefs, and to suggest that belief-formation evidently requires the application of concepts, in no way commits one to the notion that the world is not, in some important sense, "directly" perceived. The issues, it seems clear, are separate ones.

In Part Two, below, I shall advance a variety of considerations suggesting that representational theories may, in fact, be inconsistent with the notion that perception is best regarded as a species of belief-acquisition. For the moment it is enough to see that concepts need not be taken to be a form of mental scaffolding for cerebral construction projects. We attribute concepts to agents in describing the sorts of activity in which they can engage, the kinds of information they can pick up, the range of perceptual discriminations they can make, and the sorts of belief they can acquire by probing their surroundings.

Seen in this light, there is no need to be skeptical about the capacity of creatures that lack a definite language to employ concepts (though see below, chapter VIII). A concept need not be thought of as an interior word or definition, just as a belief need not be pictured as a special sort of interior sentence. This does not mean that it is a simple matter to determine what concepts to attribute to a creature that differs from us substantially. Decisions about such things require a careful and painstaking empirical investigation of the aptitudes and capacities of the creature in question.

Noticing and the Acquisition of Beliefs

Some differences in the information picked up by perceivers, then, may be accounted for by reference to cognitive or conceptual discrepancies. If you have a concept that I lack, you may be able to see more than I can see. How might one account for more humble differences in information-pickup, however, differences, for instance, in what observers *notice* about their surroundings? This topic was touched on in the previous chapter where my concern was to make a plausible case for the belief-acquisition model of perception. There it was suggested that certain apparent counterexamples to that doctrine could be dealt with if one distinguishes cases in which things are seen "in the fullest sense," from those in which things are not noticed, by reference to first- and second-order beliefs. I was inclined to link this distinction to a notion of nonconscious and conscious belief-acquisition.

Perhaps depicting matters this way is, to a certain extent, misleading. It may be that there is a continuum of cases ranging from those in which something is indisputably seen by a perceiver, to those in which a thing is in some way taken account of but not "in the fullest sense" seen (as when one makes one's way around an obstacle without "paying attention to it"), to those cases in which one utterly fails to take any account at all of a thing (and perhaps, as a result, collides with it). It is a virtue of the view at hand that it suggests a way of accommodating and making sense of such ranges or degrees of perceptual awareness.

Suppose we allow that perceiving is a matter of picking up available information, that this activity is characterizable in terms of belief-acquisition, and that it involves the application of concepts, the employment of certain cognitive skills. As an infant matures, becomes more mobile, more experienced, and more knowledgeable about its environment, it becomes increasingly adept at procuring information about that environment by means of observation. We may speak of this in terms of the infant's gaining perceptual skills or, as I should prefer, in terms of its acquiring new concepts. It seems likely, in any case, that the possession of such skills very often includes more than simply the possession of capacities to acquire beliefs of certain sorts through observation. It may include, as well, an appreciation of when and when not to exercise the skills in question.

The information that surrounds us is, we have noted, virtually limitless. Rarely is it in one's interest to pick up more than a tiny portion of all that is, at any moment, available to one. As we drive along a busy street or negotiate a crowded room, it is important that we heed certain things—obstacles in our path, for instance, things likely to interfere with or facilitate our progress. It is less important that we take note of stationary objects not in our line of travel. We *may* notice such things, of course, if they are in one way or another remarkable, if they are things of a sort in which we have a particular interest, if, that is to say, they "invite our attention."

What one notices is, we have seen, partly a function of one's concepts. A naturalist notices much about a tree that I do not; Holmes is adept at picking out clues that escape Watson. But this cannot be the whole story. There is much that we do not notice, or that we notice only very dimly, as we make our way along a city sidewalk. Yet this is not (or need not be) due to our ignorance about the urban setting. Much that we do not take note of, we simply ignore; we have, one might say, no particular *reason* to notice it.

I began by speculating that there are probably no sharp lines between cases in which things are fully attended to, cases in which they are attended to marginally, and cases in which things are simply missed altogether. Nevertheless, for diagnostic purposes it will be convenient to divide the field roughly into these three categories. In the last chapter I suggested that cases of the first two sorts—that is, cases in which one in some fashion and to some degree takes account of a state of affairs—are to be distinguished from the third sort of case by the fact that the former, but not the latter, involves the acquisition of one or more beliefs. I suggested as well that the first two sorts of case might be distinguished from one another by reference to what I labeled "nonconscious" beliefs. Now I should like to elaborate on this suggestion.

When one acquires the concept *F*, when one attains the perceptual skill enabling one to identify *F*'s, one typically learns, among other things, what *F*'s look (sound, feel, taste, smell) like. But often one learns, in addition, when it is important, or useful or appropriate to exercise this skill and when it is not. (This follows, perhaps, more or less directly from the fact that that in learning about *F*'s one learns what *F*'s are good for, how they are useful or dangerous.) If one regards perception as something passive, as the viewing, for example, of images on some analogue of an interior television screen, such a claim will seem decidedly odd. One for whom perception is passive in this way is likely to regard the failure to notice things that fall within the purview of the senses as a matter to be dealt with through the postulation of various sorts of filter or screening devices, the job of which is to remove material from the "input" before the final "processing stage."

From the point of view advanced here, however, what needs accounting for is not what one *fails* to notice but what one *does* notice. If perceiving is taken to be the skillful picking up of information, then what is not noticed (at all) is just what is not picked up. Information available to one may not be picked up either because one lacks the requisite skill or because it is, for whatever reason, not at the time taken to be in one's interest to pick it up. A significant part of what one acquires in gaining and in refining these skills is the capacity to distinguish instances in which the skill ought to be exercised from those in which its exercise would be, in one way or another, awkward or inappropriate.

If one's interest is in moving through a room, for instance, one may notice that there is a fair-sized object blocking the most direct route and, in consequence, steer an indirect course. If, in contrast, one's interest is in the aesthetic character of the room, one may notice that there is an oval table made of mahogany near its center and a green overstuffed chair along one wall. The concepts invoked and the beliefs acquired will depend—to some extent, at any rate—on motivational factors of this sort. The matter is made more complicated, perhaps, by the additional fact that one's perceptual utilities are always to some extent affected by what one encounters. Thus, the appearance of a gaping hole in the floor will, in most cases, lead to a desire to tread cautiously and, from this, to a reordering of one's attentional priorities.

It seems possible in this way to distinguish instances in which we notice states of affairs from those in which they escape us altogether (despite their being visually available to us). What about the middle category, however, that which includes cases in which one takes account of some object or event (as when one steers around it) but does not "in the fullest sense" notice it? I have suggested that when this occurs we might speak of nonconscious or first-order beliefs: information is picked up and put to use but not, as we should say, consciously. How might we make sense of this possibility?

Let us allow that the skill required for the acquisition of perceptual beliefs about F's incorporates an appreciation of when its exercise is and is not called for. Now it seems possible to make this same point about the awareness of beliefs thus acquired. That is, in exercising a certain perceptual skill, I may come to have a certain belief (call this a *basic* perceptual belief). I may, in addition, come to have beliefs about *this* belief and the circumstances under which it was acquired. On those occasions when I do not come to have a second-order belief of the latter sort, one may say that my basic perceptual belief is nonconscious. In contrast, on those occasions when I do come to have beliefs about my basic perceptual beliefs (I *monitor* them), I, in effect, recognize my having acquired certain beliefs about my surroundings. When this occurs, I may perhaps be said to be seeing "in the fullest sense." That is, I not only take account of my surroundings, but recognize as well my taking account of them.

It should be noted that the *normal* case may not be the one in which, as I have put it, one sees "in the fullest sense." Just as one may not ordinarily acquire basic perceptual beliefs without some reason for so doing, one may not come to take account of one's having acquired such beliefs in the absence of some special reason. This reverses the order of things favored by the advocate of a passive account of perception. On the latter view one is obliged to account for the *deletion* of information rather than for its selective acquisition. Theories invoking filters and similar devices seem, on the face of it, needlessly complex, though I shall not pause here to criticize them (see chapter IV, above; also Fingarette, 1969; Neisser, 1976).

There are two aspects of the view I am recommending that deserve particular attention. First, the skill involved in the picking up of information—the gaining of beliefs—is to be regarded as including not merely an appreciation of the conditions under which its exercise is appropriate but, in addition, an appreciation of the conditions under which it is useful to recognize oneself as employing the skill. Again, the latter case seems to be the special one. Much of our getting about in the world may be accomplished without our explicitly heeding or recognizing the details of our surroundings even when these have significant effects on our behavior.

Second, the view sketched here evidently allows for a regress of beliefs. If there can be second-order beliefs, beliefs about beliefs, might there not be third-order beliefs, *and so on?* I accept the notion of a regress, but deny that it is in any degree vicious. One may recognize an object and recognize that one is recognizing it *and so on.* Most of the time, of course, such activities are not pursued, although they *may* be, particularly in our more introspective, Sartrean moments. The depth to which they can be taken seems to hinge chiefly on one's patience for such things. There is no need to fear a regress, however, simply because the more basic levels of belief in no way depend on higher, less basic levels; having a belief does not seem to depend on one's recognition of the fact that one has it.

The notion that perceptual beliefs might be acquired through the exercise of a skill the possession of which includes an appreciation of those occasions on which its exercise is called for, and the further notion that beliefs about the employment of *this* skill are subject to analogous conditions, are reminiscent of the account of consciousness advanced by Herbert Fingarette in his study of self-deception (Fingarette, 1969). I have, in fact, made off with certain components of Fingarette's theory and bent them to my own ends. In so doing, I have tried to hold to the fundamental insight, namely that conscious awareness is a skillful *activity,* one that is taken up only when there is some reason for it. Reasons may be discovered in features of ourselves, our needs and interests, or in features of perceived states of affairs that make them attractive, dangerous, or seem in some other way remarkable.

I have not, of course, provided a detailed theory of the phenomenon of noticing, but merely hints of how such an account might be developed in concert with the view that perception is a mode of belief-acquisition. I want now to return to the question of the extent to which our concepts may be said to *impose* a structure on the world.

The Perceived World as a "Construct"

The notion that the perceiver's world is, in some fashion, structured in the act of perceiving is undoubtedly one of the principal underpinnings of the view that perception involves the construction and inspection of internal representations. The latter view is, at least in part, an attempt to mold a psychological theory around a particular bit of philosophical doctrine. I wish to argue that this philosophical doctrine is *philosophically* dubious, and in this way to remove at least one of the conceptual pillars on which present-day representationalism seems to rest.

It will be convenient to speak not of conceptual systems per se, but of languages. The use of language to describe states of affairs provides the clearest model we have of the activity of "conceptualizing." Further, it seems plain that there is a close connection between the capacity to employ words correctly and the possession of the corresponding concepts (those "named" by the words). To have the concept of red, perhaps, a creature need not be able to use the word "red" (or some non-English equivalent), but the possession of the ability to apply the word correctly entitles us, in most cases, to ascribe to the speaker possession of the corresponding concept. The use of language, then, may be regarded as an instance of a more general capacity to wield concepts. (The connection between language and concepts will be discussed in more detail in chapter VIII.)

In a recent book that explores the relation between the mind and the physical world, T. R. Wilkerson advances the following claim:

> . . . [W]hat really is . . . is largely a function of the way we *describe* what really is. It is grossly misleading to suppose that the world comes to us in fairly obvious pieces. It is only by describing the world that we carve it into pieces. (Wilkerson, 1974, pp. 166 ff.)

What is true for world-descriptions, seems true as well for thought. The idea is that the world, in some sense, takes on a particular form only when it is thought about or described in certain ways. Only then it is "carved up," only then does it acquire a coherent structure.

What, really, do such claims amount to? Surely it is not simply that the world cannot be *described* without the use of a descriptive medium, language (or thought about without being thought about in some particular way). That would be rather like holding that there would be nothing *called* a table unless there were the word "table," a truism with which few would wish to quibble. Yet it seems excessive to endorse the stronger thesis that saying somehow makes things so. To say—truthfully—that there is a table in the room, I must have the word, but there must, in addition, *be* a table in the room. The claim, then, seems not to concern the connection of *particular* descriptions to the world, but to concern, instead, the connection between one's *way* of talking (or thinking) and the "pieces" into which the world is "carved."

I shall not attempt to expand further on the quoted passage. I am not particularly clear which, if any, of the views I shall take up here it encompasses. I should, however, like to discuss one *natural* interpretation of that passage, and to do so without necessarily imputing that interpretation to Wilkerson.

I have in mind something that runs like this. It is naive to imagine that the world "comes" to us "pre-sliced," "ready-to-label." The divisions we make, the seams we locate in its fabric are not found but imposed. Ordinary objects and events, for example, have the boundaries they do because those are the boundaries we have (in some sense) decided on. Nothing in the nature of things forces such choices, not logically at any rate. We might have decided to draw boundaries differently, indeed there may be societies or races (on this planet or elsewhere) where this has been done. Had *we* done so, however, we should be living in a different world. Not that the world would have *changed;* for change itself is something that requires a stable background of mediating concepts and their associated boundaries. There may be, it is true, certain broad constraints on the divisions we impose. We might, for example, imagine a universe in which it would be difficult, or enormously inconvenient, or entirely pointless to employ words for what we now call events. Notice, however, that it would be misleading to put this last possibility in terms of our imagining the world as *being* different. Furthermore, we human beings may, purely as a matter of contingent fact, be constructed in such a way that certain schemes for dividing things up strike us as more natural or obvious than others. This, however, is a fact, *if* it is a fact, about us, about our modes of description, not a fact about the world we wish to describe.

For lack of a better label, I shall call this view *conventionalism*. Perhaps I have not delineated it as clearly as I might, but as anyone who has ever endeavored to discuss such doctrines is bound to discover, saying clearly what they come to is no mean task. This is perhaps due less to the circumstance that they are profoundly subtle, than that accounts of them are liable to peculiar and systematic ambiguities. This may itself be a sign of a certain underlying instability. In any case, one continual source of frustration is the difficulty of distinguishing, in language, states of affairs and *descriptions* of states of affairs. Making this distinction is manifestly easier done than said.

Nowadays conventionalism (in some form or other) pervades the air we breathe. It is accepted by many theorists as more or less obvious that the structure of our language or categories of thought determines in some interesting, non-trivial sense the structure of our world. Thomas Kuhn, to mention but one example, seems to want to defend a fairly robust form of conventionalism (see Kuhn, 1962, pp. 111, 117). I should say that, despite my attempt here to formulate the doctrine, I am not convinced that it is entirely coherent. I wish to suggest, in any case, that a certain amount of the motivation one might have for defending such a view centers on its being thought to be entailed by another, far less controversial, doctrine. The situation is complicated further by the fact that some theorists, in their eagerness to reject conventionalism, seem to feel obliged to reject as well this weaker view. I shall argue, however, that this may simply be to cast aside the basin with the bathwater.

Consider for a moment a view opposite that of conventionalism, one that I shall call, again for lack of a better label, *realism*. What there is, according to the realist, is utterly independent of our ways of thinking or talking, independent of our conceptual systems. Our beliefs about the world may change, as may our modes of speech, but the world itself is not thereby altered. Further, it is plain that there are correct and incorrect ways of describing things, not just in the obvious sense that some descriptions may be true, others false, but in the sense that in order to *be* true, a description must, as it were, *align* with the portion of the world to which it is applied. There are correct and incorrect ways of slicing up reality. It would, then, be odd perhaps, but not logically impossible, for us to discover that our *way* of talking about the world had all along been wrong.

Wittgenstein, in the *Tractatus,* seems to hold a view something like this. Consider the following passage:

Newtonian mechanics, for example, imposes a unified form on the description of the world. Let us imagine a white surface with irregular black spots on it. We then say that whatever kind of picture these make, I can always approximate as closely as I wish to the description of it by covering the surface with a sufficiently fine square mesh, and then saying of every square whether it is black or white. In this way I shall have imposed a unified form on the description of the surface. The form is optional since I could have achieved the same result by using a net with a triangular or hexagonal mesh. Possibly the use of a triangular mesh would have made the description simpler: that is to say, it might be that we could describe the surface more accurately with a coarse triangular mesh than with a fine square mesh (or conversely), and so on. The different nets correspond to different systems of describing the world. (Wittgenstein, 1921/61, 6.341)

Here the picture is fairly clear. We may choose various modes of description and these may be more or less clumsy, more or less apt. In one sense, of course, it is pointless to ask about the world independently of the conceptual structure that is fitted over it. We need a language to talk about the world because we need a language to *talk.* Nevertheless, different ways of speaking about the world are not ways of talking about different worlds, merely different ways of talking. Language embodies a system of concepts that provides something analogous to familiar coordinate systems without which we could not characterize or refer to whatever states of affairs comprise our world. But a system of coordinates does not alter the territory on which it is imposed. When we adopted a system of meridians, this changed our ways of talking about oceans, continents, and vessels at sea, but it did not thereby transform seas, continents, or vessels.

An *"Antinomy of Impure Reason"*

There is, I think, an obvious sense in which the realist must be right. Thus, it is surely true that our language "carves up" the world only in the weak sense that it is correct to say that meridians "carve up" the surface of the earth. In the style of the *Tractatus:* language can be used to depict the world only if the world has an independent structure, a definite character to *be* depicted. This much seems both clear and unobjectionable.

Rather less clear, however, is the lesson that is supposed to be drawn from this. It is sometimes thought that the world's being as it is independently of our language entails that there must be one correct (or perhaps *best)* description of that world. It is perhaps the aim of science to produce such an authoritative description. It is not obvious, however, just how the envisaged entailment is supposed to go through. Certainly it does not follow (indeed it seems to be in one way utterly inconsistent with) the line of reasoning exemplified in the passage quoted from the *Tractatus.* It may be that the belief that some such entailment holds is founded on a mistake paralleling that discussed by Kant in the first *Critique* in the course of his account of the third and fourth "Antinomies of Pure Reason" (A405/B430 ff., esp. A444/B472 ff.).

Consider the following claims:

(i) It is not the case that there is exactly one way correctly to describe the world and its contents.
(ii) What there is in the world, the way the world is, is independent of our ways of describing it.

One may, on occasion, be tempted to regard these two claims as logically connected. One might suppose, for example, that a person who advances (i) is, in doing so, committed to the denial of (ii). Similarly, one who defends (ii) may seem obliged to deny (i). It is more likely, however, that in neither case is there such a connection. This might be shown if it could plausibly be established that *both* (i) and (ii) are true. In that event, neither claim *could* entail the denial of the other; the affirmation of one of them need not commit us to any view at all concerning the other. As a matter of fact, it appears that, more often than not, theorists wishing to defend one of the claims adopt the denial of the other claim as well. They may do this for a variety of reasons, though at least on some occasions they appear to do so because they feel, perhaps vaguely, logically compelled to do so.

My suggestion is that both claims are (or certainly seem to be) perfectly true, that at least part of what realists and conventionalists want to affirm is entirely sound, although what they apparently wish to deny is false. This, it may be recalled, is roughly the vein in which Kant discusses the second set of antinomies: seemingly irreconcilable positions turn out, on examination, not to entail one another's denial. Might this be the case as well for (i) and (ii)?

I shall proceed as suggested above, namely by arguing that there are strong independent reasons for believing both (i) and (ii) to be true. If that can be established, then it will follow that neither assertion could, just by itself, entail the other's denial.

Consider, first, claim (i). Why on earth should anyone suppose it to be false? One may describe anything at all in countless ways. The object I am sitting before may be described as a desk, as a piece of furniture, as something made of metal and plastic, as a material object, as an obstacle, as a collection of molecules, and so on *ad libitum.*

What would be the point of contending that some one of these descriptions is best or privileged, that any one of them, in any sense, points more directly to what is really here before me? Of course we may, if we like, say that the desk *really is* a collection of molecules. But it really is a desk, an obstacle, a metal and plastic object, and all the rest as well. To say that the desk *really is* a collection of molecules (or to say that it *really is* anything at all) is just to say that such a description is true of it. It is not, so far as I can see, to say that it really is this *and nothing more.* The latter claim seems, on the face of it, purely gratuitous.

What is it that those who deny claim (i) mean to deny? It is not altogether clear. That it is false that I am sitting at a *desk?* Not that, surely. That it is more accurate—more *true,* perhaps—to say that the thing that I am sitting before is a collection of molecules? But why should this be so? How might one go about showing that it is so? Certainly establishing that the desk is composed of molecules would not go very far toward showing that it is not a desk.

My suspicion is that, as a matter of fact, the principal motive for wanting to deny (i) is the desire to affirm (ii) together with the tacit belief that (ii) entails the denial of (i). In the absence of independent grounds for thinking (i) to be false, however, this move is patently unsatisfactory.

Consider now assertion (ii), the claim that the world is as it is independently of our ways of talking or thinking about it. I have argued already that there is a prima facie absurdity in the denial of this claim. Again, it appears that the chief reason for anyone's wanting to deny (ii) is the conviction that (i) is true and that (i) entails the denial of (ii). If that latter belief is false, as it surely seems to be, one is left without any very good reason at all for denying (ii). Why else should anyone imagine it to be false? In what non-trivial sense *could* our way of describing or thinking about a thing make it what it is? There is, as we have seen already, the uninteresting sense in which one can "make" a certain fruit, for example, into a tangerine by calling it a tangerine. But here "making a certain fruit into a tangerine" can only mean "making it the fruit *called* a 'tangerine.' " It is true, though utterly unremarkable, that by calling a certain thing an "F," we make it a thing called "F."

The upshot seems to be that both (i) and (ii) are true, or at least our reasons for supposing them true are equally sound. It is the case both that there need not be one correct (or best) way to describe the world, *and* that the world has, for the most part, whatever properties it has independently of our modes of description. The mistake made by both conventionalists and realists lies in imagining that these claims are incompatible, that in embracing one of them, one is thereby obliged to reject the other.

Assertion (i), on examination, appears to embody a claim about language or, more generally, a claim about conceptual systems or schemes. That claim, expressed in the idiom of the *Tractatus,* boils down to the observation that there are many different coordinate systems that might be used to describe things as they are. Choice among these systems may ultimately be a pragmatic matter. It is not something determined, except perhaps in the most general ways, by the character of the world.

Assertion (ii), in contrast, merely reminds us of the fact that coordinate systems are, after all, fitted onto an independently existing reality. The system does not determine the contours of that reality, only the character of our talk about it. As in the case of Kant's third and fourth antinomies, a pair of assertions that seem, at first blush, to be in conflict, turn out, on examination, to be assertions about distinct subject matters: in the one case language, in the other, the world.

"Psychological Reality"

One is apt to lose sight of this difference because of what appears to be a general, though understandable, tendency to confuse questions about descriptions of things with questions about things described. Examples of this sort of confusion are not difficult to find. I should like to mention one in particular here for purposes of illustration. Later, in Part Two, I shall again take up these matters, although from a somewhat different perspective.

In recent years cognitive theorists have from time to time become embroiled in controversies over what has been called the "psychological reality" of various cognitive processes and structures (see e.g., Greene, 1972). The issues have been most forcefully joined in connection with linguistic rules. As it happens there are different ways of formulating the rules that "govern" the use of any particular language. This fact has led to debates about which formulations are to be preferred. Some theorists have remained content to focus on various methodological or pragmatic considerations: is one set of rules simpler, for example, or more elegant than another? Others, however, have gone on to ask whether one set of rules more adequately describes the "cognitive processes" of speakers and listeners. Such questions, of course, presuppose that the rules "governing" a language constitute descriptions of what goes on inside persons who use the language—an assumption that may strike one as dubious.

To illustrate, suppose we set out to discover what sorts of cognitive process to attribute to someone, S, who has mastered a particular natural language, L. We must begin, perhaps, by saying *what* it is that S has learned; we must, that is, begin by describing L. Here we contrive a description which, following current vogue, will consist of a set of formal rules, R, some of which "generate" an appreciable number of L sentences, others of which set out the truth conditions of these, and so on. We are then invited to conclude that S has acquired (or "internalized") R, that R is somehow embodied *inside S*.

There are perhaps many reasons why one should be wary of such ploys. For the moment, however, it need only be noticed that the reasoning underlying the quest for rules that have "psychological reality" is founded, at least in part, on an equivocation on the phrase "what S has acquired." It may be true to say that S has learned L, and it may be correct to say that R constitutes (in some sense) a description of L. But it does not follow from this that S has learned R. S has learned L, not a description of L. To confuse this point is to confuse the character of descriptions (here a newfangled sort of linguistic description) with the character of the reality described. It is to err in a way paralleling that of the conventionalist, that is, to confuse truths about descriptions with truths about things described.

This sort of confusion is, I imagine, especially pernicious in psychological theorizing where attempts are made to ascertain the character of various "symbolic processes" thought to be occurring inside the head, particularly when it is assumed that the most felicitous way to represent such processes is by modeling them on a computing machine. To set such a device to do what a person does, one must first concoct a formal description of *what is done* (this is the only sort of description that such a machine can "understand"). This description is part of what is programmed into the device; hence it does, in one obvious sense, serve to describe "what goes on inside it." But it is an enormous leap from this to the further claim that this or something "formally analogous" is what goes on inside a human being when he does whatever it is that the computing machine is programmed to simulate. (We shall return to these matters in chapter VII.)

Conceiving and Perceiving

What are the implications of all this for the view of perception I have been promoting? In the present chapter my aim has been twofold. First, I have argued that perception, taken as the acquisition of beliefs by way of the senses, incorporates a conceptual element and that it does so essentially. Second, I have tried to show that such a view does not, as it sometimes has been supposed, entail that perception is indirect, representational, or phenomenal (in some Kantian or quasi-

Kantian sense). To say that perception incorporates the application of concepts is not to say that in perceiving one imposes a form on a formless, inchoate world, or that the act of perceiving somehow colors or distorts what is perceived.

To possess a concept, I maintained, is simply to possess a capacity or skill of a certain sort, one that enables its possessor to acquire beliefs and, more generally, to entertain thoughts of a particular kind. The connection between such capacities and the ability to use a language will be explored later (in chapter VIII). For the time being one need only acknowledge that the connection, if there is one, is not obvious. I suggested, in addition, that the possession of a concept brings with it the further, though related, ability to distinguish cases in which the concept's employment was called for from those in which it is not. This led to a few heady speculations about the nature of consciousness, a phenomenon I was inclined to treat in terms of second-order beliefs.

If the possession of a concept is analyzed as the possession of an ability of a certain sort, then the claim that perception requires the application of concepts comes close to being a logical (one hesitates to say *conceptual*) truth. It becomes more interesting only when one advances the further claim that the abilities in question are employed in the extraction of information from physical stimuli, in the acquiring of beliefs by means of the senses. To complete the picture, I should have to say more about the character of the relevant psychological states and processes. In the next chapter I shall conclude my account of what it is to acquire a perceptual belief. It will then be necessary to come to some understanding of what the possession of a belief, thus acquired, amounts to. My hope is that each half of the inquiry will serve to prop up the other half and that the resulting conception will be both stable and winsome.

VI

VISUAL PERCEPTION

Perceptual States

So far I have set out what might be regarded as a collection of background conditions for an explicit account of perception. I offered a theory of the senses that tied sensing to kinds of information-bearing physical stimulation. I then advanced the view that the objects of perception—what a creature may properly be said to see, or hear, or otherwise sense—are to be determined by considering facts about the creature's sensory equipment together with facts about its conceptual repertoire. Discussion of such matters, although perhaps somewhat tedious, provides one with (at least the promise of) a principled way of connecting claims pertaining to distinct sensory modes and of relating, as well, assertions concerning creatures that differ from one another with respect either to their sensory or conceptual endowment. Unless this is done, it is difficult to see how an interesting general account of perception could get off the ground.

In the next few pages, then, I shall attempt a reasonably detailed explication of *visual* perception based on what has been discussed already. This account may, I believe, be extended to the remaining modalities (subject to those constraints discussed in chapter I), but I shall not attempt such an extension here. Further, I shall consider only cases of simple "direct" perception, cases, for example, in which we should say that Lucy sees a lemon or Henry sees a cat. Such cases instantiate the schema: "*S* sees *x* to be *F*." This insures that *F* is part of the "content" of *S*'s perception and, in light of this, it may seem that the view I wish to defend runs the risk of being, in a certain way, question-begging. I have at various times hinted at an explication of perception that is, in its essentials, neutral between cognitive and non-cognitive conceptions, yet the proposed schema seems to incorporate a definite cognitive content.

There are a number of things that might be said here. First, I am not sure that it is possible to formulate a schema of the sort required that does not in some measure reflect what mine reflects. In seeing something, a perceiver must, it seems, take account of, or be affected by, or register in *some* fashion what is seen.

Second, one might simply wish to deny that the content of F here is necessarily cognitive, although admittedly it is not obvious what a non-cognitive *content* would be. In any case, one's preference for a non-cognitive account of perception may be satisfied by simply removing the offending clause from the explication I shall produce and allowing this change to be reflected in the remaining clauses.

I shall not bother with such a project because I am convinced that perception is in fact essentially cognitive and I should like this to be captured by my account. Cases of putatively non-cognitive perception, that is, cases in which it seems true both to say that S perceives x and that S has no beliefs or thoughts of any sort in which x figures gain their plausibility from the fact that any cognitive or "intentional" state may be characterized either by reference to its content or by reference to the object or state of affairs on which it is directed. I may see a burglar yet have no beliefs at all about burglars, only beliefs about a man dashing down the street. Here my perceiving is characterized not by reference to its content but simply by reference to its object.[1] In this sense, if I see x and if x and y are identical, then

---

1. In most cases the object of a perceptual state and its cause will be identical (see the account of perceptual objects in chapter II above). The latter may have a multitude of properties of which the perceiver is unaware and, for this reason, it may be described in many ways that fail to reflect the content of his perception. One might wonder, as well, whether this content must necessarily be *propositional* or, as I have put it,

I see *y*. Far from showing that perception is non-cognitive, however, such cases seem rather to reflect a perfectly general feature of intentional states (see chapter IV, above).

I have persisted, to be sure, in describing these states as beliefs. This has seemed desirable for a variety of reasons. First, the states in question ought to be the sorts of state that can both enter into the production (hence explanation) of behavior *and* serve as justificatory epistemic *relata*. These properties are among those commonly associated with beliefs. It is beliefs, in conjunction with desires, that largely determine the course of what we should call intelligent behavior. Similarly, one's perception of one's surroundings is a crucial determinant of one's intelligent negotiation of those surroundings. Further, as we have noted already, one is, on occasion, inclined to justify beliefs about how things stand by linking these to what one has seen, heard, or felt.

Causally, then, and justificatorily, perceiving is on all fours with believing. Another notable similarity arises from the evident fact that perception, like belief, need not be fully *conscious*. One may drive through traffic while conversing with a companion and not be altogether aware of one's surroundings. In such cases one sees things, as it were, without noticing them. One steers clear of obstacles and obeys traffic signals (and, in this sense, sees them), yet fails in any more interesting way to take account of them: one *may* do so, but one need not.

Perceptual states, then, resemble beliefs on several dimensions, so much so that I have been moved to regard them as *kinds* of belief. The important thing, perhaps, is not that one agree with this terminological maneuver, but that one feel comfortable with my characterization of the intentional and

---

cognitive. To say that mental contents are propositional is just to say that they represent, and that their content mirrors that of a proposition in having a certain definite sense. They may have, in addition, further properties (phenomenal ones, perhaps, or non-phenomenal, physical ones) that are, it seems, inessential to their representational characteristics (though cf. Searle, 1980). From this point of view, the notion of an ineffable, nonpropositional mental content makes no clear sense. If this is correct, then, if one takes "percepts" to have content, one thereby takes them to be cognitive.

causal properties of perceptual states. Again, I invite the reader to substitute some other, more congenial expression for "belief" in the account I shall give if that seems, for whatever reason, preferable.

Components of Visual Perception

What, then, must be the case in order for it to be true that S sees x to be F? First, of course, x must *be* F. Unless this condition is satisfied, one has only a case of *supposed* or *presumed* perception. Given that x is F, however, it must be the case as well that S *believes* x to be F. That is, it must be the case that S is in a certain state with a certain content, a state that I have elected to call a belief.

Third, x's being F must be (part of) what causes S to believe x to be F.[2] This causal condition provides a basis for distinguishing perceptual states from states of other sorts. One may come to believe x to be F because one has *seen* x to be F, or for some other reason—perhaps one merely guesses or has a hunch, perhaps one has been told this by a friend. The causal condition insures the presence of an appropriate linking mechanism, then, but it does more than this. It introduces, as well, the right sort of "counterfactuality" into the account. Thus, if it were *not* the case that x were F, S could not *see* x to be F.

This feature provides a way of bypassing certain sorts of counterexample in which S comes to believe (truly) of x that it is F, although x's being F is, in one way or another, irrelevant to S's having this belief. One might imagine, for example, S's brain being tampered with in such a way that when he next opens his eyes the first thing he gazes on will produce in him the belief about that thing that it is F. If it should now happen that, on opening his eyes, S is confronted by x, and x is F, then it is true

---

2. Or, at any rate, part of what "causally sustains" this belief; see below. The causal role of x's being F requires, of course, that x *be* F, hence this first-mentioned condition need not be included among those finally settled on below. Indeed, the causal role of x's being F will itself be incorporated in a more complex condition to be discussed.

that x is (part of) what causes this belief in S, but it is not (or, at any rate, need not be) true that x's being F is efficacious in the right way. The same belief would have been produced in S even if x were not F.

Because of the central importance of this counterfactual element, one may be tempted to include it as an explicit (although perhaps redundant) rider on the causal condition: if x were not F, then S would not on this occasion have been brought to believe about x that it is F. Such a condition, however, is a good deal too restrictive. There are undoubtedly cases in which a visually induced belief would be held even if its object, hence its causal support, were absent. Lucy may see a lemon and, at the same time, be told by her companion, Henry, that there is a lemon present. Further, Henry may be disposed to testify to the presence of lemons (and Lucy to adopt the corresponding belief on the basis of this testimony) even when there are no lemons in the vicinity. If this were so, then it would not be true of Lucy that she would not have come to believe that a lemon is present had one failed to be present. Nevertheless, she sees a lemon.

The trick is to formulate a causal condition strong enough to be interesting without making it too narrow. Presently, it will be suggested that what is required is some notion of *sustaining* causation. It is important to recognize, however, that complications of this sort attach to causal analyses generally. Their cropping up here should occasion neither surprise nor alarm.

The inclusion of a causal requirement among those conditions seemingly necessary for cases of visual perception, obliges one, as well, to formulate an account of the envisaged causal mechanism in a way that is both suitably general and sufficiently constrained so as to rule out various sorts of "wayward" causal chain. This seems inevitably to require an appeal to some vague, unanalyzed notion of *standard causation:* we shall want to insist that S's belief (or percept) is caused by the right *sort* of mechanism, *and* that it is caused by that mechanism in the *right way*.

Imagine a case in which S is wired to a device, $D,$ a machine perhaps used to monitor neural goings-on in S's brain. On some occasion the technician charged with the operation of D places on top of the device a hot cup of coffee. The heat from the cup causes D to short-circuit and "backfire" so that a charge is sent to S's brain that causes him to have the belief about the cup of coffee that it is hot. Here S's belief is caused by the right sort of thing (the cup's being hot), but it is caused in a way that seems to rule out our saying that S in any sense *perceives* the cup to be hot.

I doubt that the difficulty here has anything to do with the fact that S's normal sensory equipment has been bypassed. I, for one, might not be reluctant to describe S as perceiving x to be F were S connected to a device of the *right sort* that produced in him the appropriate beliefs. In chapter I, considerable time was devoted to the discussion of one such device, the TVSS.

What principle, then, determines that a causal chain is, with respect to perception, "wayward"? My suggestion is that the critical link in the chain of causes is not to be located amongst the "transducers," devices that "convert" an incoming pattern of stimulation into a percept or belief, but rather in the character of that stimulation itself. Thus S's seeing x to be F depends crucially on the presence of specifically *visual* stimulation—light radiation—structured by x's being F. We may put this by saying that the causal mechanism, M, responsible for the production of S's belief includes, as an essential component, light radiation that carries information for x's being F.

We are still not out of the woods, however. Imagine S listening to T describe a sunset over the telephone. S may, in this way, come to have certain beliefs about the sunset, beliefs perhaps indistinguishable with respect to their content from those had by T as he gazes from his window. Further, the beliefs acquired by S will be traceable to the right sorts of visual stimuli, namely those responsible for T's seeing the sunset. I want to resist the temptation to rule out such cases on the grounds that S's beliefs come by way of his ears rather than through his eyes. As our discussion of the TVSS indicated, vision cannot usefully be pinned down to some anatomically distinct "channel" or neural pathway. My hunch is that the present example fails to count as a case of visual perception chiefly because an essential mediating component of the causal mechanism connecting the sunset with *S*'s beliefs about the sunset is a certain intentional state, in this case *T*'s perception of the sunset. *S*'s beliefs about the sunset are mediated by his understanding of certain meaningful utterances, by his (correct) ascription to *T* of certain (corresponding) intentional states. To the extent that *S*'s beliefs about the sunset depend on his detection and identification of such states, those beliefs cannot correctly be described as perceptual.[3]

A similar point could be made if we imagine a case in which *T* is replaced by a computing machine, one built and programmed so as to produce "descriptions" of its surroundings. So long as *S*'s beliefs about the sunset depend on his acquiring beliefs about distinct intentional states (or mechanistic analogues of such states), we cannot say that *S* sees (or otherwise perceives) the sunset.[4] And this, of course, is as it should be. We want to distinguish perception from hearsay, "direct" apprehension from knowledge at secondhand. It is not that in perceiving one may not be dependent on other people or on various devices. It is rather that the causal chain running from perceived state of affairs to perceiver cannot run *through* the intentional—more particularly, perceptual—states of others. This may perhaps be formulated as follows: the causal mechanism, *M*, that produces in *S* the belief about *x* that it is *F* does not include, as an essential component, the prior detection by *S* of some intentional

3. I am not, of course, denying that in conversing with *T,* there is much that *S* perceives. He hears, for example, *T*'s voice. His understanding of *T* depends, perhaps, on his appreciation of *T*'s communicative intentions. I am simply ruling out *S*'s perception of those states of affairs on which *T*'s beliefs are directed, insofar as *S*'s beliefs about those states of affairs are dependent on mediating beliefs about *T*'s intentional states, *T*'s beliefs or perceptions.

4. The case imagined here is one in which *S* depends on *descriptions* produced by a computing machine, sentences that *S* is obliged to interpret in a particular way. Such cases are to be distinguished from those discussed earlier, those, for example, in which *S* relies on a TVSS, a sonar device, or a weather satellite (see chaps. I and II).

state the content of which is comprised of the ascription of F to x.

One may object to the use in this formulation of the notion of "detection." "Detect" is, after all, a cognate of "perceive," hence ought not appear in what purports to be an explication of visual perception. The clause in question, however, is designed merely to rule out certain sorts of cases as instances of certain species of perceiving. It would not do, for example, to rule out *tout court* the presence of intentional states in perceptual causal chains. One wants only to exclude intentional states that play a particular role. I may be dependent on the skills of a lens grinder, hence on a variety of intentional states, if I am to see the rings of Saturn.

It is not, then, the mere presence of psychological states of a given sort in the causal chain leading from a state of affairs to the acquiring of beliefs about that state of affairs that prevents S's coming to have beliefs about the sunset from counting as an instance of perception. Rather it is the particular role played by T's intentional states in the causal sequence that connects S's beliefs about the sunset to the sunset. A moment ago I put this by saying that this causal chain could not *run through* some intentional state. S's belief about the sunset cannot depend upon his having the belief that T believes (or perceives, or whatever) certain things about the sunset.

It might be noted that S and T need not be distinct perceivers for this to be so. If S's belief about some state of affairs is dependent in the way described on another of S's beliefs, then S's being caused to have the former belief is not a case of S's perceiving that state of affairs. The distinction here is just that between S's perceiving something and S's beliefs about his perceiving something. The latter may be causally connected to a perceived state of affairs, but they are not themselves perceptions of that state of affairs.

Perhaps all this may be reformulated in the following way: the causal mechanism, M, that produces S's belief about x's being F does not incorporate as an essential component S's holding a belief about a distinct intentional state (belief, percept, or whatever) that includes x's being F in its content. The condition, put this way, allows S to have independent beliefs about x's being F ("background" beliefs, for example; see chapter IV) without this ruling out his seeing x to be F. All that is required is that these independent beliefs not play a certain role in the causal mechanism responsible for S's coming to have (or continuing to have), on this occasion, the belief about x that it is F.

This is an exceedingly murky topic, one difficult to discuss in a straightforward way. I am, in fact, not completely satisfied with the way in which I have put the matter, but it would border on the perverse for me to go into greater detail here. Whether or not I have succeeded in correctly formulating the principle, I trust that the idea behind it is, in a general way, clear. The perception of states of affairs occurs when one is caused in the right way to have beliefs about those states of affairs, not when one is caused to have beliefs about beliefs about those states of affairs.

One potential source of embarrassment for any causal account of visual perception stems from the fact that light radiation travels at a finite velocity. This allows for a temporal "gap" (or "time lag") between the time at which x is F and the moment at which the information that x is F reaches the perceiver. So long as one considers only the perception of terrestrial things and events, of course, this temporal gap is vanishingly small (although this is not so for cases of audition). Distant objects—stars, for instance—might seem to present special difficulties. One may wish to describe S as *seeing*, at t, a certain star that in fact exploded thousands of years earlier, hence does not cause, at t, anything at all, much less anything in S.

Such considerations have, on occasion, been regarded as decisive by theorists wishing to defend one or another version of representationalism. Thus, to some it has seemed natural to move from the notion that there is a "gap" between an object's being a certain way and one's perceiving it to be that way, to the notion that what one *really* perceives is not the object but some mediating state or event contemporaneous with one's perceiving.

Moves of this sort ought, however, to be regarded with suspicion. It seems equally "natural," for example, to describe one's visually perceiving a very distant object as a case in which the latter is perceived as it was at the time it initiated the causal sequence that culminates in the perception (see Pitcher, 1971, pp. 48 ff.). This way of speaking is familiar enough when applied to audition: one hears the rumble of a distant thunderclap moments after it occurs.

It is perhaps worth mentioning that, far from making difficulties for the account of visual perception being suggested here, apparent complications of this sort seem to fit nicely with that view. One's seeing (at t) x to be F was said to depend causally on x's being F, but not on x's being F *at* t. Rather it is the operation of a certain mechanism, M, a mechanism the character of which is determined in part by x's being F, that must act on S at t. Strictly speaking, then, objects and events are not seen as they are at the time when they are seen but as they were when they structured the light radiation that reaches the perceiver.

Note that it would be misleading to put this by saying that in cases where there is a nonnegligible temporal gap between the time at which x is F and the time at which light radiation bearing this information reaches one's eyes, one "sees into the past." It is less objectionable, surely, to say that one may see (certain) very distant objects as they were at some past time. In the same way, one's hearing a distant thunderclap moments after it occurs is not a matter of one's "hearing into the past," but merely a matter of one's hearing something that occurred at some slightly earlier time.

I now turn to what I hope is a simpler matter. Consider the following case. Lucy, looking about the kitchen, sees a lemon. She then closes her eyes but, not surprisingly, continues to believe that there is a lemon in the kitchen. Here Lucy has the right kind of belief, caused in the right way, yet it is surely false to say (once she has closed her eyes) that she any longer *sees* the lemon.

Cases of this sort are distinguished by the fact that one is inclined to imagine that perceiving occurs only so long as one's perceptual state—one's beliefs—are being causally sustained or "propped up" by the perceived state of affairs. Once one's eyes are closed, it may remain true that one's beliefs about a state of affairs *were* brought about by that state of affairs (via a suitable causal mechanism, M), but it is no longer true that they are *sustained* by it. Beliefs related to states of affairs in this way are taken to be *memories* rather than perceptions.

Perhaps cases of this kind are excluded by some version of the causal condition discussed earlier. When Lucy shuts her eyes, her belief about the lemon is no longer in the right way counterfactually dependent on the presence in her vicinity of the lemon or, for that matter, on the operation of the causal mechanism that connects Lucy's belief to the lemon. This is correct, certainly, nevertheless the causal condition as it has been formulated pertains only to the cause of a belief, not to the continued operation of that cause. Thus it may be true of Lucy with her eyes *closed* that she would not believe what she does had it not been for the functioning of a certain causal mechanism. One needs to add a further condition, one requiring the mechanism in question to be operating in such a way that it continues causally to sustain Lucy's belief. Once it ceases to play this role—because Lucy shuts her eyes, or because the light is turned off, or because the lemon is removed or occluded—one cannot any longer say that Lucy sees the lemon, regardless of the character of her beliefs or their particular causal origin. To count as an instance of perception, a belief must be dependent on the operation of a proper mechanism at the time it is held. One way of putting this is as follows: S's belief about x that it is F is causally sustained by the mechanism, M, described already.[5]

5. I am aware of difficulties surrounding the notion of a sustaining cause. It has been noted already that Lucy may come to believe, quite independently of her

It is unlikely that the condition can be made stronger than this. One could not, for example, require that the dependence be such that S would no longer believe what he does were the mechanism to cease operating. Perceptual beliefs characteristically "linger" in just the way Lucy's belief about the lemon does when she closes her eyes.

One may suppose that I have ignored an obvious and much simpler possibility. Imagine, for example, that one is in Lucy's shoes. One first looks at the lemon, and then shuts one's eyes. Granted that one continues to have beliefs about the lemon, there remains an enormous *phenomenological* difference in the two conditions: *looking* at the lemon is nothing at all *like* entertaining thoughts about the lemon with one's eyes closed.

I wish, however, to resist this move. In the first place, what is here characterized as a "phenomenological difference" is not a difference in the character of the relevant beliefs. Beliefs seem not to have any particular phenomenology except *per accidens*. One's beliefs about the lemon when one's eyes are open and one's beliefs about the lemon that remain when one's eyes are closed need not differ in any way at all. We do not discover anything very interesting about our beliefs by attempting to scrutinize them introspectively and noticing what they are *like*. These remarks, of course, pertain to the beliefs one has, not to what one may wish to describe as the "experience of perceiving." By contending, earlier, that sensation and perception must be sharply distinguished, I have tried to reinforce the suggestion that perceptual states are, strange as it may at first sound, essentially cognitive or doxastic. If these states have other properties, the latter seem not essential to their being *perceptual* states.

perception, that there is a lemon in the kitchen. Here her belief is caused by something other than the perceptual mechanisms mentioned. Further, this belief might be sustained independently of those mechanisms. Nevertheless she *sees* the lemon. This suggests that we need in some way to weaken still more the condition just formulated. I am not sure how to do so, however, and still preserve the intuition that underlies it.

It would, in any case, be a mistake to confuse features of perceptual states with properties of perceived states of affairs. When Lucy sees a lemon, the yellowness of the lemon, its shape and size are not properties of her perceptual state. They are ordinary properties of the lemon detectable by Lucy when she opens her eyes and looks about the kitchen. Certain features of Lucy's perceptual state are informed by the lemon's being as it is; indeed this is what occurs when she *sees* the thing. Further, the fact that a honeybee or a Jovian might detect a different range of properties need not cast suspicion on those seen by Lucy. It merely reminds us that, given our constitution, there is much that we cannot tell about a lemon simply by looking at it in the usual way.

Perceptual Experience—Again

As we look about ourselves, we are put into contact with our surroundings by way of the "ambient optic array." When we close our eyes, we shut out this array. In so doing we cease to perceive visually, not because our perceptual states suddenly fade or lose their coloring, but because we have, as it were, broken off contact (in this case, visual contact) with the world about us. In theorizing about characteristics of perceptual experiences, philosophers (and, one suspects, psychologists as well) seem often to have in mind things and properties that in fact appear to belong (if anything does) to the "external world." The latter are objective, public, and perfectly real. Difficulties arise when these are regarded as belonging solely to the perceptual *states* of perceivers.

My discussion of perceptual states, the suggestion that these are cognitive, is apt to sound outrageous only if one fails to appreciate this point. I have, to be sure, systematically oversimplified the content of ordinary perceptual states, but not in the sense that I have made them colorless and dull. They are *already* colorless—or rather their color has, so far as one can

tell, nothing much to do with their *content*. My oversimplifica-
tion has consisted in speaking as though ordinary perceptual
states had, as one might put it, a single, simple content, that *x* is
F, for instance. In fact, a perceptual state may more closely
resemble a complex, dynamic *mass,* something that one would
find it difficult to spell out in any detail.

It is easy to be scandalized by such a characterization of
perceptual states if one persists in the belief that in seeing
something one is confronted by a "sensible manifold," a collection of sensations or "appearances." This is a picture I wish to
reject. I am doubtful, of course, that there are any knockdown
arguments available to philosophers that force abandonment of
the doctrine that, in perceiving, one is (immediately) aware only
of private subjective states and episodes. Nor, however, do there
seem to be any cogent arguments obliging one to accept such a
doctrine. Special perceptual states and episodes are most often
postulated to account for the discrepancy between how things
appear and how we imagine them to be in reality. My
suggestion is that this discrepancy may be better explained, in
the case of visual perception, by reference to features of the
"optic array."

In any event, it seems to me reasonably clear that the
ingredients of what philosophers might wish to identify as the
sensible manifold are, in the main, not sensations or sensation-
like states at all, but ordinary public features of the world.
Colors, shapes, and the rest can be photographed, measured,
and observed by anyone with the right sensory equipment.
Appearances of ordinary objects (that square towers at a
distance "seem round," that round coins "look elliptical," that
railroad tracks "appear to converge" at the horizon) can, as we
have seen, be explained by reference to perfectly objective
characteristics of the "optic array." The latter determine, as
well, the images on a strip of photographic film and the
vibratory patterns of a TVSS.

Again, I suspect that many of the difficulties one associates
with the way I have elected to describe perceptual states are

misplaced. If I am asked to report all that I see as I gaze from my window, I should regard this as a request, not for information about the content of my perceptual state at the moment the request is made, but rather as a request for information about the scene in front of me. What I report in complying with this request is, it is true, a manifestation of my perceptual state, but it is a state that is constantly changing as I scan from one thing to another in (what is by all accounts) a systematic fashion. One's perceptual state at any moment evidently reflects only a tiny portion of the information available to one at that moment.[6] It seems likely, in fact, that information is picked up or ignored in an orderly, principled way. As we saw in the previous chapter, one does not typically notice what one does not need to notice about one's surroundings.

It is sometimes thought that in order to account for this sort of "selective attention," one must suppose that perceivers first take everything in, then filter out whatever they may not, at the time, happen to need. It is possible, certainly, that this is what occurs, but it seems equally possible that the "filtering" takes place at an earlier stage. The latter suggestion troubles some theorists because it seems to require, paradoxically, that one first take account of something in order to decide that the thing taken account of does not merit attention: one excludes items from one's awareness only by first ascertaining that they are the sorts of item one has reason to exclude. Reflections of this sort give rise to theories in which noticing or attending occurs at two levels: one first "takes in" everything, but tags only those items that are in one way or another notable; one then "brings to consciousness" just those items previously tagged.[7]

6. One way of appreciating this point is by looking briefly at the photograph of a reasonably complex scene, then covering the picture, and trying to recall all that one can about it. Doing this may provide *some* idea of the disparity between one's perceptual state (at a given time) and the information available to one (at that time). Admittedly, this technique confounds perceptual and memorial tasks, nevertheless it provides a rough idea of what I have in mind.

7. On such a theory, one may regard perceiving as occurring at *either* level. Thus, one may elect to distinguish *perception* (as what occurs at the lowest—input—level) from *cognition* (what is derived at the second level). This seems close, in fact, to the view

It is significant that filter theories of the sort envisaged begin with the supposition that what needs to be accounted for is that which is *not* noticed by the perceiver. Failure to notice is taken to be a form of excluding or rejecting, activities that seem to require a measure of reflection, a level at which one examines an item and determines by means of some test that it should be ignored. The metaphor here is that of an inspector on an assembly line sorting items as they move past.

Suppose, in contrast, one begins, as was suggested in the previous chapter, with the notion that what needs accounting for is what *is* noticed. On such a view, a perceiver might function so as to attend only to those items that were in some respect worthy of attention. Imagine, for example, a device constructed so as to register the presence only of items with a certain property, *P.* A device of this sort, one supposes, might be built so as to "take in" everything presented to it, then to examine all of these "inputs" testing for instances of *P,* putting these in a special file or bin, and tossing out everything lacking *P.* A device of the sort imagined might, however, be built much more simply by arranging it so that it responded only to things exhibiting *P.*

Ordinary perceivers are, of course, very much more complex than this, but I doubt that this fact alone rules out the possibility that they function in ways analogous to the simpler of the two devices just described. We are not "built" to register the presence of one sort of thing; rather our capacities in this regard seem flexible, determined, perhaps, by our appreciation of our circumstances and by our passing needs and interests. This, anyway, is a possibility, one that happens to mesh nicely with the account of visual perception I have been trying to piece together. In particular, it enables one to make sense of the disparity between the richness of the information that confronts us as we look about ourselves, and the relative austerity of the resulting perceptual states.

advanced in Dretske, 1981. One may, in contrast, hold that the first level is not "in the fullest sense" perceptual. I shall not further discuss these options.

Summary

The aim of the present chapter has not been to provide an analysis of perception, but merely to sketch a tentative account of what it is to see something, an assemblage of conditions that are, at any rate, prima facie necessary. For convenience I shall set out below the central ingredients of that account.

At t, S sees x to be F only if:

(i) at t, S believes x to be F;

(ii) The causal mechanism, M, responsible for S's belief about x that it is F includes as an essential component light radiation that carries information that x is F (and does so in virtue of its being structured by x's being F);

(iii) M does not include as an essential component S's holding a belief about a distinct intentional state (belief, percept, or whatever) that includes x's being F in its content;

(iv) S's belief about x that it is F is "causally sustained" at t by M.

PART TWO
Cognition

In Part One, I attempted to sketch an account of ordinary perception. My suggestion was that perceiving is best regarded as a causal process, one leading from some perceived thing or event to a belieflike cognitive state via a chain consisting of information-bearing physical stimuli and sensory mechanisms. One may wish to disagree with various details of this account without wishing to abandon its broadest features. Thus, one may be skeptical about the cognitive character of perceptual states as I have elected to describe them. One may, on the other hand, be suspicious of the notion that "physical stimuli" bear information in the way suggested. I have tried to show that these, and related, features of my explication are less objectionable than one might suppose; still, I admit that there is substantial room for informed disagreement.

In Part Two, I wish to explore a set of issues that takes on a special significance in light of what has been said thus far. The issues in question seem to me to arise not only from the way I have elected to characterize perception, but from any account of perceiving that takes seriously the notion that perceivers come to be in certain "mental states" as a result of purely physical events occurring both inside and outside their bodies. The difficulty, in part, is to explain the relation between physical occurrences, broadly conceived, and psychological ones. I shall assume, without arguing the point, that sentient creatures in general, and human beings in particular, are physical systems, and that our psychological features are in some way dependent on certain of our physical characteristics.

There are many questions to be asked about such matters,

and I shall raise only a very few. I shall be concerned, for example, with psychological states and events only insofar as these are representational. I shall say nothing about sensations or "feels." It is not that such things are unimportant, it is merely that they are of no particular concern for the project at hand. I have argued already that the having of sensations is not essential to perception. Even one who rejects this contention, however, will at some point be obliged to face the issues I shall discuss here, namely the character of those cognitive or representational states that one associates with perception.

VII

MENTAL REPRESENTATION

Computation and Cognition

Perception, I shall henceforth suppose, involves the production in a perceiver of certain cognitive states. I have argued that such states are best thought of as beliefs, but the important point, at present, is that, whatever they are, they are *representational*. One may if one likes subscribe to current fashion and refer to psychological states of this sort as *mental representations*. Introducing a label for a phenomenon, however, ought not to be confused with offering a coherent account of it. The fact that, to many theorists, it now seems *obvious* that intelligent creatures are brimming with mental representations should not blind one to the potential such notions have to blur important distinctions and muddy the waters of inquiry. In this chapter I shall try to say briefly (and without much originality) what mental representations might be and what they probably are not, and in this way to detach my view of perception from ones that it might otherwise superficially resemble.[1]

I have said that representational cognitive states are produced "in perceivers." This seems to imply that mental representations are interior inscriptions, marks, or episodes, and that one can speak unproblematically of *internal* representations. I suspect that this is a mistake, a deep, longstanding error in our ways of picturing various psychological features of sentient creatures. In saying this I am setting myself off from practitioners of what is

---

1. The discussion will be sketchy because the topic is hideously complex. A satisfactory theory of mental representation evidently awaits an explanation of representational phenomena generally.

nowadays called information-processing psychology and, in some quarters, "cognitive science." Theorists who identify their disciplines in this way typically pride themselves in having overcome earlier, unfashionable reductionisms: talk about mental states and processes is no longer thought to be reducible to, in the sense of "translatable into," talk about either physiological goings-on in the nervous system or behavior.

One may applaud the demise of these brands of reductionism, but it is not obvious that the newer appeals to internal representations are, at bottom, any less reductionistic or otherwise objectionable. At present, the most prominent view has it that talk about psychological states may be replaced by talk about *computational* states of the creatures to whom the states belong. Computational states and processes, in turn, are thought to be characterizable *formally,* that is, they consist in the end of elements and relations definable syntactically (merely by reference to their *shapes)* and similarly definable operations over these (see e.g., Fodor, 1981, p. 277; cf. Smith, forthcoming).

The notion that cognition is in the last analysis nothing more than computation has been most forcefully defended by Jerry Fodor, but it is, I think, implicit in most recent cognitive theories. It is important to be clear on what this sort of "computationalism" (as I shall call it—following John Searle; see Searle, 1980) involves and what it denies. When it is said, for example, that a computing machine "manipulates symbols" (or that ordinary thought is in this way "symbolic") it would be wrong to imagine that the machine (or brain) *literally* reads, or interprets, or understands symbolic goings-on in its interior. On the contrary, it reacts to those goings-on not in virtue of their meaning, but solely in virtue of their intrinsic (non-representational) characteristics. The representational content of interior episodes (if any) is thought to be determined not (or, at any rate, not entirely) by their internal roles, but by their contribution to "overt" behavior or response to "inputs." Thus, if a particular circuit fires (perhaps in concert with many other circuits) when, and only when, a device's sensors are confronted with a tomato, it may seem plausible to regard the circuit (or its firing) as *representing* tomatohood (or something of the sort).

The representational content of a computing machine (or a brain) is determined, on such a view, by causal relations partly external to the device. Significantly, this content plays no role in the operation of the device. One may imagine a simple mechanism that, when a certain circuit is activated, prints (or "utters") the English sentence, "Lo, a tomato." The mechanism need not—indeed it had better not—depend on an *understanding* of anything at all.

The operations of computing machines are all, it seems, characterizable in this way. If we wish such a device to "understand" a sentence, for example, we must provide it with a way of analyzing the sentence syntactically and relating it to other "stored" syntactic objects. In saying that the machine "understands" the sentence fed into it, then, we are saying only that the device acts on (in the sense of "behaves appropriately toward") the sentence in a way resembling the ways in which you or I might act on it (Fodor, 1981; Searle, 1980). The question is whether this, "suitably extended," is all there is to understanding a sentence.

It is undeniable that it is enormously *convenient* to ascribe psychological predicates to computing machines (Dennett, 1978; Smith, forthcoming). It is still possible to wonder, however, whether there is anything more to it than convenience. There are two thoughts here that incline one in opposite directions.

In the first place, there is the notion that human beings (in understanding sentences, for instance) *must* operate in pretty much the ways in which computing machines operate. Thus, it is held that in understanding one another's utterances we "process" those utterances internally as syntactic, formal objects. This may involve (as Fodor, 1975, suggests) linking sentences heard to "wired-in" sentences in one's "internal representational system," or it may involve something else. In any case, on such a conception all that goes on in the realm of understanding can be set out (at least in principle) in a series of rules specifying purely formal operations over syntactic entities. The staunchest advocates of this picture have argued that something like this *must* be right. There is, they insist, simply no other way to account for our higher-order psychological faculties. To suppose, for example, that at some basic level human beings operate on "inputs" in virtue of their *meaning* (as distinct from their physical "shape"), is to make such processes mysterious. The appreciation of *meaning* (as distinct from the response to shape or form) requires, it seems, an intelligent *interpreter*. And it is no good attempting to explain my capacity to understand what I hear by postulating inside me one or more "understanders," ultimately little men or homunculi, the operation of which one is now obliged to explain.

Pulling in the opposite direction, however, is the conviction that interesting psychological states and processes inevitably resist formal reductions. This point has been made excruciatingly clear in the disappointing performance of computer programs designed to empower machines to "recognize" written letters or numerals, or identify familiar objects presented to them via a television camera—in general, tasks involving what has come to be known as "pattern-recognition" (see Dreyfus, 1979). In this domain there do not seem to be any interesting ways to characterize formally even simple, apparently well-defined patterns like letter-shapes and typefaces, much less the shapes of ordinary natural objects like cats and lemons, or artifacts like tables and spectacles.

One may continue to insist that human beings *must* recognize such things in virtue of some set of defining formal characteristics, on the grounds that this is, at bottom, the only sort of explanation that makes any clear sense.[2] In contrast, one may suspect that the notion that psychological states and processes

2. This is the line Fodor, for example, repeatedly takes; see e.g., Fodor, 1975, p. 52. For a sharply contrasting point of view see e.g., Rosch, 1977, 1978.

are formally characterizable is no less a modern myth (though really one with a long and depressing philosophical history; see Dreyfus, 1979) than earlier physiological and behaviorist reductionisms.

Part of the problem, I shall suggest, is that mental states appear to be conceptually interdependent, linked together in countless ways, and identified largely by their relations to other, similarly linked, states. Beliefs, for example, cannot sensibly be ascribed to a creature separately, one at a time, but only in concert with other beliefs. My believing, say, that grass is green (as distinct from my merely emitting noises resembling an utterance of the English sentence "Grass is green") requires that I have beliefs about certain plants and their colors. Were I to lack such backgound beliefs, my (foreground) belief would not be about *grass* at all. It might be about anything, or nothing. Beliefs about plants and colors require, in their turn, other, related beliefs, *and so on*.[3]

Now one might suppose that these points are perfectly consistent with the computational perspective. Beliefs, or at any rate, propositions believed, seem the sorts of item one might expect to be characterizable formally. So long as a belief-system is finite, there may be no particular reason to doubt that it might be somehow reducible to a definite set of sentences (or similar, appropriately syntactic objects).

It is not obvious, however, that systems of beliefs *are* in any interesting way finite—at least if one regards finitude as incorporating countability. More troubling, in any case, is the possibility that belief-systems themselves float on a non-propositional sea (or "background") consisting of abilities, propensities, attitudes, skills and the like, characteristics of agents irreducible to "propositional" ones (see e.g., Dreyfus, 1982). The latter require for their realization not merely further "propositional attitudes," not merely the possession of or assent to a large

---

3. This is a theme discussed in Davidson, 1973*b* and elsewhere; see below. See also, Kierkegaard, 1846/1941, p. 174.

number of formulae, but something very like the body of a sentient creature. They are, in Keith Gunderson's instructive phrase, "program resistant" (see Gunderson, 1971). I shall not attempt to argue these matters here. They go well beyond the concerns of this essay and, in any case, they have been discussed at length by others elsewhere.[4] I wish only to detach my view from those that take beliefs and similar states to be computational features of creatures possessing them and, in virtue of being computational states, to be internal representations. Thus, when I say that beliefs are "in" a believer, I do not mean that they are (thereby) computational (or neural) states of the believer. Beliefs are in believers rather in the way beauty is in a painting, or sadness is in a melody, not in the way (for example) an electronic circuit is in a computing machine, or a collection of neurons is inside a skull.

Admittedly, none of this is particularly helpful. I have said only what I think beliefs (and similar representational states) are not. It is far from obvious that I have done much to advance an account of what they *are*. Rather than confront such a massive topic head-on, however, I should prefer first to examine those intuitions that, as I have suggested, incline us toward a certain picture of mental representation.

The Assumption of Physicalism

First, I shall suppose that we (and other terrestrial creatures) are physical systems functioning in response to a physical environment. I want to make this supposition, not because my account of cognition requires it, but for the opposite reason: it is this assumption, shared it seems by most of us, that occasions the *sort* of view I wish to endorse. The assumption (I shall call it, somewhat grandiosely, the "assumption of physicalism"), whatever we may wish to say about it philosophically, is based

4. See e.g., Dreyfus, 1979; Fodor, 1981; Gunderson, 1971; Haugeland, 1981; Pylyshyn, 1980; Searle, 1980.

in part on the simpleminded conviction that the activities of human beings and other creatures are all mediated *in some sense* by our respective physical constituents, more particularly by our nervous systems, those parts of us that seem designed expressly for this purpose.

I should say very quickly that, in embracing this assumption, I do not mean to be prejudging any questions about such difficult and elusive topics as the nature of consciousness and its place in psychological theorizing. I am not, for example, suggesting that all that can be said about the activities of intelligent creatures (and perhaps especially about the activities of human beings) can be *translated* into or replaced by talk about neurophysiological goings-on. Such views seem to me fairly obviously mistaken. Rather, I am merely calling attention to the seemingly evident fact that whatever actions we perform, our bodies are mobilized by physical occurrences. Reductionists may wish to add that there are definite, principled relations between actions described in the usual ways and the physical processes underlying these. This, however, is an article of faith that I do not care to endorse. I want only to advance the assumption of physicalism in its most innocuous and trivial guise, a guise with which even the staunchest antireductionist may feel comfortable.

The assumption of physicalism is worth making explicit because without it many of the puzzles underlying the present essay would simply cease to be puzzling. If Descartes had been right, if intelligent actions were the products of a non-spatial, *non-biological* entity, then there would be no need at all to worry about the relation of psychological and physiological accounts of behavior, no need to worry, for example, about how the nervous system *could* support representations, or appropriately representational elements. Such matters strike us as perplexing only when we start from the supposition that intelligent creatures, creatures to which a variety of interesting psychological properties belong, are, at bottom, physical mechanisms operating in accordance with ordinary (and relatively dreary) physical principles. If the physicalist assumption is false, then, it will not follow that the view I wish to defend is false. The account would be, as it were, lobotomized; much of its motivation would have been removed.

One suspects that many (arguably, *most)* of our present-day philosophical questions about minds and mental properties stem from the assumption of physicalism, or rather from attempts to reconcile this with our ordinary, commonsensical picture of mental states and processes. We regard ourselves as biological systems that are intelligent. This leaves us with the difficulty of understanding how a system could be *biologically* engineered so as to perform intelligent actions. It is, I believe, in attempting to come to grips with this puzzle that many have been attracted to the use of the computing machine analogy or, more abstractly, to the notion that all intelligent behavior is ultimately "computational." Computing machines are, after all, mechanical systems engineered in a certain way. Despite this fact (though really, of course, *because* of it), such machines seem capable of being set to perform a range of tasks that have many of the earmarks of intelligence. So far as anyone can see, there is no compelling reason to suppose that such machines could not one day be constructed so as to mimic intelligence in the fullest sense (once it is decided, one hastens to add, what intelligence in the fullest sense *is;* see e.g., Bennett, 1964, pp. 32 ff.).

At present, however, an appeal to computing machine modeling seems apt more to confuse the issues discussed here than to illuminate them. The tendency to move from facts about what one must do in order to program a computing machine to perform a certain task, to the claim that the task is performed in some analogous way by biological entities, is evidently widespread. In chapter V, I suggested that machine analogies could be positively pernicious (see also, Heil, 1981). Programming a computing machine to perform various tasks is too closely tied to the need for us first to make clear to ourselves the character of the tasks performed, and then to convey this information to the machine. There seems no reason at all, however, to suppose that biological mechanisms must perform in ways even remotely analogous to the ways in which we happen to find it convenient to formulate descriptions of particular processes and activities (see Runeson, 1977*a*).

It is perhaps the case that computing machine enthusiasts in psychology (devotees of so-called *artificial intelligence*) are those who have found it possible to cope with the assumption of physicalism by adopting, as an article of faith, the belief that certain physical systems operate on *psychological* principles. (I say psychological principles because the requirement of clarity and explicitness requisite for the writing of a computer program are, in a certain sense, psychological requirements. They reflect the fact that for a computing machine to do what we want it to do, we must first make explicit *what* we want done.) But of course not even computing machines work this way. They operate exclusively on mechanical principles. We may, if we like, describe the activities of such machines using a vocabulary borrowed from the language of intelligence, but the reason we can do this need not be that these machines operate in accordance with a special, distinctively highbrow set of principles (they do not). Rather, we have stage-managed them in a certain way with our programs. We are apt to lose sight of such homely facts because our contact with computing machines is mostly at a somewhat elevated level of abstraction. We forget that these abstractions have different values for the machine than they do for us.

I could be wrong in all this. It could turn out that the biological mechanisms underlying intelligent behavior are more closely analogous to the programmed mechanisms that drive a digital computer than I imagine. The issue is, after all, an empirical one (a fact that both detractors and champions of artificial intelligence are prone to forget). I could be wrong, too, though I doubt it, about the assumption of physicalism. These considerations are not, in any case, necessary constituents of the view of mental representation I want now to spell out. Nevertheless, the view in question fits such points nicely and that, perhaps, is something in its favor.

The Biological Basis of Intelligence

A corollary to the assumption of physicalism is the notion that the character of a creature's responses to its environment must be due ultimately to features of its physical constitution. Like the assumption of physicalism, most of us most of the time seem to believe that this is the case, at least "in some sense." (And *that* sense, whatever it may be, is the sense I hereby intend.)

The difficulty faced by the psychologist concerned with explaining the mechanisms of intelligent behavior, however, is that such behavior seems often to be directed toward aspects of the environment that cut across the natural categories of physics, chemistry, or biology. We seem, that is, to have the capacity to "behave selectively" toward things and events as members of classes that have no discernible connections to biological (or physical or chemical) categories (see Armstrong, 1973). One responds "appropriately," for example, to objects that are *valuable,* even though the class of valuable things is unlikely to correspond to anything *naturally* characterizable. (It includes, for instance, stock certificates, coins, paintings, vases, Big Macs, old baseball cards, and real estate, items that appear not to have any interesting physical properties in common.)

All this seems clear enough. Now, however, one is confronted with a new puzzle, for it is far from clear how a biological device could be built so as to interact with features of the environment that themselves seem to have no particular biological legitimacy. One response to this, the response of the reductionist, is just to insist that the classes in question *do* have some natural basis. A somewhat different (but still, I think, ultimately reductionist) response is that offered by computationalists. Classes of objects may be somehow formally specifiable.

Both sorts of response may strike one as nothing more than wishful thinking—*implausible* wishful thinking—and as such they are irrefutable. Perhaps the best one can hope for is an account of how the assumption that intelligence is biologically determined does not, despite appearances, require that one embrace such doctrines. As I see it, the task of setting out an adequate account of mental representation is that of showing how such general assumptions as that intelligent behavior is biologically based can be squared with the evident fact that the components of such behavior—beliefs, desires, intentions, and the like—incorporate non-biological, *representational* properties. The sticking point is that beliefs and desires appear to be representational essentially, whereas the biological determinants of behavior seem, on the face of it, to lack any such property or, for that matter, even an analogue of any such property. Theories of behavior, then, that make use of representational states or occurrences would seem to be *intrinsically* inadequate, at best provisional. In order to get clear on these matters, it will be necessary to scrutinize the criteria employed in attributions of representational states to intelligent creatures, and the relation of these to criteria used in ascriptions of non-representational, biological characteristics.

Descriptive Strata

Any thing or event at all, it seems, may be described in a variety of ways. I may describe the object in front of me, for example, as an apple, as a spherical fruit, as a collection of molecules, a delicious morsel, a red surface. All these ways of speaking may be perfectly correct, although some may generate more controversy than others. If you dislike fruit, you may doubt that apples are correctly described as delicious. On matters of taste we are, for this reason, inclined to hedge and add the relativizing qualification, "for me." Thus, in saying that the item on the table is "delicious for me," I do not obviously come into conflict with you. It may be that differences in tastes of this sort are largely explicable by reference to dispositional properties or causal powers of objects. My saying that the apple is delicious, then, might be understood as a way of saying that the apple has, or is likely to have, a certain effect on me, one that it might well fail to have on you.

These are matters perhaps better discussed by metaphysicians. Here I wish only to introduce a simple reminder: from the fact that some state of affairs may be described in a number of ways, it does not, or at least need not, follow that our descriptions are descriptions of items in different *realms*— "material bodies" and mental representations of these, for instance. Things and events are singled out by reference to their properties and, if we allow for relational and causal properties as well as ordinary categorical ones, there is no obvious limit to the number of properties a thing can have.

This is not to say that any description one might settle on is as apt as any other. There is always a possibility of error (the thing is a tomato, not an apple; it is not red, but merely illuminated in a special way; it is not sweet but sour). Nor are all descriptions equally informative for all observers. If your description of something depends on my picking out a property of the thing described, I must in some way recognize, or at any rate be capable of recognizing, that the thing *has* the property in question. Anything may possess countless properties that I know nothing about, hence there may be descriptions applicable to it that I cannot appreciate. An apple on the table in front of me may have a worm in it, but unless I know (or at least suspect) this, the description "the thing with the worm in it" will not help me identify the apple.

The issues here have been widely discussed by philosophers of language, and they involve a variety of complexities that we can, for the moment, safely ignore. I wish, instead, to take up the notion of what may be called *descriptive levels*. This notion, in common with many others that we routinely employ, seems simple and obvious so long as one is content to regard it casually. Difficulties arise, however, when one attempts to make it clear and unambiguous. My strategy will be to begin with a simple case and then to move on to matters that are perhaps less transparent.

Consider a particular work of art, *W*, a painting, for instance. *W* has a multitude of properties, and it is in virtue of these that we can say a variety of things about it, more particularly, that we can describe *W* in many different *ways*. Here are a few representative descriptions:

(i)   *W* is Flemish.
(ii)   *W* was painted by *S*.
(iii) *W* is in Paris.
(iv)   *W* depicts a bowl of fruit.
(v)   *W* is highly realistic.
(vi)   *W* is composed of oil pigments.
(vii) *W* is reflecting light radiation of frequency *F.*
(viii) *W* weighs *n* grams.

To keep matters as simple as possible, I shall suppose that all these things are true of *W*. What is important to notice here is that such descriptions may be said to belong to several different (though related) *ways* of talking about *W*. Thus, it is not merely that there are different things to be said about *W*, but that there are as well different points of view or perspectives from which *W* may be regarded. One way to distinguish these ways of speaking about *W* is to think of the aims or goals of speakers. Thus one may be concerned with *W*'s history, and concentrate on its historical properties. One may, in contrast, be concerned with *W* as an aesthetic object, or as an object with a certain chemical constitution.

It is no more possible exhaustively to catalogue the ways we have of talking about *W* than it is possible to set out a complete list of things that might be (truly) said about *W*. This does not mean, of course, that there are no constraints on the sorts of things one might say about *W* or that there are no useful distinctions to be drawn among the *kinds* of description one employs. In the first place, one may speak of and distinguish aesthetic descriptions from historical ones, and these from chemical descriptions, and so on. The idea is that the descriptions we offer comprise families or classes, collections with both prototypical or central members and less central, borderline members (Rosch, 1977, 1978). Thus, "*W* is highly realistic" seems to belong exclusively to the aesthetic family of descriptions of *W*. In contrast, "*W* is in Paris" may belong, perhaps, to a set of historical descriptions of *W*, but it might belong, as well, to a family of descriptions focusing on *W*'s "purely physical" properties.

Second, although certain things one might say about *W* may be logically related to other things one might say about it (if, for example, *W* depicts an apple, then it thereby depicts a fruit), there are in general no logical relations of this sort between (what I have been calling) *ways* of talking about *W*. This is not to say that there are *no* relations between the ways one has of describing *W*, only that these relations are not, for the most part, logical.

One needs to say "for the most part" here because there is, as we have seen, a certain amount of overlap among our descriptive classes. In any case, the idea is simply that one cannot, in general, infer purely aesthetic truths about *W* from chemical or historical truths about *W*, and vice versa. Of course, from the fact that *W* depicts a bowl of fruit, one might infer that *W* is a physical object or that it was probably not painted by a resident of Lapland. But this is another matter, one depending on one's beliefs about paintings and Laplanders, not on one's scrutiny of *W*. What I wish to resist is the notion that ways of talking are in some fashion *reducible* to or derivable from one another in principled ways. The absence of such logical connections is, I think, something approaching a criterion of whatever distinct *ways* of talking about *W* there may be. It is not a particularly useful characterization, perhaps, owing to the fact that our descriptive schemes lack anything like sharply defined boundaries. Nevertheless, it may be clear enough for the use to which it will be put.

By *ways of talking* I mean roughly what I take people to mean when they speak of such things as "levels of description." One may prefer to speak of descriptive *schemes* rather than descriptive *levels* because the former suggests that alternative ways of talking may be "ontologically" on a par, while the latter implies that these may be *arranged* or ordered, perhaps hierarchically. I shall use the expressions interchangeably, however, in part because the hierarchical picture seems to me not altogether inappropriate.

What is crucial for present purposes is that such schemes or levels are not distinguished by reference to their denotata, the things and events that fall under them, but in other ways. All the descriptions cited above are descriptions of a single individual, *W*, they mention features or properties of the very same particular, they constitute, as one says, different ways of talking about the same thing. Failure to appreciate this point occasionally leads to doctrines in which special levels of *reality* are postulated, theories in which properties mentioned in distinct descriptive schemes are assigned to distinct particulars. Thus one finds theorists holding that colors, for instance, do not "belong to" material bodies, but merely to minds. I do not wish to claim that philosophical problems about colors or, more generally, problems about the proper referents of descriptions can be solved with a wave of the hand (see e.g., Averill, 1982). Nevertheless, there is something to be said for accounts that oblige us to postulate fewer kinds of individual thing.

We have, then, some notion of descriptive schemes, strata or levels. In the main, these seem to be founded on classes, or collections, or families of properties that exhibit certain relations to one another (see Kim, 1978, 1979). Thus, in general, predicates belonging to a single level evidently possess internal, conceptual relations to others at the same level but, at best, nomological relations to those at a different level. Further, families of properties picked out at one descriptive level may, at least in some cases, be said to *supervene* on classes of properties picked out at a lower, "more basic," level. The aesthetic properties of a painting may, in this way, be said to supervene on its purely natural, physical properties (on a certain distribution of pigments, for instance); and these in turn may be taken to supervene on further, "lower level" chemical or molecular properties of the painting. Two paintings with the very same physical and chemical properties, that is, two paintings exactly alike with respect to their physical constitution, would, it seems, be aesthetically indistinguishable. The converse, however, appears not to hold. Two paintings may represent a bowl of fruit (even the very *same* bowl of fruit) without sharing any interesting physical features. Similarly, two paintings may be beautiful, or tacky, or maudlin despite the fact that they differ widely from one another in respect to their physical constituents.

The notion of supervenience, like that of descriptive levels, is difficult to specify precisely (see however Kim, 1978, 1979). It seems a simple matter to think of instances of supervenience, rather more difficult to say in detail what it is that *makes* these instances of supervenience. The same of course is true for descriptive schemes. One may, if one likes, characterize these by reference to "families" of predicates or properties as I have suggested, though it is not obvious that in doing so one does very much at all to clarify the intuitive notion with which we began. It does, perhaps, endow the latter with a trace of respectability. I propose, in any case, to employ both the notion of a descriptive level and the related notion of supervenience in what follows simply because these, whatever their faults, seem best suited for the formulation of the perspective I shall defend.

Psychological States and Representational Content

Let us characterize psychological states and processes as those states and processes (attributable to intelligent creatures) that have *intentional* or *representational* content essentially. (In putting it this way I do not mean to be ruling out in advance the possibility that computing machines might turn out to have, or be capable of having, psychological properties. I wish the term "intelligent creature," then, to be interpreted broadly.) Examples of psychological states are beliefs, desires, wishes, fears, doubts, intentions, and memories. Such things, and many others besides, possess some intentional or representational *content*, they are, that is, directed beyond themselves, they are *about*, or *for*, or *of* some actual or possible state of affairs. If one takes representational content to be in some sense *propositional*, then we may follow philosophical custom and refer to such psychological states as *propositional attitudes*. I *believe* that it is raining, *wish* that it would stop, and *fear* that it will not. One may have different attitudes toward the same proposition (as one may believe, wish, or fear that it will rain), or the same attitude toward different propositions (one may believe that it will rain and believe, as well, that today is Tuesday).[5]

All this is familiar, well-trod territory. Few would doubt, for example, that one is often correct in ascribing propositional attitudes to oneself and one's fellows. We frequently find it convenient to extend this practice to nonhuman creatures and, perhaps, to sophisticated computing machines engaged in chess-playing routines and the like. Whether this extension is warranted or whether it is merely a *façon de parler*, a rampant form of anthropomorphizing, is a topic I shall leave aside for chapter VIII. For the present I wish only to discuss those cases in which we are, if we ever are, entitled to attribute representational states, propositional attitudes, to human beings.

Consider a case in which one (correctly) ascribes a belief to *S*, the belief, say, that there is a tomato on the table. I have suggested already that it can make sense to attribute such a belief to *S* only if one is prepared to ascribe to him a host of other beliefs (and perhaps non-propositional "background" attitudes and skills as well; see Dreyfus, 1982). Beliefs in this

5. I leave aside consideration of both of those states that seem to lack appropriate representational content ("undirected" fears, anxieties, and the like) and of those states whose representational content may be nonpropositional (mental images are perhaps of this sort). I leave aside, as well, consideration of sensations (see note 10, chapter I, above).

way resemble locations in a coordinate system, places on a map, for instance. A coordinate point is realizable only within a whole *system* of coordinates. Further, as Donald Davidson has argued at length, belief-attributions require that we employ an internal standard of coherence and rationality (see e.g., Davidson, 1970, 1973a). Beliefs are individuated, they can have a determinate content, only insofar as they fit into some *coherent* pattern of beliefs.

This is not to say that one cannot hold or ascribe irrational or anomalous beliefs to an agent, merely that the holding of such beliefs can make sense only against a predominantly rational background. Consider the parallel possibility of a *mistaken* or incorrect move in a game. One can make a bad or mistaken move in playing chess, for instance, only if one ordinarily and for the most part does not make such moves. If one consistently moved pieces "incorrectly," one would not be playing *chess* at all, hence not playing bad or mistake-ridden chess. Belief-ascriptions, in the same way, evidently require the presence of patterns of behavior that may be interpreted as manifesting coherence and order.

It seems likely, as well, that one must regard systems or complexes of beliefs as being not only internally coherent but, in addition, as being mainly *true*. In practice this means that one must suppose that the beliefs of others generally match one's own (which, of course, one imagines to be true). Again, this is a conceptual point about the determination of *what* is believed by a given agent. Imagine a case in which we are deciding what beliefs to ascribe to *S*. We interrogate him, observe his circumstances, his reaction to these, and try to fit these observations with what we have noticed about *S* on other occasions. This requires not merely that we assume a measure of consistency with respect to *S*'s beliefs, but also that this consistency be pegged to what is *in fact* occurring in *S*'s vicinity. Perhaps we wish to say that *S* believes that tomatoes are edible because *S* seizes and eats a tomato from the plate in front of him. It is possible, of course, to ascribe a different, apparently anomalous belief to *S* provided we are willing to make adjustments elsewhere in our assessment of *S*'s psyche. We might, for example, suppose that *S* wishes to ingest something that will make him ill. But such adjustments can make sense only if they serve to bring *S*'s whole system of beliefs (and desires) into better alignment with the facts—or, at any rate, with the facts as we see them.

These matters are difficult and considerably more complex than such simple examples suggest (see Davidson, 1973*a*, 1973*b*, 1974, 1975, for further detailed discussion). Nevertheless, it may be possible to draw from them a number of tentative morals.

First, ascriptions of representational psychological states (beliefs, desires, and their brethren) are necessarily *holistic*. They cannot be made, as it were, one at a time, but only against a background of related representational states. In this regard mental representations resemble points in a coordinate system, or perhaps sentences in a language.

Second, representational complexes must be regarded as coherent and, where beliefs are at issue, mainly true. Irrational desires and false beliefs are possible only against a backdrop of otherwise rational and appropriate desires and beliefs. Here what is significant is the apparent fact that correct ascriptions of psychological states involve appeals to standards of rationality and truth that belong to a particular level of description; indeed they may be constitutive of that descriptive level. Whether or not a creature's brain is in a certain state, whether its body moves in this way or that way, are matters to be determined by criteria founded on neurophysiological or perhaps Newtonian principles. Whether or not a creature holds a particular belief, however, will depend, at least in some measure, on the extent to which that belief fits a certain coherent structure of beliefs (desires and the like), all manifested in patterns of action over time. Ascriptions of psychological states, then, are founded on considerations that seem to have no place in the determination of physiological or (purely) behavioral states and processes. I shall return to this point presently.

Third, given the determining grounds of belief-attributions, one might suppose that all such attributions are provisional, tentative. If, that is, one's ascription of psychological states to a creature involves finding in that creature's behavior certain patterns and characterizing (or, in Davidson's terminology, "interpreting") these patterns in certain ways, it might be possible to devise alternative characterizations, each with its own *internal* coherence, but each differing from the other with respect to its precise composition.

This worrisome prospect may be appreciated if one considers the possibility that S's ingesting a tomato may be regarded as manifesting, say, his belief that the tomato is edible, together with a desire to ingest something edible. One might, however, equally take S's action as manifesting a different belief-desire pair (the desire to be ill, perhaps,' together with the belief that the tomato is poisonous). Of course, if one confronts a creature's activities over a significant stretch of time, many of these and similar indeterminacies will fade or be rendered implausible in virtue of their unmotivated complexity. Nevertheless, there is no a priori guarantee that there is a single *best* way of characterizing a creature's mental complex, even if one is privy to *all* the creature does (or says). Given the labyrinthine character of interrelations among psychological states and processes, it seems always possible to regard two (or more) utterly distinct psychological interpretations of a creature's deeds as equally fitting the data. What are we to say about such cases?

One may feel that here a distinction must be introduced between attributional criteria (roughly, what determines the warrant of one's ascriptions of psychological states) and criteria of possession (whatever it is that, in reality, constitutes a creature's being in, or possessing such a state). Indeterminacy of attribution, if it obtains, seems to apply only to the former. Thus (it might be thought) one could have every reason for ascribing to S the belief that p (given one characterization of S's psychological constitution) and the belief that $not\text{-}p$ (given a distinct, but equally plausible and coherent characterization of that constitution). Yet it must be the case that S holds *either* p or $not\text{-}p$. *(S* may, of course, hold inconsistent beliefs, but that is a different matter. The sort of case I have in mind is one in which there is no question of S's holding both p and $not\text{-}p$, but of his holding one belief and not the other.)

Such a worry, however, largely misses the thrust of what has been said already. The thesis is that, in the end, there *can be* no fundamental distinction between the psychological states one is ideally entitled to ascribe to a creature and those actually possessed by the creature. This is not a matter of verificationism (or "instrumentalism"), nor a matter of our being limited in our methods of discovering what states a creature is in. It is a matter, rather, of what *counts* as having or being in a given psychological state. If the criteria for the application of psychological predicates leave open the possibility of a degree of indeterminacy, then that indeterminacy is as much a "fact about the world" as it is a feature of our way of speaking (see Quine, 1960).

This is both more and less startling than one might suppose. It is, on the one hand, more startling because it suggests that there is no smooth "mapping" of psychological expressions onto either behavioral or physiological—or, for that matter, ectoplasmic—ones. It is, on the other hand, less startling if one takes into account all that has been said thus far. If one compares psychological talk to the use of a coordinate system to describe a certain geographical region, this becomes plain. There are numerous coordinate systems that might be employed in the description of a particular locale. The surface of the earth, for example, may be described using Mercator or polar "projections." It makes no sense to insist that only descriptions framed in one such system correctly describe the relative locations of geographical places. In the same way, psychological characterizations, when taken as wholes, may be regarded as essentially equivalent (again, as wholes) despite their very different appearances. One is apt to miss this point if one attends only to *local* phenomena, just as one is apt to be fooled by the apparent size of Greenland if one compares a Mercator with a polar projection of the earth's surface. Is Greenland *larger* on a map employing a Mercator projection, than it is on one determined by a polar projection? The question betrays a confusion about projective techniques and, in consequence, makes no clear sense. Just so with the attribution of beliefs, desires, and the like. Do S's beliefs about tomatoes, given one global characterization of S's beliefs and desires, differ from his beliefs about tomatoes given a distinct global characterization? This question, too, seems to lack a clear sense. It presupposes what is surely false, namely that beliefs and desires can be (individually) held constant while their background conditions are altered.

A Map Analogy

Much of what I have been struggling to say clearly may perhaps be brought into some sort of focus by considering the proposed analogy between complexes of psychological states ("mental complexes," for short) and mapping systems. We know that it is possible to describe features of the surface of our planet by projecting onto that surface a system of coordinates. Using this system one may locate various places, calculate their distances from each other, their relative sizes, and the like. All these things may be put into a map which one may then use to find one's way about and to tell others how to reach places that they might otherwise be unable to locate.

One notable feature of this technique is that it would be useful only on a planet the surface of which consisted of more or less easily identifiable and persistent landmarks. On a planet whose surface was as smooth and featureless as that of a billiard ball, or on one that was gaseous and unstable, it would not take one far. A similar point may be made concerning belief-attributions. It is useful to ascribe beliefs to creatures only if they are capable of a relatively wide and interesting pattern of actions and only if they show signs of being able to adapt their behavior in the face of changes in their environment. Otherwise the mechanism of belief-attribution is mostly idle. It seems, for this reason, perfectly natural to attribute beliefs to a monkey or a rat, rather less felicitous to ascribe them to a caterpillar or a shrimp, and entirely pointless to speak of them in connection with the activities of tiny, primitive creatures whose behavior is limited and rigid. (The legitimacy of extending belief-attributions to nonhuman creatures will be taken up in chapter VIII.)

Maps, as we have noted already, resemble mental complexes in another respect as well. One cannot speak of a single location on a map without implicitly invoking the whole system of coordinates in which that location is embedded. In speaking of propositions in "logical space," the author of the *Tractatus* advances a similar thesis: "A proposition can determine only one place in logical space: nevertheless the whole of logical space must be already given by it" (Wittgenstein, 1921/61, 3.42). Mental complexes evidently function analogously. They provide a scaffolding or backdrop against which attributions of particular beliefs and desires make sense and without which such attributions would be impossible. To ascribe a particular belief to an agent is to single out one aspect of his mental complex, an aspect that may be of particular interest or significance to those concerned with the agent's activities at the time (including, of course, the agent himself).

This brings to mind another, previously mentioned, respect in which the parallel between beliefs and maps seems illuminating. Two maps employing different modes of projection, different coordinate systems, may be used to describe a particular stretch of terrain. Assuming that each of these is accurate, both may be said correctly to depict how things stand geographically. This will be so even if isolated bits of one map seem to be nothing at all like isolated bits on its counterpart. Whether a certain cartographic region on the one corresponds to a particular region on the other is not something that could be determined simply by comparing, piecemeal or in isolation, the two regions. Rather, one must discover how each region is embedded in the whole map of which it is a part.

In the same way, the impression that distinct interpretive schemes might, with equal warrant, assign incompatible beliefs to some intelligent agent owes its plausibility to our tendency to treat beliefs as solitary and detachable bits of psychological paraphernalia. Before representational states may be compared, however, they must be identified. And this requires more than attention to discrete behavioral episodes (linguistic or otherwise); it requires, as well, a determination of the place of those episodes in a comprehensive and ongoing pattern of deeds and utterances.

Maps can tell us how things are laid out, what to expect when we travel from one place to another, and how far we need to go to reach a particular destination. They cannot, however, tell us much about what is beneath the surface of a particular region, what its hidden geographical characteristics are, what brought about its special topography. If we wish to know about such things, we shall have to put down our maps and take up picks, shovels, and other implements suitable for geological exploration. In the same way, our knowledge of mental complexes provides us with a way of describing, accounting for, and predicting behavior, but little in the way of an understanding of the underlying physiological mechanisms presumably responsible for that behavior. One's supposing that there is a simple relation between features of mental complexes and features of these underlying mechanisms would be rather like one's assuming that meridian lines on a map correspond in some simple way to geological features of the planet. One's imagining a one-to-one correspondence between beliefs and internal structures parallels the mistake of a child who supposes that the equator is a groove running around the circumference of the earth. The notion that a scientist could "read off" a person's beliefs simply by inspecting his brain is analogous to the notion that one might discover one's latitude and longitude by carefully analyzing the soil of the terrain on which one is standing.

We are able to use belief-attributions to describe and predict the behavior of intelligent creatures, not because such attributions happen to match up straightforwardly with particular goings-on (or types of going-on) inside those creatures, but simply because the notions of belief and desire provide us with a framework within which behavior that we regard as intelligent may be sorted out. Similarly, maps are useful to us, though not because our planet evolved geologically in accordance with certain geometrical principles. The boring truth is that the geology of the earth has been, until recently anyway, determined exclusively by geological factors. The use of maps enables us to say certain things about the world that we should find it enormously difficult, perhaps impossible, to say otherwise. The same may be said for belief.

It would not do to push the analogy between maps and mental complexes much further. I have introduced it only to provide some measure of clarification for the view of representational mental states that I have been laboring to develop in the present chapter. I have no intention, however, of implying that ascriptions of beliefs, for example, are arbitrary in quite the way maps may perhaps be thought to be arbitrary. Nor do I mean to suggest that agents "don't really" have psychological states. Of course they do. Such states are not, for example, "convenient fictions." We need, however, to be clear about what it means— and what it does *not* mean—to say that a creature possesses them.

Supervenience and Psychological Autonomy

How does this emerging picture of psychological states fit with earlier remarks on supervenience and "levels of description"? We may suppose that talk of psychological states— mental representations—belongs at a certain descriptive level, a level distinct from that at which talk of purely behavioral or neural properties finds a place. Psychological properties may, even so, be regarded as *supervening* on the latter. Thus, psychological properties are in some fashion determined by (though not reducible to) "lower level" non-psychological properties of the creatures to whom such properties are attributable.

I have suggested already that aesthetic features of a painting may be regarded as supervening on various of its non-aesthetic, physical properties. To say this is, I take it, to say that the painting has whatever aesthetic characteristics it has in virtue of certain of its ordinary physical characteristics. This need not mean, however, that the former are *reducible to* the latter, that aesthetic predicates are in some way *analyzable into* or *inferrable from* non-aesthetic ones.

These points are nicely illustrated in R. M. Hare's characterization of moral properties as supervenient:

> Suppose we say "St. Francis was a good man." It is logically impossible to say this and to maintain at the same time that there might have been another man placed in exactly the same circumstances as St. Francis, and who behaved in exactly the same way, but who differed from St. Francis in this respect only, that he was not a good man. (Hare, 1952, p. 145)

St. Francis has, one supposes, whatever moral properties he has in virtue of (certain of) his non-moral properties (but of course not vice versa). It need not follow, however, that moral properties are merely fictions, or that they are "eliminable," or that moral predicates are in any sense reducible to naturalistic, non-moral ones. What does seem to follow, rather, is that moral discourse belongs at a different descriptive level than talk about non-moral states and processes.

One ought not be misled by these examples into imagining that supervenience relations are intended to hold only between "normative" and "natural" properties (or families of properties). Something's being a table, for example, appears to supervene on its being a certain molecular configuration. Identical configurations will result in identical tables, yet tables may result, as well, from widely different kinds of configuration. Tables in this sense may be "nothing more" than collections of molecules even though it is (at least) enormously unlikely that "criteria of tablehood," specifications of what could and what could not count as a table, might be framed in terms of molecules and their properties. The relation between particular tables and their "underlying" atomic constituents, then, may be one of identity, without its being the case that tables are reducible to, definable in terms of, or logically derivable from anything more "basic."

I am not certain that the notion of supervenience can, in the end, be made to work or whether, even if it can, the relation between the mental and the physical ought properly to be regarded as one of supervenience. Suppose one grants, however, that representational psychological states, mental representations, are (or at any rate might be) supervenient in the way envisaged on ordinary physical features of intelligent creatures. What follows?

In the first place, we shall want to be clear about *which* non-psychological properties of an intelligent creature might determine that creature's mental properties. Could mental states be taken to supervene, for instance, exclusively on certain neural configurations? Or only on these together with additional, extra-neural bodily features? Those who imagine that brains kept alive *in vitro* are unproblematically capable of thought seem committed to the former notion. Those embracing what Stephen Stich (1978) has called "the principle of psychological autonomy" require at least the latter.

Imagine that a technology were available which would enable us to duplicate people. That is, we can build living human beings who are atom for atom and molecule for molecule replicas of some given human being. Now suppose that we have before us a human being . . . and his exact replica. What the principle of autonomy claims is that these two humans will be psychologically identical, that any psychological property instantiated by one of these subjects will also be instantiated by the other. (Stich, 1978, pp. 573 ff.)

The intuition here is that psychological explanation, properly speaking, ought to be concerned just with those internal (that is, nonrelational) features of agents that direct their intelligent behavior.

... [T]he principle of psychological autonomy states that the properties and relations to be invoked in an explanatory psychological theory must be supervenient upon the *current, internal physical* properties and relations of organisms (i.e., just those properties that an organism shares with all of its replicas). (Stich, 1978, p. 575, emphasis in text)

In insisting that only "current, internal physical" properties of agents are "psychologically relevant," the principle of autonomy

... decrees irrelevant all those properties that deal with the history of the organism, both past and future. It is entirely possible, for example, for two organisms to have quite different physical histories and yet, at a specific pair of moments, to be [psychological] replicas of one another. (Stich, 1978, pp. 575 ff.)

It is not, of course, that intelligent creatures, or for that matter, intelligent creature *parts*, lack all sorts of interesting relational properties, or that external goings-on play no role in their development or behavior. Rather, such properties and occurrences are *psychologically* irrelevant, they fall outside a purely *psychological* specification of an intelligent creature. Goings-on outside the skin are relevant to psychology only indirectly, only via their internal *effects*.

There is something of a parallel between the requirements of an autonomous psychology and those governing the explanation of the functioning of a computing machine by reference to its program. Computing machines have a multitude of relational properties and are affected in a variety of ways by what goes on outside their metallic skins. Yet, if our aim is to explain a machine's operation by reference to its program, we are perforce debarred from invoking such goings-on. To say that a computing machine is inverting a matrix because its operator, *S*, has a passion for such things, or that it has blown a fuse because of a wayward electrical surge, is to explain its operation (on a particular occasion), but to do so in ways that are in one obvious sense or another irrelevant from the point of view of the programmer.

The computing machine analogy is not meant to suggest that programs provide descriptions of the internal physical mechanisms that drive such machines. On the contrary; program-level properties are to be regarded as somehow *supervening* on such mechanisms. Those properties are realized (one supposes) by the machine in virtue of its electrical and mechanical features, and the very same properties (one is assured) might be realized in utterly different sorts of devices. Further, an explanation of a computing machine's function in terms of its program is not distinguished from other sorts of explanation just by the fact that programs mention only *interior* features of the machine; a purely mechanical explanation might do the same. It seems, rather, that the predicates associated with programs are at a *higher level* than those belonging to the accounts of an electrical engineer.

Similarly, one cannot distinguish psychological explanations of behavior from biological or physiological accounts solely by reference to autonomy. One must add that psychological explanation is distinctive in virtue of its being couched in terms of those (supervenient) properties of agents that are properly *representational* (beliefs, desires, and the like). Biology and physiology may deal with neural mechanisms on which psychological states might be thought to supervene, but such accounts make no use of the *representational* features of those mechanisms. Thus psychological theory is meant to be autonomous in a second sense: it is not interchangeable with physiology or biology.

If one couples the principle of autonomy with the doctrine

that representational states supervene on internal, physical states, one generates what may be called the principle of *representational autonomy*. According to this principle, representational properties, or at any rate those with psychological interest, must be determined by (supervene on) internal, nonrelational features of the creature instantiating them, just those interior features that would be shared by a creature and its "atom for atom and molecule for molecule" replica.

One powerful intuition embodied in the doctrine of psychological autonomy is that the psychological states of a creature and its replica, despite substantial divergence in their relational properties (they may, for example, have been brought about in very different circumstances), must share a common representational *content*. Further, this content must be determined just by states and goings-on inside each of the two creatures; this is the principle of representational autonomy.

Such a view obliges one to distinguish sharply between the "purely representational" properties of mental states and certain of their *epistemic* properties, ones pinned, for example, to the truth and falsity of their propositional content. Imagine that S and T are "atom for atom and molecule for molecule" replicas, although S and T have enormously different histories. S was born in Philadelphia in 1950, T was manufactured last week in a laboratory in Tijuana. Thus, although both S and T (it would seem) believe they witnessed the fifth game of the 1958 World Series, S, having been there, *remembers* watching Gil McDougald hit a home run, while T merely believes (falsely) that he saw the same. The principle of autonomy requires that in explaining the behavior of S and T we appeal only to their respective beliefs. The truth and falsity of those beliefs, or their epistemic warrant is, from the perspective of psychological explanation, utterly irrelevant.

On such a conception, S and T must be regarded as psychologically identical even though their beliefs differ widely in truth-value (indeed, virtually all of T's beliefs about his past will be false). This, however, seems a mere complication, hardly grounds for doubting the principle of psychological autonomy.

One may feel less sanguine about the fact that the latter principle requires, as well, that one ignore differences in the referential and indexical features of beliefs. *S*'s belief that he, *S*, is standing upright, seems to differ crucially from *T*'s belief that he, *T*, is standing upright. *S*, in addition, has countless beliefs about the house in which he lives and his dog, Spot. How is one to characterize *T*'s supposedly corresponding beliefs? Are they beliefs about *S*'s house and dog? Or are they, rather, false beliefs about non-existent dogs and houses? If one considers the possibility that *S* and *T* are, respectively, inhabitants of Earth and Twin-Earth, a planet "atom for atom and molecule for molecule" identical to Earth, then virtually all of their beliefs about particulars will differ in these ways.

Consideration of such cases suggests that if autonomous psychology is to be made to work, a way must be found to distinguish an *autonomous mental content* (what *S*'s and *T*'s beliefs, despite differences of the sort illustrated above, have in common) from non-autonomous (hence "psychologically irrelevant") features of mental states. It is not easy to feel optimistic about this possibility. Stich suggests that in stripping away from beliefs all that seems, in the sense envisaged, non-autonomous, one may be left with something that cannot properly be described as a belief, hence something that could not play the role of belief in a suitable psychological theory. If what was said earlier about belief-attribution was on the right track, it seems clear that by pushing ahead into such matters, one leaves behind the notion of representation altogether and thus jeopardizes the prospects of an autonomous psychology in a different and perhaps unexpected way. Peeling away the nonrelational properties of psychological states evidently leaves one not with pure, autonomous representational content, but instead with states drained of their representational properties altogether, hence ones of no interest to a proper *psychology*.

The conception of psychological state attribution I have been defending is in one sense compatible with the notion that such states supervene on neurophysiological states and processes but not, on that account, with the (much stronger) doctrine of psychological autonomy. St. Francis's moral properties may supervene on various of his non-moral features, but the latter must surely include more than occurrences in the interior of St. Francis. In the same way psychological characterization depends on much else besides neural occurrences, it depends on (what Hare calls) "circumstances" and on patterns of behavior over time. One who continues to insist that S and his replica, T, must, at any rate, act "just the same," imagines that there is some way of specifying what counts as *the same* that does not require appeal to essentially relational (situational, historical) features of agents. There is, perhaps, such a criterion of sameness, but it pertains neither to ordinary descriptions of deeds done nor to representational psychological states, but only to non-intentional, Newtonian descriptions of bodily motions and the like. If S and T are physiologically indistinguishable, one may suppose that they will, in virtue of this fact, make similar noises when they are prodded or interrogated. This, however, does not entail the rather stronger notion that those sounds thereby have the same *sense*. Precisely the same point can be made for S's and T's beliefs, desires and the like. S's behavior on a particular occasion may manifest his belief that p. If T's bodily motions, on the same occasion, match S's down to the last muscle contraction, it does not follow that T's behavior manifests this same belief (or that it manifests any belief at all). (On this see Davidson, 1973a, 1974, 1975; see also Putnam, 1981, chap. 1.)

The Computational Level of Description

This way of regarding psychological states and processes, I have suggested, runs counter to views that take these to be "internal representations" (the doctrine championed, for example, in Fodor, 1975). One way of setting off the differences here involves returning briefly to the notion of descriptive levels. On the view I have been recommending, there are two relevant descriptive levels, the psychological and the neural-behavioral.[6] One may wish, in any case, to divide the field further by distinguishing a purely behavioral level of description from the neural. Such a division complicates, but does not fundamentally alter the picture I wish to sketch.

In contrast to this view, those who speak of internal representations in the special sense in which Fodor does, evidently have in mind an intermediate descriptive level. Thus, lying between and connecting talk about psychological states and processes and talk about neural goings-on, is a *computational* stratum. If one prefers to speak of properties and supervenience rather than of descriptive levels, then this point may be put by saying that psychological properties of intelligent creatures are "realized in" certain *computational* features of those creatures, and these, in turn, are determined by their neural make-up (or, more generally, by their "hardware"). Psychological properties, on such a view, supervene on computational properties, and the latter themselves supervene on various strictly physical (presumably structural), internal properties of intelligent creatures (or devices).

The question is, why should one suppose that there is such an intermediate, computational level—whether of properties or descriptions? In one sense, perhaps, the supposition is innocuous. If it is true, as has been claimed, that anything at all instantiates *some* computational program or other, then the claim that agents to whom psychological states are ascribable do indeed realize some such program is true but uninteresting (see Searle, 1980). The stronger claim, namely that intelligent creatures come by whatever psychological states they have solely in virtue of their instantiating a certain computational program,

---

6. By "behavioral" here I mean only to be referring to what are sometimes called "bodily motions," not to what is ordinarily labeled "behavior." In the latter usage, beliefs, desires, intentions, and the like are implicit (see e.g., Davidson, 1971).

seems, in contrast, interesting but dubious. Such a program would, at best, determine physical responses and motions, not psychological interpretations of these. The latter depend on, among other things, situational and historical occurrences that are altogether external to the logic of interior mechanisms. Seen in this light, Fodor's advocacy of "methodological solipsism," that is, his contention that cognitive psychology *must* be autonomous in roughly the sense discussed earlier, amounts to what Davidson has called "changing the subject" (see Fodor, 1980; Davidson, 1970). If we limit our inquiry to occurrences (whether physiological or computational) inside the skin of intelligent agents, there seems no prospect of appeal to representational states.

One matter remains to be discussed, however. I have recommended a causal account of perception. Perceptual states have been described as *resulting from* a complex causal chain, each link of which is itself a particular physical event. It is enormously tempting, given such a view, to identify perceptual states with those neural states produced by this process. This makes it appear that beliefs, for example, are (genuinely) interior states, namely those physiological states (perhaps those with certain "syntactic" features) in perceivers brought about by a particular causal process. How else, one may wonder, can we entertain thoughts of a *causal* account of perception?

I have taken considerable trouble to show that one need not—indeed ought not—regard beliefs and similar representational psychological states as interior, possibly neural, configurations. But if this is so, how is it possible to account for their causal role? Beliefs are, in many cases, brought about by ordinary physical events and lead, often, to deeds that are themselves comprised of ordinary bodily events. The significance of our appeal to beliefs in the explanation of intelligent behavior seems to depend on these causal, mediating properties. I have suggested that beliefs supervene on "lower level" properties of believers, but their role as mediators of behavior suggests that their "supervenience base" must be strictly neural (see Kim, 1978, 1979, 1982).

Consider, however, what is implied by one's holding one property to be supervenient on others, when, for instance, some aesthetic property of a painting is held to supervene on certain of its non-aesthetic features. Such conceptions seem plausible not because there are correlations between aesthetic and non-aesthetic properties, but simply because one imagines that any particular instance of, say, beauty, will be realized in *some* purely physical distribution of ink or pigment.

The same is true of psychological states and processes. One may suppose (or, if one accepts the assumption of physicalism, one must suppose) that every particular, dated psychological state or process is realized in *some* physical state or process. Further, one may (or must) hold that it is in virtue of this fact that the psychological state or event finds a place in the causal nexus. What would be wrong, of course, would be to move from these claims to the view that there are causal laws connecting physical and psychological events (in the way that there may be causal laws connecting, for example, retinal and electromagnetic ones). It is this that makes the notion that psychological states— mental representations—are internal states enormously misleading. It is undoubtedly true that neural events make a difference here. But this is only to say that a different sequence of neural occurrences (and their attendant behavioral effects) might force a change in psychological assessment. If one tampers with the distribution of pigments on a canvas, the result may be a painting with very different aesthetic properties. From this, however, it would be unwise to conclude that aesthetic properties were pigment properties.

If beliefs have causal properties, then, this may be (and almost certainly is) due to the fact that creatures to whom particular beliefs are attributable have certain sorts of complex interiors. It does not, however, follow that talk about beliefs is really talk about those interiors (even talk about those interiors at an elevated—computational—level of description). Psychological descriptions of persons and their activities depend upon one's being able to interpret or characterize things done and said in light of a rational, coherent, and appropriate scheme. This requires appeal to much that lies outside the skin of the agent, much that goes on at a temporal remove from the present moment. Psychological states of the sort I have been discussing are individuated only by the place they occupy in an edifice comprised of further, similar psychological states. They fit an agent not individually, one by one, but only as a structured whole. These constraints on belief, desire, and the like evidently block attempts to regard such states as purely internal features of the creatures to whom they are ascribed.

Concluding Remarks

These observations, of course, depend on my earlier discussion of the conditions licensing the attribution of such things as beliefs and desires. In the absence of a knockdown argument in favor of that conception, one may remain skeptical about my dismissal of the notion of internal representation and the cognitive psychological theorizing that evidently relies on that notion. On matters such as these, however, it is perhaps unreasonable to expect decisive proof or refutation. Instead, one is confronted with alternative approaches to a subject-matter. Admittedly, such approaches differ not merely in point of view or perspective, but substantively as well. This may lead us to expect lines of battle to be clearly drawn, opposing positions to be sharply set off from one another.

Philosophical differences, however, are not often like this. Disagreements over one matter are traceable to disagreements elsewhere, and these to still further differences. This is one reason that philosophical views are rarely shown to be demonstrably false. Rather they come and go, grow more or less fashionable depending on changes in background circumstances or *Zeitgeist* that serve to set off or to blur issues in the foreground.[7] My goal in the present chapter has been to sketch a plausible alternative to the conception of mental representation that has come to dominate "cognitive science." I have wished to suggest that it is possible to invoke representational mental states in explanations of cognitive phenomena without, on the one hand, dragging in some notion of internal systems of representation or, on the other hand, falling back on one or another species of reductionism. More particularly, I have spoken of perception as the production "in us" of certain belieflike cognitive states without wishing simultaneously to embrace the view that such states *must* be understood as interior computational or syntactic configurations.

Now I shall direct attention to a question that has repeatedly come to the fore: to what extent is the having of representational psychological states dependent on linguistic ability?

7. This is not to say that there is no progress in philosophy, only that progress cannot be calculated incrementally. To imagine that the issues that nowadays excite our interest are the very same issues that puzzled our philosophical ancestors is as misleading as imagining that present-day physicists' concern with the ultimate constituents of matter are pursuing the very same questions as those pursued by the Milesians.

VIII
LANGUAGE AND THOUGHT

There are a large number of words differing from each other in almost all respects, but having this point in common, that they are not the plain English for what is meant, not the forms that the mind uses in its private debates to convey to itself what it is talking about, but translations of these into language that is held more suitable for public exhibition. We tell our thoughts, like our children, to put on their hats and coats before they go out; the policeman who has *gone* to the scene of the disturbance will tell the magistrate that he *proceeded* there; a minister of the Crown may *foresee* the advantages of his policy and *outline* it to his colleagues but in presenting it to Parliament he may *visualize* the first and *adumbrate* the second. These outdoor costumes are often needed; not only may decency be outraged sometimes by over-plain speech; dignity may be compromised if the person who thinks in slang writes also in slang. (Fowler, 1965, p. 208)

Thought and Speech

What is the connection, if there is one, between language and thought? To what extent are thoughts themselves linguistic entities or episodes? When one thinks does one engage necessarily in some form of inner speech, *sermo interior?* And, if so, is there a special "language of thought," a dialect perhaps distinct from and prior to ordinary spoken language? Might creatures that lack a language nevertheless be said to have thoughts?

I propose to draw a bead on these questions—and certain related ones as well—by examining two very different accounts of thought, ones advanced by D. M. Armstrong and Donald

Davidson.[1] Very generally, Armstrong wishes to deny that in order to possess thoughts a creature must, in addition, be conversant in some language. In contrast, Davidson holds that only creatures capable of employing a full-fledged language are capable of thought.

I should perhaps say a word at the outset concerning the two notions under discussion: thought and language. By "language" I intend something more than the simple capacity to *communicate*. Many things may be said to communicate, but it would be implausible to regard them, in virtue of this fact alone, as linguistic. Your dripping umbrella tells me it is raining out-doors, the cry of an infant informs us that it is unhappy, the squeak of the garden gate provides eloquent testimony that its hinge needs oiling. From the fact, then, that creatures are often linked together communicatively, it need not follow that they are employing a language. This is a small point, but one sometimes overlooked in discussions of so-called animal languages (see Heil, 1982). In any case, I wish to reserve the term "language" for activities more sophisticated, varied, and interesting than those that are merely communicative. These matters will receive further attention presently.

With respect to thought, I shall, in what follows, narrow the topic somewhat and discuss only one species of thought, namely belief. This may seem unwise. Thus, one may feel that what holds true for belief may well fail to hold, for example, for various sorts of "occurrent" thought. I concede this, but doubt that it poses a serious difficulty for the matters of concern in the present chapter.

If one considers thoughts to have two fundamental compo-nents, (i) some intentional or representational mental *content* or other, together with (ii) an *attitude* (of acceptance, hope, fear, longing, doubt) toward that content, then it seems clear that most of the difficulties one has in determining the relation

---

1. I shall concentrate here on views set out in Armstrong, 1973, and in Davidson, 1975. Parenthetical references will be to these sources unless otherwise noted.

between language and thought, the reticence, for example, one may feel in ascribing thoughts to dumb animals, center on the former component, thought *content*. And it is this that is common to all (or, at any rate, most) sorts of thought. The real issue seems to be whether one can justifiably ascribe such mental contents to beings that lack a capacity for speech, beings that I shall henceforth refer to as *mute creatures*.[2] If one thinks of beliefs, for example, as acceptances or endorsements of particular representational contents, then it is easy to regard beliefs as an especially primitive or basic form of thought. Thus, if Davidson were right in arguing that mute creatures could not have beliefs, then it would not be unreasonable to suppose that the very same arguments would lead to the conclusion that such creatures could not engage in other, subtler forms of mental activity either.

Finally, it is perhaps worth reminding ourselves that representational states were introduced in Part One as components of perception. There I suggested that perceptual states were best regarded as beliefs. In any case, I threw myself behind an account of perception that included, as an essential element, belieflike cognitive states. I committed myself, as well, to the idea that such an account could be smoothly extended to creatures other than human beings, ones presumably lacking a recognizable language. In so doing, I implicitly embraced the view that at least certain sorts of thought can correctly be ascribed to mute creatures. The present chapter constitutes an attempt to extend and vindicate this claim.

Armstrong's Account of Belief

In order to understand Armstrong's views about the connection of language and belief, it will be necessary to examine in

---

2. I do not mean to suggest that mute creatures are incapable of making noises, or of communicating (as birds do) with sounds, or of mimicking human speech. Examples of mute creatures are rats, dogs, parrots, chimpanzees, and human infants. (See Heil, 1982.)

some detail his conception of belief-content. The latter conception seems to me, in certain respects, seriously defective, and it seems so for roughly the same reasons that theories that rely on the postulation of internal representations seem, generally, to be defective. I shall, on that account, take the time to point out what I consider to be its flaws. My hope is that, in so doing, I shall provide some additional, if indirect, support for the view of belief endorsed in the previous chapter.

According to Armstrong, then, beliefs are internal states of a special sort. It is likely, he thinks, that these states will turn out to be identical with states of believers' brains, though they *might* not (the issue, he suggests, is an empirical one). It may turn out, for example, that the sorts of property required of ordinary "belief-states" could not be had by any imaginable brain-state. If that were so, we should have to ask whether the properties in question might be had by something other than a brain, an immaterial mind perhaps, an organ with special irreducibly intentional properties. We should, however, do well to be suspicious of theories that *begin* with the assumption that beliefs (or representational states in general) are what they are in virtue of their possession of some special non-physical property. In this regard, the use by certain theorists of the property of "intrinsic intentionality," seems especially ad hoc (Armstrong cites Brentano, 1874/1960). It may be that there are such properties, but this is a conclusion to which one should be driven, not a datum with which to begin an investigation.

In any case, "belief-states," considered as a species of representation, are said, by Armstrong, to exhibit "an inner complexity which mirrors the complexity of the proposition which is believed" (p. 50; see Wittgenstein, 1921/61, 4.121). They are, in this respect, like maps of a particular region, but for one crucial difference. Ordinary maps represent states of affairs *conventionally*, they must be *interpreted*, given a sense. A map may be *applied* correctly or incorrectly, it may be *taken* one way rather than another. One can use a map only if one has some prior grasp of established mapping conventions, and an understanding of the particular conventions (typically set out in a *key* or *legend)* employed by its maker. Such things cannot be the case for belief-states, however. One does not interpret one's beliefs, and decide what they are about. To apprehend one's belief-states *is* to apprehend them as being about this or that state of affairs. Belief-states, then, must represent *of themselves, naturally,* not conventionally.

The point here is a familiar one. If a belief-state did not represent naturally, we should expose ourselves to an unpalatable regress. If belief-states, like maps, had to be interpreted, we should have to postulate something further that imposes the interpretation, an item that, in effect, stipulates: "Belief-state *B* represents *R*." This "something further" must itself either (i) represent what it does (somehow) naturally, or (ii) represent in virtue of some further interpretation. One is driven, in this way, to postulate what H. H. Price has called *natural signs* if one is to avoid a representational regress (Price, 1946).

The notion of a natural sign is the notion of an entity that represents whatever it does simply because of the way it is, just in virtue of its own internal properties. To apprehend such an entity *is* to apprehend what it represents. Armstrong suggests that belief-states are natural signs of this sort:

> If belief-states are "maps" then they are maps in their own nature. Nothing outside themselves, and in particular not conventions, make them into maps. (p. 54)

Consider a particular belief-state, *B,* a belief about some state of affairs, *A*.[3] We shall say that *B,* in addition to whatever causal properties it may have, has certain representational properties as well: *B* represents *A*. That *B* represents *A* rather than some other state of affairs is due, according to Armstrong, to the fact that the structure of *B* matches the structure of *A,* to-

---

3. *B,* of course, must be a state of some believer, *S.* Throughout this exposition I shall use the term "belief" to stand for a particular, dated state, one possessed by some particular doxastic agent. My interest here is in how it is that believers embody or *realize* such things as beliefs.

gether with the fact that the elements comprising B "reach out" to the constituents of A in a certain way. Let us leave aside for the moment difficulties with the notion that elements "reach out" somehow of their own accord and grant, provisionally, that this picture is satisfactory.[4]

Consider a simple example: Moscow's being to the east of Smolensk, a state of affairs, and its representation on a map in the usual way. Moscow may be represented by a particular jot, Smolensk by another jot, and the relation to-the-east-of by the relation to-the-right-of on the map. Here, if one wishes to speak of elements of the state of affairs, one may say that these include a pair of particulars, Moscow and Smolensk, which bear a certain geographical relation to one another. The corresponding elements in the cartographic representation of this state of affairs are a pair of jots, appropriately labeled, that bear to one another a corresponding spatial relation.

Suppose now that S holds the belief that Moscow is to the east of Smolensk. According to Armstrong, this would involve S's being in a particular belief-state, one that, among other things, incorporates representations of Moscow, Smolensk, and the relation to-the-east-of in a way formally analogous to the map. If this were all there were to the theory it would be of little interest. So far we have been given no account of the mechanisms that enable the constituents of belief-states to "reach out" to constituents of states of affairs. Armstrong, however, argues that it is by way of *ideas,* the elementary components of beliefs, that such reaching out occurs. Ideas are representational atoms; beliefs are structures, molecular complexes that represent what

---

4. It is perhaps worth mentioning that one may allow that what a sign represents is determined by the sign's structure, without necessarily committing oneself to the further notion that representation is *simply* a matter of structure (as in Palmer, 1978). Thus, "xRy" may represent a state of affairs distinct from "yRx," and this difference may be due to a structural difference in the two signs. It is one thing, however, to hold that the structure of a sign can make a difference in what it represents, and quite another matter to imagine that representation is entirely explicable in terms of structure. Structure, one might say, makes a difference *given* a system of representation. (See McLendon, 1955; Heil, 1981).

they do in virtue of the ideas that comprise them. The character of ideas, then, is crucial, and it is to these that I should now like to turn.

Ideas and Concepts

Armstrong begins by developing a distinction between (what he calls) concepts and ideas.[5] Ideas are, as we noted, representational elements, items that represent both the constituents of states of affairs and the relations obtaining among these. Ideas themselves are particulars, they come and go, resemble one another in various ways, and so on. Concepts, in contrast, are not like this. To possess a concept is to possess a certain skill or ability, the ability, namely, to form ideas that correspond to the concept (p. 52). If I have the concept (of) X, then I have the capacity to entertain ideas about X's.

> . . . [I]f a child has the concept of "dog," he is capable (given that other conditions are also satisfied) of forming beliefs and having thoughts in which dogs figure. Contrariwise, if he can form beliefs and have thoughts in which dogs figure, then it is entailed that he has the concept of dog. Each such belief-state or thought-episode will have a structure, one element of which will be the Idea of dog. (p. 52)

Capacities of this sort are dispositional, at least in the sense that they may be had without ever being put to use.

Belief-states, as we have had occasion to observe already, must possess the property of "self-directedness":

> Beliefs are to be thought of as maps which carry their interpretation of reality within themselves. Of their own nature, apart from any conventions of interpretation, they point to the existence of a certain state of affairs (though there may be no such state of affairs). They have an intrinsic power of representation. (p. 4)

---

5. In fact he employs the capitalized form "Ideas," a practice that I shall not follow except in direct quotations.

Armstrong prefaces these remarks with a quotation from the *Tractatus:*

> The pictorial relation consists of the correlations of the picture's elements with things. These correlations are, as it were, the feelers of the picture's elements, with which the picture touches reality. (Wittgenstein, 1921/61, 2.1514-2.1515)

Wittgenstein's idea, roughly, was that the components of a "picture" (or in the case of a proposition, a special sort of picture, the constituent *names)* were linked of their own accord to particular elements of reality. Different arrangements of pictorial components produce different pictures, pictorial representations of distinct states of affairs. The latter may be depicted only by configurations of elements, but the *linkage* between depictions and depicted states of affairs is accomplished at the level of elements.

It is, in fact, here that the "picture theory" of the *Tractatus* seems to break down, for Wittgenstein provides no clear account of the capacity of pictorial elements to attach themselves to their referents. Armstrong's theory may be seen in this light as an attempt to remedy this Tractarian omission.

The property of "self-directedness" possessed by beliefs may be explained, says Armstrong, if one can account somehow for the self-directedness of the simplest ideas. That a thought has a sense is owing to its being constructed of these elementary bits; that it has one sense rather than another is owing to the manner in which its elements are configured. Again, the map analogy seems useful. Maps contain an assortment of "non-relational elements related in various ways" (p. 55). One may imagine, for instance, marks representing schools, bridges, and highways. These marks are related to one another spatially, and their being in a given spatial relation means that a certain geographical region is laid out in a certain way.

Such analogies suggest that "there must be a set of *primitive* or *fundamental* elements and relations. Given the interpretation of the whole set, then it will be determined 'what the map asserts' " (p. 55). Beliefs resemble maps in being composed of "fundamental 'representing' elements and relations" (p. 55). These are simple ideas, self-directed elements that represent *intrinsically.*

The suggestion that simple elements are intrinsically representational need not commit one to the view that, just by themselves (that is, in isolation) they represent any state of affairs. On a map, for instance, a given jot can represent a particular locale only when it appears together with other symbols (see *Tractatus* 3.3: "Only propositions have sense; only in the nexus of a proposition does a name have a meaning"). A school symbol, just by itself, doesn't *say* anything at all (any more than an ordinary proper name—"Nebraska," for example—says anything when it stands alone). To understand or grasp the significance of such a symbol is to understand the range of things that it can, when combined with other symbols, be used to represent (see e.g., *Tractatus,* 2.012-2.0124, 3.201-3.203). All this is meant to be true as well of simple ideas.

Given a preliminary notion of what constitutes a simple idea, one may proceed to characterize *complex* ideas as concatenations of simple ideas.

> They are built up of simple Ideas in the same way that, in a map, complex representations are built out of primitive or "simple" representational features. . . . [L]ike the complex representations on a map, complex Ideas can be analyzed *without remainder* in terms of simple Ideas. . . . The logical analyses of concepts produced by philosophers . . . would seem to be attempts to lay bare to reflective consciousness the structure of our complex concepts. (p. 59)

All mental representation, then, comes down to the representational properties of the simplest ideas.

The plausibility of such a view hinges on whether anything can be made of the notion that certain ideas are self-directed, that they possess an "intrinsic power of representation." It is this that, in the end, enables thoughts to *have* a sense without having been *given* a sense.

In the case of a map, once the "interpretation" of the simple mapping features is fixed, the "interpretation" of the map is fixed. That is to say, if we know how to interpret these simple features, we can read the whole map. The "interpretation" of the simple mapping features is in turn fixed by the semi-iconic mapping conventions. But this brings us face to face with our problem. For the interpretation of our simple concepts and Ideas is not conventionally fixed. They have an intrinsic interpretation. Of their own nature they point in a certain direction. (p. 60)

This intrinsic "directionality" is, according to Armstrong, to be explained by reference to features of simple *concepts*. The latter, he suggests, may be regarded as "certain sorts of selective capacity towards things that fall under the concept in question" (p. 60). It is this that "constitutes their self-directedness" (p. 60).

Suppose that *S* possesses the concept of redness and suppose that this concept is a simple one. In that case, when, "in suitable circumstances," a red object "acts upon the mind" of *S*, *S*'s mind will come to be in a certain state. "This state is a capacity of *[S]*'s which he can exercise if he so desires, to act in a selective fashion towards the red object" (p. 61). In general, then, to possess a (simple) concept, *C*, is to possess a capacity to "act selectively" toward whatever exemplifies *C*, to react to things as members of the class *C* (p. 61).

S, we are imagining, has the concept of redness. Because of this, when a red thing "acts upon *S*'s mind," it creates a simple, internal map. The latter

... must register the *redness* of the object, that is, the map must contain a feature which gives a capacity for selective behavior towards the thing *qua* red thing. But equally, the map must contain something which will register *where* the object is relative to *S*. For if this is lacking, *S* will not be able to come into relation with the red object. (For instance he will not be able to point in the right direction.) (p. 61)[6]

6. At first one may be inclined to question the inclusion of the latter feature. Why, after all, does *S* need to be *told* where the red thing is? It is right *here*, "acting on *S*'s

The creation of a map of this sort inside S in effect endows him with the rudimentary belief that "this thing here is red." Such a belief has two components, an instance of the idea of red, and a "referential component," the idea of "this thing here" (p. 62). One must now ask whether this theory sheds light on the crucial property of self-directedness, that feature of simple ideas that is regarded as underlying all mental representation.

Self-Directedness

A creature, S, may, on Armstrong's view, be said to possess the concept, C, if S has the capacity to acquire beliefs of the form "this x is C" on those occasions, for instance, when S perceptually encounters an x that is C. The belief, thus acquired, has two components, one representing C-ness, and one representing "this thing here" (that is, x). It is the second component, the idea of "this thing here" that allows the belief to be *about* a particular state of affairs.

It is not clear, however, how any of this is supposed to help one understand the puzzling property of self-directedness. One is told that certain thoughts incorporate elements that *are* self-directed, and that this is due to their in some sense embodying the idea of "this thing here." But how, exactly, is this supposed to work? What is the *mechanism* of self-directedness?

Armstrong's answer is incorporated in his suggestion that the mind has the capacity to "respond selectively" to elements of the world as members of various classes. The problem (or, anyway, *one* problem) for such a view, as we saw in the last chapter, is to understand how this could be possible, in particular how it could be possible for classes that are, at the physical or biological level, ill-defined. Thus, one can perhaps imagine a

mind." This way of putting the matter, however, is misleading. What S acquires is a *belief* about a red object, the belief, namely, that "this thing here is red." It is not that S must *consult* his belief to discover the whereabouts of the red object. His discovery of its location *is* the acquisition of that belief. (Here and elsewhere I have used the designation S, where Armstrong uses A.)

device that "responds selectively" to particular wavelengths of light radiation. But can one, with equal ease, imagine a device that responds in this way to things in virtue of their being *valuable,* or *interesting,* or *morally praiseworthy?* In one sense, of course, it is simple to imagine such devices, namely *people! We* respond constantly to things as members of classes that seem impossible to characterize in any very clear way. Armstrong's account, however, purports to explain this capacity, not merely to call attention to it. And the "explanation" seems just to be that we are able to do this because we have inside us some mechanism or other, very probably a neural mechanism, that enables us to do it. Further, one component (at least) of that mechanism is *representational,* and it is this latter component that undergirds the capacity to realize *any* mental representation.

Like the author of the *Tractatus,* Armstrong takes representation to depend on some ultimate level of signs (simple ideas) whose representational characteristics are *intrinsic* to them, ones whose sense is determined somehow from *within.* Such signs are described as "reaching out" beyond themselves of their own accord. They generate their own significance in virtue of the fact that they are "switched on" in the right ways, they, as it were, *resonate* in the way a tuning fork resonates when it is "acted on" by the right sorts of vibratory occurrence.

There is, unfortunately, no obvious way to extend this model beyond the most elementary levels. And unless one supposes that our higher-level concepts and categories of thought are (literally) analyzable without remainder into concepts applicable at the most basic physical level, the theory is no help at all. Armstrong begins by pointing out that attempts to explain representational states by postulating special properties tailor-made for the task are "exposed to the suspicion which attends every attempt to solve a metaphysical problem by postulating a unique and irreducible entity or property" (p. 54). Yet it is far from clear that his own account comes to very much more than this.

My suspicion is that these difficulties are perfectly general, that they cover all theories that seek to explain representation "from the inside out." If this is so, if representational states are dependent on the sorts of social and behavioral patterns discussed at length in the last chapter, then it is not difficult to see why an account of the sort advanced by Armstrong is bound to disappoint one's expectations.

Armstrong on Linguistic Ability and Belief

Let us for the moment bracket these concerns and turn to a consideration of Armstrong's views about the connection between a creature's having a language and its having beliefs.

I have contended all along that there is nothing whatever objectionable in the ordinary practice of attributing beliefs to mute creatures, creatures that, so far as we know, lack linguistic ability. Certainly we ascribe beliefs to infants and to pets as readily as we do to professional colleagues. We explain, for example, Spot's barking at the foot of a tree by attributing to Spot the belief that the tree is occupied by a squirrel. This seems to make perfect sense. Our ascribing to Spot possession of this belief helps to explain his behavior in a way that we should not be able to do otherwise: why the *barking?* Why *this* tree? Tabby's vigilance outside a hole in the baseboard is chalked up to her desire for the mouse inside.

Just as in the case of human activities, the behavior of lesser creatures is illuminated by the attribution to them of beliefs and desires (and intentions: consider a tiger stalking its prey). Indeed, it is difficult to see how we could possibly come to understand their behavior otherwise. True, attempts have been made to forgo such mental intermediaries, notably the efforts of old-line behaviorists to replace talk about beliefs and desires with talk about stimuli and reinforcement histories. But in the absence of some special reason to the contrary, the attribution of a belief to a key-pecking pigeon or a desire to a barking dog seems both natural and useful.

One snag in this comfortable view appears when one is

challenged to say what it is precisely that a mute creature believes. Spot hears a noise and runs, wagging his tail, to the front door. We smile and say that Spot believes that his master is at the door. But even granting that Spot is acting on a belief of some sort, how can one be sure that it is *this* one and not, say, the belief that *Smith* is at the front door (assuming that Smith is Spot's master; but then who else but *Smith* would name his dog *Spot*?), or the belief that the stocky man who sets food out is at the door, or any of countless extensionally similar beliefs? How, in other words, is one nonarbitrarily to characterize the *content* of Spot's belief?

Armstrong suggests that, although such a task is difficult, it is by no means impossible: "generations of work by animal psychologists may be necessary before the exact content is known" (p. 27). This matter is made more complicated by the fact that belief-content is constrained by, among other things, the *concepts* one happens to possess. However we may wish to regard Spot's concepts, they need not be very like ours. But even if they were rather similar to ours, we should have difficulty in determining *which* of them Spot was invoking in cases of the sort just described.

The fact that the determination of belief-content for a mute creature may be a delicate business, however, need not lead to undue pessimism. When Spot fixes his gaze on something across the garden, we may wonder whether it is best to describe him as seeing Tabby, as seeing a cat, a furry gray animal, or a foe. On the one hand, we are at liberty to characterize what Spot sees "transparently," just as we do when we say that an infant sees a stethoscope or a carburetor. On the other hand we may, in time, come to appreciate Spot's stock of concepts, and thus the sorts of belief he can acquire as he noses about his habitat. Perhaps he behaves differently toward cats than toward other, similarly furry animals. We may note that his dislike for cats is not in any way general but reserved for two or three neighborhood brutes who particularly torment him. Discoveries of this sort may enable us to narrow down the range of theories that plausibly and economically make sense of Spot's activities. There is, or so it seems, no more difficulty in principle in ascertaining the content of beliefs of mute creatures than in coming to appreciate the significance of expressions in a language other than one's own.

Considerations of this sort, at any rate, lead Armstrong to the conclusion that there is "no necessary connection between the having of beliefs and having the capacity to express them linguistically" (p. 28). Even granting this much, however, we seem faced with two further puzzles. First, one might wonder whether there could be beliefs that, for whatever reason, could only be *expressed* linguistically. Second, as Armstrong puts it, "if there are such beliefs, is it possible for a being without the necessary linguistic competence to hold such a belief despite the fact that he cannot express it?" (p. 31).

Might Spot, for instance, secretly harbor a belief about Goldbach's conjecture, or a belief about the incommensurability of Einsteinian and Newtonian conceptions of mass? Again, even if we allow that Spot can believe that Smith is at the door, is it equally sensible to say of Spot that he believes that Smith will appear at the door the day after tomorrow (see Wittgenstein, 1953, p. 174)? Why should this strike us as somehow less plausible? Has it anything to do with Spot's apparent inability to express such a belief linguistically?

Having and Expressing Beliefs

At first glance, the class of beliefs requiring linguistic expression seems enormous. This, Armstrong contends, is deceptive. The class in question is "very much smaller" than one might suppose. "A little ingenuity can often produce descriptions of behavior which are plausible candidates for non-linguistic expressions of quite sophisticated beliefs" (p. 32). Imagine that it is customary for Spot's master, Smith, to be away on two-day excursions to some remote place. We observe Spot and notice that on the first day after Smith's departure he behaves in his usual indolent manner. On the second day, however, he becomes "restless and expectant." In such a case, Armstrong suggests, we might be warranted in saying of Spot, on the day of Smith's departure, that he believes that his master will return "the day after tomorrow."

> Admittedly, the belief involved is still quite simple. It is hardly comparable with a dog's believing the truth of Goldbach's conjecture. But it may be that one could work up through a series of ever more complex cases culminating in the providing of behavioral but non-linguistic expressions of beliefs in the truth of abstruse mathematical hypotheses. (p. 32)

Even if this could not be done, however, Armstrong argues that it is another matter altogether to contend that creatures that lack a language (and therefore, perhaps, the capacity to express certain "abstruse" beliefs) could not secretly *harbor* such beliefs.

One difficulty, of course, lies in the whole notion of what is to count as the *expression* of some particular belief. In chapter VII, it was argued at length that beliefs are never manifested "one-at-a-time," but only in concert with other beliefs, desires, hopes, and fears. Thus, on some occasions, my doing nothing at all could constitute an expression of my beliefs about Goldbach's conjecture. (This might be so, for example, if I were a member of an audience listening to a speaker who, before going on to make some complicated point, wishes to know whether anyone present believes Goldbach's conjecture to be false.) It is a mistake, then, to imagine that belief-expressions can be pinned down to simple performances—or even a range of these. Virtually *any* performance can express *any* belief, given a suitable background of related beliefs and desires.

Nevertheless, despite the fact that any particular segment of behavior might be construed as expressing almost any belief, patterns of behavior over time severely constrain the range of permissible belief-attributions. Thus, if one wishes to attribute a certain belief to *S*, there must be things that *S* does or says that lend themselves to one's interpreting his behavior in this light. It is possible, for this reason, to speak loosely about behavior expressing a given belief. In speaking this way, one need only bear in mind the fact that very similar behavior in different circumstances might count as expressing an utterly different belief. The point is not that every belief has a characteristic behavioral manifestation, but that some behavior in some situations may be characteristic of one who holds a particular belief. It is the *sort* of behavior that would warrant the attribution of the belief in question.

The issue now before us is whether we might imagine a creature holding a certain belief, yet never *doing* anything at all that we should regard as characteristic of one who holds such a belief, never giving us the slightest *reason* to ascribe this particular belief to him. When I speak, then, of the expression of a given belief, this is what I have in mind—and what, I shall suppose, Armstrong has in mind as well. His claim, seen in this light, might be put as follows: a creature might harbor a particular belief even though there is nothing whatever that the creature *could* do that would warrant us in ascribing the belief to him. Such a view, of course, runs utterly counter to the thesis of chapter VII, and it is, for that reason, worth considering in more detail.

Armstrong offers three arguments in defense of the claim that there is a conceptual gap between the having of beliefs and the possession of the corresponding belief-expressing capacity. These are, first, that if we subscribe to the notion that beliefs are (in some sense) identical with states of a creature's nervous system, it ought to be possible to have a certain belief (that is, be in a certain neural state), whether or not that belief is appropriately linked to behavior-producing mechanisms. Perhaps this is unlikely—who knows? But it might be possible for a neurophysiologist to discover beliefs, as it were, *directly,* by scrutinizing one's brain. Once discovered, a belief might be "isolated" from one's "output" system, in the way that the operation of a computing machine may be cut off from its output mechanisms.

Second, long ago William James discussed the case of a deaf-mute, Melville Ballard, a man who was said to have possessed in childhood an impressive repertoire of metaphysical and scientific beliefs despite the fact that he was, at the time, quite unable to express those beliefs or, for that matter, even to understand linguistic expressions of them (James, 1890). James himself made much of the Ballard case, arguing that it provided an affirmative answer to the age-old question "whether thought is possible without language" (James, 1890, p. 266).

Third, all of us, from time to time, find ourselves having to "grope successfully or *unsuccessfully* for words" that aptly express some thought or belief: "we say that the words which we do utter quite fail to capture what it is that we believe, yet we may not know what better words to utter" (p. 32). These cases all suggest a chasm between belief and expressive capacities. Let us consider each of them carefully.

Ascertaining Beliefs by Inspecting the Brain

Imagine a scientist examining the brain of S and attempting to determine whether or not S holds a certain belief, B. What is the scientist to look for? What sort of neural doodad or state will be allowed to *count* as S's belief? Perhaps S's beliefs are "neurally encoded" in some fashion. What would such a neural code resemble? One might suppose that the code consists in sentencelike configurations of neurons. The scientist perhaps has learned to read these so that he is able to browse about in S's brain rather in the way one browses through the *Wall Street Journal*. What, however, would he have to read in S's brain in order to conclude that S holds B? It would not be enough simply to discover a tiny inscription, "B." For what would make this inscription a belief as distinct from a mere neural curiosity, no more significant than a birthmark that happens to resemble the numeral "2"?

Even if it were in some manner established that the configuration had something to do with S's state of mind, how could one conclude that the configuration instantiated a belief as distinct from a mere thought or fleeting idea? It would not, of course, advance matters much if the scientist discovered the neuralese inscription, "I hold *B*," for this itself could be an idle thought or a mere curiosity. (On these and related matters, see Collins, 1979; Putnam, 1981, ch. 1.)

What seems required here is that the investigator connect somehow the neural inscription to things *S* does. Thus, a particular inscription could be regarded as a candidate for the belief *B*, only if it were connected to mechanisms responsible for the production of behavior that, we should say, expresses the belief *B* (in the very broad sense discussed above). Now, however, the notion that the belief is identifiable with the "inscription" begins to look, on the whole, rather less plausible. *B* is determined, not by features of this inscription, but by the behavior it produces (and, of course, much else besides).

One might imagine that this need not always be so. Suppose, for example, that the neural state mentioned above (call it *N)* were connected only with *S*'s "inputs," that is, *N* came into being when and only when *S* gazed at a red object, but *N* itself was not connected in any obvious way with the production of behavior (verbal or otherwise) on the part of *S*. Mightn't one say here anyway that *N* is the "neural realization" of *S*'s belief that "this is red?"

In the discussion of perception in Part One, I distinguished what might be called the *registering* of information, from the bare sensitivity to information-bearing stimuli. Eyeballs and photocells respond to electromagnetic stimulation, but they do not pick up or *register* information. The picking up of information involves the capacity to respond intelligently to what is picked up, to *make sense of* or *appreciate* it. And this is just to say that behavior is produced that fits into a certain pattern, a pattern suggesting intelligence. It is this that is missing in the case of eyeballs and photocells and missing, as well, in the case of the neural state, *N*. Just as there is no single thing that *S* might do that would unequivocally express his belief, *B,* so there is no single part or state of *S* that it could make sense to identify as this belief. At best eyeballs and neural states (and perhaps photocells as well) are components of intelligent creatures, that is, creatures whose deeds merit the attribution of beliefs.

Belief-Attributions and Parsimony

In the previous chapter I suggested that the attribution of beliefs (and other psychological states) is founded on the assessment of patterns of behavior. The latter in turn seems to require the application of standards of coherence and rationality. It requires, in addition, considerations of parsimony. Given that any particular segment of behavior may be explained by reference to countless mental complexes, one seems obliged to postulate the simplest collection of beliefs and desires consistent with the "data." Simplicity is, in part, at one with rational construal, but it is not reducible to the latter.[7]

When I explain *S*'s refusal to skate on the pond by reference to his belief that the ice is thin, I invoke a relatively straightforward mental complex. If, in contrast, I explain his refusal by reference to a belief that the ice is perfectly safe, I shall be obliged to suppose that *S*'s related beliefs and desires are, in one sense, more complex than they appear. (Perhaps he wishes to impress *T* by skating on ice that is obviously dangerous because he suspects that *T* doubts his courage.) Of course, given *S*'s past (and subsequent) actions, the simplest, most straightforward attribution might well turn out to be the second of those mentioned. The point, however, is not that parsimony provides a test for the attribution of a belief on an occasion, but that simplicity, relativized to whole mental complexes, is to be preserved.

---

7. An early application of the principle of parsimony in the attribution of mental complexes to mute creatures may be found in Morgan, 1894: "In no case may we interpret an action as the outcome of the exercise of a higher psychical faculty, if it can be interpreted as the outcome of the exercise of one which stands lower in the psychological scale" (p. 53).

Such matters are particularly important when one considers beliefs attributed to mute creatures. Imagine a species of fish whose members return to the stream where they were hatched to spawn. Finding the proper stream, one may suppose, requires such fish to negotiate substantial distances across open water, locate the river to which the sought-after stream is a tributary, and distinguish that stream from other, similar, streams nearby. One might try to account for this apparently complicated range of activities by imagining that such fish possess a host of sophisticated beliefs about tidal patterns, the use of the stars in navigation, underwater landmarks, and the like. One might make their beliefs more complex still by supposing that the fish have less obvious interests. They wish, perhaps, to relive childhood memories or to punish themselves for dimly recollected infantile sins, and they believe that these aims might best be served by returning to their earliest environment.

Suppose, however, one discovers that small streams have distinctive "odors," that streams differ not simply in their geographical characteristics but also in respect to this single, very simple feature. If one now determines that the fish one is observing can detect such odors and discriminate among them, one has the makings of a much more parsimonious explanation of the spawning behavior described above. Such an explanation would require the attribution of a far simpler set of beliefs to the fish and, in light of this, it is an account we should prefer.

Idle and Necessarily Idle Beliefs

Part of the plausibility of the notion that a creature might hold a certain belief while lacking the capacity to in any way express that belief hinges on the fact that all of us harbor beliefs that we may never have occasion to express. Let us call a belief held but never, for whatever reason, expressed an *idle* belief. I may believe, for example, that truculent bears can be driven away by clapping one's hands and whistling. I never have occasion to mention this belief to anyone and never find myself in a position where I am threatened by bears. My belief is, in an obvious sense, idle. It makes no appreciable difference at all in anything I do or say. No one could conclude, just from watching me go about my daily affairs, that I believed what I do about bears, for *ex hypothesi* nothing that I do depends in any way on my having the belief. From this it seems to follow that Armstrong is right, that a creature's failure to manifest a belief is no sign at all that the creature lacks the belief.

Putting the matter this way, however, conflates a number of points that are better kept separate. My belief about bears is idle, but it is the sort of belief that I might come to manifest given appropriate circumstances. So long as the belief remains idle, you are not warranted in attributing it to me, but there are conditions under which you would be so warranted. It is not, then, senseless for you to imagine that I have such a belief.[8]

This is what seems to distinguish my case from that of the dog depicted by Armstrong as secretly believing in the truth of Goldbach's conjecture. Let us suppose that the dog lacks any means of expressing or in any way manifesting this belief: given the dog's behavioral repertoire, no pattern of "behaviors" he might engage in could ever entitle us to attribute this belief to him. In that case, the belief for him would be *necessarily* idle. That is, it is not just that the dog does not care to express the belief, or that the proper occasion never presents itself, but that there is nothing at all the dog *could* do that would count as an expression of this belief. In such a case, it is not merely that we have no reason to attribute a belief about Goldbach's conjecture to the dog but that we *could* have no reason to do so. What would it mean to insist, even so, that the creature nevertheless has or might have the belief?

This is not a matter of being skeptical about the mental states

---

8. I have said that the belief never affects anything I do, but this may well be an exaggeration. If the belief *is* a component of my mental complex, then it will make a variety of (perhaps subtle) differences in what I do and think about. I may, for example, react differently to pictures of bears or stories about them than people who hold different beliefs.

of dumb animals. There is, I have repeatedly suggested, nothing at all odd about our attribution of beliefs and desires to creatures other than human beings.[9] Similarly, it is not just our inability to "verify" the dog's alleged belief about Goldbach's conjecture that makes the thought that he might have it so strange. My belief about bears or Spot's belief about a bone buried in the garden may, after all, remain unexpressed, hence undetectable (particularly if I am kept away from bears or if Spot loses his teeth, hence his interest in bones). The difficulty is that the ascription of a belief to a creature that utterly lacks the wherewithal to express that belief makes sense only if one imagines beliefs to be interior states characterizable solely by reference to certain of their internal properties. We have seen already that such a conception is mistaken.

Groping for Thoughts

What is the significance of the fact that we are by no means uniformly successful in expressing our beliefs, even on those occasions when we wish to do so? It is tempting to suppose that one is *aware* of the belief, that it is inwardly present to one in some fashion or other, but that one falls short in one's efforts to communicate it felicitously, to extract it. One can tell, after all, that one is putting it badly, one recognizes one's failure. This suggests that one is privately comparing one's utterance against a non-defective standard and finding it wanting.

Consider, however, a parallel case. It sometimes happens that I try to whistle a tune but always, at a certain point, get it wrong. I recognize my mistake, catch myself, and begin again. Still, however often I try, I continue to err (though perhaps in different ways). I am, as it were, groping for the tune. I know the tune, at least in the sense that I know how it *ought* to sound, and I know that I am getting it wrong. Must one say, however, that I have inside my head a *correct* version of the tune guiding

9. A somewhat different perspective on this matter may be found in Griffin, 1976.

my reproduction, but that I nevertheless manage somehow to botch the latter?

One may feel that this is so on the grounds that I know, after all, I have got the thing wrong, and I could know that only if I were in some way comparing my results to a mistake-free version.[10] Since I do not have access to an "overt" instance of the tune, I must be consulting a covert, internal copy of it. The tune is *there*, I just cannot manage to get it *out*.

Consider another example. You and I are looking at a recently painted protrait of a mutual friend. We both see that the painting is a bad likeness. In seeing this, must we compare the image on canvas to another image of our friend, one we carry, perhaps, in our pocket? This need not be the case. We know what our friend looks like, we can recognize him when we see him, and we can see that this portrait does not look the way he would look. The same seems true for my attempts to get the tune right. I know how the tune is supposed to sound, and I know that *this* is not it. The ability to recognize a tune whistled evidently differs from the ability to whistle it (though these are no doubt connected in some important way), just as the ability to recognize a decent likeness differs from the ability to fashion such a likeness.

One may suspect that such cases are not at all like groping for a thought. That may be so, although they do, I think, show that attempts to "say what one thinks" need not be described as attempts to reproduce outwardly an articulated something-or-other stored inside one's head that one, in some manner, consults. If the consulted item itself were vague, we should not know how to account for our ability to recognize its expression as faulty. If, in contrast, the item were clear and explicit, one's inability to reproduce it accurately would be even more puzzling than it is.

---

10. Compare this line of reasoning with that used by Plato *(Phaedo,* 73-75) to show that one's ability to recognize imperfect beauty, say, or lack of wisdom, entails one's acquaintance with perfect exemplifications of these.

In any event, it is likely that cases of groping for thoughts are not uniform, that they do not represent a single phenomenon. Sometimes when one struggles to express a belief, for example, one may simply be unsure *what* it is one believes. It is not that the belief is there, stored away inside one's head, and that one is just at a loss to translate it into English, but that *what* one wishes to express is itself unformed or tentative.

At other times, one's inability to say what one believes may take on a pathological cast. Self-deception and the sorts of odd phenomena that turn up chiefly in the experiments of social psychologists seem to provide examples of this (see e.g., Bem, 1972). Thus we sometimes catch ourselves doing or saying things that we find difficult to reconcile with our espoused (or self-acknowledged) beliefs. When this happens, we may fish about for some belief that would allow us to maintain a unified front. I find myself at the office Christmas party flattering Smith, a colleague I have always detested. Later, in reflecting on the episode, I may succeed in convincing myself that, after all, Smith is not so bad, or that I have never *really* disliked him. I may take to recommending his company to others. Here, perhaps, some account of self-deception is required (see Fingarette, 1969).

Finally, I may find it difficult to express a certain belief simply because my audience is ill-equipped to understand me. There is no mystery in one's having trouble explaining to a five-year-old one's thoughts on nuclear fission or Hegelian logic. The difficulty in such cases is in putting things that are extremely (or perversely) complicated in a simple way. This may prove enormously difficult or even, at times, impossible.

From the fact, then, that we are sometimes obliged to grope for a thought, it need not follow that thinking runs along inside us quite independently of our actions. More particularly, such cases do not show that the having of beliefs is not related conceptually to expressive capacities in the way suggested in chapter VII.

The Saga of Melville Ballard

I want to look at one further attempt to show that sophisticated, "abstruse" beliefs can be held in the absence of a capacity to express them. The case I shall discuss is that of Melville Ballard, a nineteenth-century deaf-mute who has achieved some measure of philosophical and psychological fame. I shall say more about Ballard, perhaps, than absolutely needs to be said to make the point I wish to make about the relation of language to thought. The matter is, however, worth dwelling on if only because the accounts of the case that have been preserved in the philosophical mythology seem so far from the truth. What follows, then, is a brief contribution to the history of ideas.[11]

Ballard, it may be recalled, claimed to remember having, as a child and before he acquired a mastery of English, complicated thoughts and beliefs. James cites his case as evidence for the view that thinking is not conducted in language, that thought is not a form of inner speech. Armstrong, in contrast, mentions Ballard's testimony in order to support his contention that it is possible to have beliefs, even complex and abstract beliefs, without having the capacity to *express* those beliefs. James and Armstrong each take it as obvious both (i) that Ballard's reports of his having, as a child, thoughts on such heady topics as the origin of life and the creation of the universe are reports of episodes that did in fact occur, and (ii) that Ballard had no linguistic facility during the period in which he claimed to entertain these ideas. Each of these assumptions may be questioned.

So far as one can tell, there is no reason to suppose that Ballard, in reminiscing about his New England childhood, was engaging in any sort of deliberate fabrication. But it does not follow from this alone, from the fact that Ballard seems

---

11. Ballard's case is discussed as well in Wittgenstein, 1953. All references to the testimony of Ballard are taken from James, 1890. A more complete account of Ballard's life may be found in Porter, 1881.

altogether *sincere* in describing how he felt and what he thought about as a child, that his recollections are accurate. The phenomenon of "childhood amnesia" and, more impressively, the prevalence of what Freud calls "screen memories" should make one wary of accepting at face value the testimony of adults concerning even (or, perhaps, *especially*) their most vivid childhood memories.[12]

The point of view of an adult differs markedly from that of a child. This disparity must be particularly pronounced if the adult is linguistically competent and the child is mute. At best, an adult sees his childhood experiences at a distance, filtered through the categories and expectations of an adult, categories and expectations often utterly alien to the child who underwent the remembered experiences. If this is true in the ordinary case, if there is anything to it *at all,* how much more must it be true in the case of Ballard? One need not doubt Ballard's sincerity to raise questions concerning the way he has elected to characterize the thoughts that occurred to him as a small boy.

The existence of screen memories and related phenomena is, I gather, well documented. This, of course, does not prove that Ballard *must* have been wrong in his childhood recollections. It does, however, make clear the fact that Ballard's testimony, just in itself, does not go very far toward establishing what either James or Armstrong takes it to establish. This becomes increasingly vivid when one examines more closely the details of Ballard's early life.

In the first place, despite James's and Armstrong's hints to the contrary, Ballard was not congenitally deaf, but lost his hearing "in infancy" (according to Porter, 1881, when he was nineteen months old). From this alone, it is impossible to know how far his linguistic competence might have developed before the onset of muteness (a condition with which he was afflicted as the result of a fall). This is perhaps noteworthy, for there is

---

12. See "A childhood recollection" and "Screen memories" in vols. 4 and 5 of Freud, 1956; also Erdelyi and Goldberg, 1979.

evidence to suggest that there are important and pronounced differences in the cognitive and linguistic capacities of children born deaf and those of children who have had some exposure to language before losing their hearing (see e.g., Lenneberg, 1966). More significantly, it is far from clear what Ballard's limitations really amounted to: "I could convey my thoughts and feelings to my parents and brothers by means of natural signs or pantomime, and I could understand what they said to me by the same medium" (p. 266). This remark seems at odds with Armstrong's contention that Ballard lacked any means of expressing his thoughts linguistically (unless we wish to deny that the use of "natural signs or pantomime" is linguistic in an important sense). The significance of this point is brought home by other of Ballard's remarks:

> It was during those delightful rides, some two or three years before my introduction into the rudiments of written language, that I began to ask myself the question: "how came the world into being?" (p. 267)

Here we are told by Ballard only that he lacked a facility in *written* language. But of course most young children and, in some locales, large numbers of adults, lack this facility. Nothing of particular interest seems to follow from that fact alone.

Compare these reflections with another passage from Ballard's memoir:

> ... I believed that man would be annihilated and there was no resurrection beyond the grave,—though I am told by my mother that, in answer to my question, in the case of a deceased uncle who looked to me like a person in sleep, she had tried to make me understand that he would awake in the far future. (p. 267)

This strongly suggests that little Ballard had at least the capacity to frame *questions* about death and immortality. It is surely rash, then, to hold with Armstrong and James that he lacked all linguistic capacity in this regard.

Notice, too, that the phrase "she tried to make me understand that he would awake in the far future" is importantly ambiguous. It is not clear from the context whether Ballard's failure to understand his mother was due to some linguistic deficiency or to the fact that such notions may be difficult for a small child to understand. His failure to do the latter would hardly be surprising.

Nor is it by any means clear how one ought to regard Ballard's description of the *content* of his childhood beliefs. He describes one of these by saying that he "believed that man would be annihilated and there would be no resurrection beyond the grave." This suggests a picture of a small child with a theory about survival—or rather the lack of it—after death. Such a description, however, might well be taken to typify a point made earlier, namely the tendency to redescribe one's childhood musings in light of one's (often very different) adult beliefs and attitudes. It is at least plausible to suppose that little Ballard had no views at all about resurrection, that such a thing never occurred to him. And it might be perfectly natural for a pious nineteenth-century New Englander to describe this frame of mind as one embodying *disbelief* in resurrection. Do Bushmen believe that there is no Christian God? An evangelical missionary might say this, but in saying it he might just mean that Bushmen, never having considered the matter, altogether lack such beliefs.

To repeat a point mentioned earlier, I am not here trying to establish that Ballard had or lacked one or another of the beliefs he attributes to himself as a child. I am merely offering the reminder that what Ballard's testimony establishes is far from obvious. It provides evidence that might be taken in a number of ways, hardly the sort of foundation on which one might be entitled to erect a theory concerned with the relation of thought to language.

The difficulties I am pointing to are reinforced by remarks such as the following: "One day, while we were haying in a field, there was a series of heavy thunder-claps. I asked one of my brothers where they came from" (p. 268). On another occasion, Ballard recalls his mother telling him about "a being up above":

> When she mentioned the mysterious being up in the sky, I was eager to take hold of the subject, and plied her with questions concerning the form and appearance of this unknown being, asking if it was the sun, moon, or one of the stars. (p. 268)

The picture that begins to emerge is hardly one of a solitary child, brooding secretly over deep abstractions without any benefit of linguistic commerce with others.

It seems clear, in fact, that from *Ballard's* point of view, the remarkable character of these excursions into religion and cosmology is due, not to their having been conducted in a communicative vacuum, but to their having occurred at such an early age—before, even, he began his formal education. His precocity in this regard is what he seems most proud of in the following passage (and, indeed, throughout the memoir):

> I think I was five years old, when I began to understand the descent from parent to child and the propagation of animals. I was nearly eleven years old when I entered the Institution where I was educated; and I remember distinctly that it was at least two years before this time that I began to ask myself the question as to the origin of the universe. My age was then about eight, not over nine years. (pp. 267 ff.)

It is fair to conclude, I think, that there is no reason at all to regard the childhood recollections of Ballard as establishing much of interest concerning the connection between language and belief.

"Language-Dependent" Beliefs

Where does all this leave us? We have seen that Armstrong's claim that there is no necessary connection between the use of language and the having of beliefs is plausible up to a point. That is, it is prima facie reasonable to attribute certain beliefs to creatures that lack any linguistic facility at all. We have also seen, however, that the attempt to show that there is no connection between the having of a belief and the capacity *in some way* to express that belief apparently fails. The question remaining to be answered is this: Are there beliefs that could find expression *only* in a language? And, if there are such beliefs, how numerous are they?

Armstrong's contention, as we have seen, is that the class of beliefs requiring language for their expression is "very much smaller" than we think. Given "a little ingenuity" it is possible to "produce descriptions of behavior which are plausible candidates for non-linguistic expressions of quite sophisticated beliefs" (p. 32). It might be that we "could work up through a series of ever more complex cases culminating in the providing of behavioral but non-linguistic expressions of beliefs in the truth of abstruse mathematical hypotheses" (p. 32).

The point is important for, if this were so, if, that is, it were possible to envisage some non-linguistic means of expressing virtually *any* belief, however "abstruse," then even if I am right about the holding of a belief requiring some means of expression, it would turn out (since any belief would in principle be expressible by any creature with a reasonably varied behavioral repertoire) that virtually any belief might sensibly be attributed to every such creature. A creature's never doing anything to express the belief might be taken to show only that, if the creature in fact held it, it must be idle. This, however, is the very point that seems to me wrong. What needs to be shown, then, is that, contrary to Armstrong's claim, the class of beliefs that require a language for their expression is larger (and larger in an interesting way) than he supposes.

Let us look again at Armstrong's example of a dog that is taken to entertain the belief that its master will return home "the day after tomorrow." How is the dog to express this belief given that it cannot speak? This *seems* a simple matter. We imagine the creature observing its master's departure; then, perhaps contrary to its usual practice, letting forty-eight hours pass before showing signs of "restlessness and expectancy."

The example, however, is anything but obvious. We are seeking grounds for attributing to the dog what one may call a *tensed* belief, a belief about a state of affairs at a moderate temporal remove from the time of attribution. The question should be, what can the dog do *now* to express the belief that its master will return the day after tomorrow? The dog's becoming restless and expectant just at the time when its master returns does not (or, at any rate, need not) express *this* belief, but rather the belief that its master is (or is about to be) at the door.

Most of us at one time or another have been regaled with stories of pets capable of anticipating the return home of schoolchildren or adults at a particular time every day. If Spot becomes restless and expectant just as the children are due home from school, we may be entitled to attribute to him the belief that the children are due home "at any minute." But are we similarly entitled to say of Spot, hours earlier as he wanders about the kitchen, that he believes the children will arrive three hours hence?

Spot's behavior is, to be sure, *consistent* with his holding such a belief. But plainly his doing anything (or, for that matter, nothing) at all would be consistent with his holding this belief. As we have seen, one needs more than consistency with behavior to warrant the attribution of a particular belief. And, in the present case, there are surely more parsimonious attributions available to us.

My stomach may begin rumbling just at lunchtime every day. In this way, we may say, I manifest my hunger, the fact that I am (or take myself to be) hungry. But it would be odd, surely, to hold that my stomach's complacent state at nine o'clock in the morning manifests my *future* hunger, the fact that I shall be hungry three hours hence. To be sure, my stomach's mid-morning silence is, in some sense, *consistent* with this possibility, but so, I think, is its doing anything at all. Far simpler is the notion that my stomach's mealtime rumbling is due to certain fairly uncomplicated things going on inside it *at the time*. It is to those things that we must turn in explaining the rumbling, not to descriptions of my stomach as, three hours earlier, manifesting future hunger.

Similarly, it is more parsimonious to explain Spot's daily routine of expectation by reference to things happening in or around Spot at the time.[13] As a result of these, one may, if one wishes, say that Spot comes to have the belief that the children are due. Perhaps he hears the bus or familiar footfalls, perhaps he is sensitive to the time of day in some special and interesting way. This belief, however, is not tensed, nor does there seem to be any reason at all to attribute a tensed belief to him. Nothing Spot does warrants our ascription to him of such a belief, nothing he does requires such a belief for its explanation.

The same may be said of the dog in Armstrong's example. By endowing it with a tensed belief one provides *an* explanation of its behavior. This, really, is why it may seem plausible to suppose that the dog might have such a belief. But it seems clear that the dog's behavior upon its master's arrival does not in fact express the (tensed) belief that its master will return the day after tomorrow, but only (if anything) the belief that its master has returned or that his return is imminent. This, coupled with the fact that the creature's behavior seems far simpler to explain by reference to present stimuli (and beliefs, if any, associated with these) than by reference to on-going "belief states," means that one has no reason at all to attribute to the dog the belief in question. My stomach lets me know that it is lunchtime, though it has no beliefs at all, certainly no mid-morning beliefs that lunchtime is three hours hence. The dog may have many beliefs, but there is no reason to suppose that any of these are, in the manner required by Armstrong, tensed.

So long as it lacks a language, it is not clear how a dog, how-

13. One must not underestimate the extent of assorted "Clever Hans" effects in such cases (see Pfungst, 1911/1965).

ever clever, *could* express beliefs of this sort. We have seen that the possibility of belief is tied to the possibility of its finding expression in some pattern of behavior. From this it seems to follow that one has no reason at all to suppose that the dog could have beliefs about temporally remote states of affairs. The expression of beliefs about such things evidently requires the use of an appropriately tensed language. The same is true, perhaps, of beliefs incorporating modal notions (that the children *might* be late today, that it is *impossible* for them to be two places at once). It is plausible to suppose that the expression of all such beliefs is "necessarily linguistic" (Heil, 1982). If this is so, and if the account of belief given thus far is correct, then beliefs involving modal notions, too, are beyond the range of mute creatures.

Mathematical beliefs, insofar as these incorporate the notion of implication and necessity, must go the way of modal beliefs. Beliefs about spatially remote states of affairs, too, seem language-dependent and for roughly the same reasons that tensed beliefs seem to require linguistic expression. A belief about a distant state of affairs could be manifested by a mute creature only by its first traveling to the distant spot. This, one may suppose, would take some *time*. To say now of Spot that he believes something about a place far away seems, then, to involve one's indirectly attributing to him a tensed belief (roughly: "When I arrive at P, I shall observe X"). For a mute creature, then, beliefs about spatially noncontiguous states of affairs would be "fused" to tensed beliefs in a way that ought to arouse suspicion.

It is a truism, though perhaps one worth trotting out in the present context, that the ascription of beliefs, desires, intentions, and the like to nonhuman creatures always runs a certain risk of excessive anthropomorphizing. Spot's behavior, after all, may not appear so different from the behavior of a clever adolescent. But it cannot be concluded from the fact that two activities, in some respects, *look* the same that they *are* the same (or that one is a "primitive form" of the other). A child aimlessly moving pieces on a chessboard may *look* like a competent player polishing his game. The differences, however, are significant. One may teach faithful Spot to move pawns about with his nose. It would, however, be wrong to describe him as playing chess or playing "primitive" chess (or even, I think, as moving pawns— if one means by this what one means in speaking of the actions of a chess player). Spot's behavior overlaps that of chess players, but only in a tiny way and only accidentally.

Davidson on Language and Thought

In chapter VII, I defended an account of belief that was intended to be close to that offered by Davidson. I wish now to distinguish my view from Davidson's. The differences turn mainly on the latter's insistence that belief and language are *conceptually interdependent* (p. 8; see note 1, above, for reference). I have suggested that this is indeed the case for a significant number of beliefs, but that it is not so for every belief. What seems essential is that a creature possess the capacity to express the beliefs it holds, and to the extent that certain beliefs are expressible only in a language, such beliefs are attributable only to creatures with appropriate linguistic capacities. I shall try briefly to set out Davidson's arguments against the aptness of belief-ascriptions to mute creatures and then to suggest where these seem to go wrong.

Consider, first, ordinary explanations of action that invoke beliefs and desires, "teleological" explanations as one may call them. *S* raises his arm because he wants to attract the attention of *T*, and he believes that by raising his arm he will do so. Such an explanation, according to Davidson,

> explains what is relatively apparent—an arm-raising—by appeal to factors that are far more problematical: desires and beliefs. But if we were to ask for evidence that the explanation is correct, this evidence would in the end consist of more data concerning the sort

of event being explained, namely further behavior which is explained by the postulated beliefs and desires. Adverting to beliefs and desires to explain action is therefore a way of fitting an action into a pattern of behavior made coherent by the theory. (p. 11)[14]

One need not suppose, of course, that beliefs and desires are nothing more than "patterns of behavior, or that the relevant patterns can be defined without using the concepts of belief and desire" (p. 11). The central idea is that teleological explanations of this sort "supervene" on behavior "more broadly described." Belief-ascriptions depend on the discovery of coherent patterns of behavior, patterns of the sort discussed here and in chapter VII.

On such a view, any action expresses what I have dubbed a "mental complex," that is a constellation of beliefs, desires, intentions (and perhaps other, less easily characterizable psychological traits as well, those belonging to the "background"). If this is so, how is one to disentangle such attributions?

For any agent, there are, it seems, countless distinct mental complexes available. We have seen already that there is bound to be some measure of indeterminacy here, but in the absence of speech, these indeterminacies, according to Davidson, multiply unreasonably.

A man who takes an apple rather than a pear when offered both may be expressing a preference for what is on his left rather than his right, what is red rather than yellow, what is seen first or judged more expensive. (p. 15)

Further observation may make certain of these attributions more plausible than others, "but the problem will remain how to tell what he judges to be a repetition of the same alternative" (p. 15).

14. Here "theory" means nothing more (nor less) than an assessment of beliefs and desires, an interpretive scheme. The necessity of such a scaffolding in attributions of psychological states was defended in the previous chapter.

What is needed, Davidson suggests, is a theory of interpretation to supplement one's theory of action.

> If we think of all choices as revealing a preference that one sentence rather than another be true, the resulting total theory should provide an interpretation of sentences, and at the same time assign beliefs and desires, both of the latter conceived as relating the agent to sentences or utterances. (p. 15)

This leads to the view that belief-attribution "must go hand in hand with the interpretation of speech" (p. 15). "The . . . reason is that without speech we cannot make the fine distinctions between thoughts that are essential to the explanations we can sometimes confidently apply" (p. 15).

This was a matter discussed earlier when the issue of *what* belief to ascribe to Spot (that his master is at the door? that Smith is at the door? that the man who sets out food is at the door?) was first raised. "We have," says Davidson, "no real idea how to settle or make sense of such questions" (p. 16). He continues,

> It is much harder to say, when speech is not present, how to distinguish universal thoughts from conjunctions of thoughts, or how to attribute conditional thoughts with, so to speak, mixed quantification ("He hopes that everyone is loved by someone"). (p. 16)

Behavior that does not include speech, on this view, could never provide sufficient reason to attribute "fine-grained" thoughts to creatures whose activities one wishes to understand. In such cases, belief-attributions seem to be largely anthropomorphic excesses.

A notable difficulty with this line of reasoning, however, is that it appears to show only that one is not entitled to attribute certain *sorts* of thought to mute creatures. And this, of course, is perfectly consistent with the view I have been setting out in the present chapter. It does not follow from the fact to which Davidson alludes that one is never entitled to attribute *any*

beliefs at all to creatures who do not engage in speech. When one sets out to interpret the behavior of Spot, there may be much indeterminacy in the beliefs and desires postulated. If, however, one eliminates from consideration those sorts of belief express-ible only in speech (including, almost certainly, those mentioned by Davidson in the passage just quoted), and if one observes Spot over a sufficient period of time, one may come to feel that the threatened indeterminacy is no more serious in Spot's case than it would be in the case of Smith, his master.

I am not suggesting that a satisfying account of the contents of beliefs attributable to mute creatures is a simple matter. Fortunately, we can avail ourselves of that feature of beliefs that enables them to be identified by reference to the states of affairs on which they are directed, their "transparency." Admittedly, this way of picking out beliefs cannot provide us with an entirely satisfactory way of explaining behavior (given that teleological explanation appeals essentially to belief *contents*), but it can at least push us off dead center and move us in the right direction. To explain Spot's frantic barking by reference to his belief that there is an "intruder" in the vicinity, may not be entirely felicitous, but it is not thereby entirely inappropriate either. Indeed, our use of the expression "master" to describe the contents of mute creatures' beliefs about those persons who direct their lives seems to have evolved precisely because it comes very close to capturing something underlying the pattern of relationships one finds in such cases.

I conclude, then, that Davidson's observations about the connection of belief-contents and linguistic behavior do not show that belief-attributions in every case depend on language. Again, one may agree that we are severely limited in the sorts of thought that can reasonably be attributed to creatures that lack a capacity for speech. When we consider perception, for example, we shall want to take care in attributing content to the perceptions of mute creatures. This does not mean, however, that in such cases there *is* no mental content or that we are helpless in these matters. Naturalists, ethologists, and those who study animal behavior are the most likely source of illumination on such points.

Belief and the Concept of Belief

Davidson introduces one additional argument in support of his claim that it is wrong to ascribe thoughts to mute creatures, an argument that I shall discuss only briefly because I find it somewhat puzzling and, on the face of it, unpersuasive. The argument may be summarized as follows (see p. 22):

> (i) A creature can have a belief only if it can have the concept of belief.
> (ii) A creature can have the concept of belief only if it is a member of a speech community, only if it has a language.
> (iii) Therefore, only creatures with a language can have beliefs.

One may, I think, be willing to concede the second premise here but remain skeptical about the first. What is there to say in its favor?

Davidson argues that a person "cannot have a belief unless he understands the possibility of being mistaken, and this requires grasping the contrast between truth and error—true belief and false belief" (p. 22). And this, in effect, forces one to include among the beliefs of any creature capable of having such things, beliefs about beliefs. One cannot have beliefs about beliefs, beliefs in which beliefs figure, without having the concept of belief.

I am prepared to concede that, if this were so, if (i) were correct, we should not be entitled to attribute beliefs to mute creatures. But I cannot see why we should suppose that it *is* so. Why does having a belief require having, as well, an understanding of "the possibility of being mistaken"? And why does the latter require that one have a language (and with it the capacity to interpret the utterances of those who qualify as members of one's speech community)?

A creature whose behavior is suitably adaptive, one that does not continue to respond inappropriately and rigidly when conditions change, is just the sort of creature to which belief-attributions seem apt. Perhaps this is in some measure due to the fact that we regard such behavior as, on occasion, manifesting a willingness to give up certain beliefs. This, however, does not support Davidson's strong claims about the necessity of attributing beliefs about beliefs to any creature to which one is warranted in ascribing any beliefs at all.

I conclude, therefore, that it seems right to suppose that the having of beliefs does not require the possession of a language—either an interior language in which those beliefs are "encoded," or an exterior mode of speech in which they may be expressed. It would be wrong, however, to conclude from this that the having of beliefs is detachable from one's having the means to express those beliefs in some fashion or other. Further, certain beliefs, as we have discovered, evidently require a linguistic expression. If this is so, then such beliefs could be held only by creatures endowed with a capacity for speech.

Finally, I have suggested that the range of beliefs expressible only by means of language is large, large enough, certainly, to be interesting. It includes (at least) beliefs concerned with temporally remote states of affairs, those involving modal notions, and those incorporating mixed quantification. It seems likely that other sorts of belief are "necessarily linguistic" in this sense: beliefs, for instance, about states of affairs spatially remote, beliefs ranging over principles, laws, precepts. In all such cases, Davidson's observations about the relation of thought and language seem on the mark.

The upshot is that it is possible to acccept the notion that perception is, as I have suggested, cognitive, that in perceiving one comes to be in a certain state that in many ways resembles belief, without thereby limiting perception to creatures possessing a language. If perceiving is (in a certain way) believing, then perceivers must be capable of forming and holding beliefs, but they need not in all cases be capable of expressing those beliefs linguistically.

IX

CONCLUSION: PERCEIVING AND COGNIZING

In the course of this essay I have advanced a two-pronged thesis. First, I have argued that perception is cognitive, epistemic, that perceiving is best regarded as the acquiring of beliefs (or, at any rate, belieflike cognitive states) by way of the senses. The environment in which we find ourselves is saturated with ambient physical "stimuli"—light radiation, pressure waves, and the like—structured by the objects and events comprising that environment. A creature equipped to detect this structure is capable of gaining information about its surroundings borne by it, and acquiring, thereby, reliable beliefs about its world. My suggestion has been that it is this activity of information-pickup, belief-acquisition, that constitutes perceiving.

The picking up of information in the manner described requires not only that a creature be equipped with gangs of receptors sensitive to a particular source of stimulation. It requires as well that the creature possess appropriate concepts. To see all that the botanist sees in looking at a shrub, I must know what the botanist knows. The information that I can pick up in looking at, listening to, sniffing, tasting, and feeling about in my habitat will depend both on my sensory endowment and on my cognitive equipment, my beliefs about the world. In defending this view, I have rejected the notion that perception is essentially the having of sensations or phenomenal percepts, if these are taken to be noncognitive states or episodes. Such experiencings may occur, indeed they may (although I doubt it) be essential stages in the causal processes that lead to our acquisition of perceptual beliefs, but their occurrence is not sufficient for perception.

I have wished to suggest further that the notion that perception incorporates in this way a conceptual or cognitive element lends no support either to the doctrine of representationalism or to that of epistemological relativism. Thus, from the fact that what one is capable of perceiving depends in some measure on beliefs one already possesses, it does not follow that perception consists in the imposition of structure on an inchoate "pre-conceptual" sensory mass. The information embodied in structured light radiation or in pressure waves is objectively real. Different observers may, of course, sample different portions of the information available to them. Some may be blind to large segments of it, either because they are physically insensitive to its presence or because they lack the necessary cognitive background.

It is a large step from these points, however, to the claim that perception is ineluctably subjective, that there is no such thing as an objective perceiving, that perceptual worlds are, in the final analysis, incommensurable. Relativism of this sort, I argued, depends on a gratuitous move from the innocuous claim that there is no *single* correct view of things, to the apparently outrageous claim that *no* view is in any objective sense correct. A botanist and I may well "see things differently" (that is, in gazing at a shrub, acquire different sets of perceptual beliefs), but it does not follow from this that we see different things, or that the beliefs we acquire could not, for the most part, be objectively true.

Nor, I think, ought such considerations lead us to some form of representationalism, the view that our perceptual contact with the world is inevitably indirect, that perceiving consists not in the awareness of states of affairs in the world, but in an awareness of one sort or another of perceptual intermediary. In order for me to see the tree in front of me, a number of things must go right, a complicated causal sequence must occur. If all goes well, I may, as a result, obtain a certain amount of information (acquire various true beliefs) about the tree. If we wish to speak here of awareness, I may, in the case described, be said to be directly aware of the tree despite the fact that this awareness seems to depend upon a causal sequence that, from my point of view, may be altogether mysterious. Representationalism requires that awareness be restricted to a postulated intermediate event in this sequence.

Such a move, however, involves a dubious conflation of epistemological concerns about what constitutes a "perceptual object" with empirical concerns about the causal mechanisms underlying perception. The ordinary person is perfectly correct in supposing that he is, in looking about the world, perceptually aware of middle-sized physical objects, and in imagining that those objects, for the most part, possess the properties he takes them to possess. The physiologist's account of the causal determinants of perception cannot cast doubt on this supposition. On the contrary, the physiologist provides a partial explanation of it in detailing the physical conditions that give rise to one's perceptual awareness of trees, lamps, and lemons.

Psychologists of perception, in focusing attention on the character of an assortment of postulated sensory mechanisms and processes, are apt to lose sight of the simple notion that, in perceiving, creatures come to learn about the world. Perception is epistemically basic, at least in the sense that it constitutes one of the foundations of intelligent, appropriate behavior. An empirical theory of perception may perhaps be regarded as a function from environment to beliefs reflecting that environment. But the environment perceived is one comprised of perceptual objects and events, not one readily characterizable at the level of physics and chemistry. To lose sight of this fact is to render perceiving even more mysterious than it is.

The second prong of the essay's thesis consisted in a lengthy discussion of the notion and character of certain sorts of cognitive states: "mental representations." I have, in general, wished to suggest that such things are not best regarded as internal configurations with a certain formal structure. My motives for going on as I have about representation are mixed. In the first place, I have wanted to show that it is possible to take perception to be the acquisition of beliefs without, at the same time, incurring a commitment to the existence of computational states or *internal* representations. Admittedly, others may not share my distaste for such esoterica. My hope, however, is that I have said enough to show at least that perceptual theories, if not psychological theories in general, can manage perfectly well without them. Indeed, if my suggestions on these matters are well founded, then I may perhaps be entitled to the stronger claim that such things *can* do no work at all in theories purporting to explain intelligent behavior.

When S believes that p, what constituent of S (what neural state, say) incorporates the content of S's belief, what portion of S realizes p, what component or subcomponent of S has *these* representational properties? My answer was that, in an important sense, nothing does. We may say if we like that S, in holding the belief that p, realizes certain representational properties. We may say that he does so because his nervous system drives him in certain ways. But it is to S-*thus-driven* that we are warranted in ascribing the belief that p, not to some component of S.

The point here is not merely a verbal one about the nature of "belief talk." It is rather that beliefs are connected essentially to patterns of behavior, even though they are not in any sense reducible to such behavior. It is in virtue of these connections that beliefs have whatever content they have, it is here that the notion of mental representation finds a place. Such representations require for their realization, not simply computational media, but agents capable of manifesting them.

The idiom of perception, incorporating as it does talk of information and belief, is a pragmatic idiom. Predicates belonging to this domain apply to creatures in virtue of certain characteristics of those creatures' activities and talents. The latter are determined, we may suppose, biologically. But this fact, if it is a fact, does not require anything like a principled relation between biological and psychological predicates. Indeed it may be positively dangerous to mix categories appropriate to one idiom—those involving representation, for example—with those belonging to the other domain—"hardware" predicates, say, applicable to neural states and processes. I do not say that this is done often, but it *is* done, and with unfortunate results. One aim of this essay has been to show that such theoretical level-confusion, despite the contentions of those who take the notion that mental states are computational states in deadly earnest, can be avoided. And, given that it can be avoided, it ought to be.

X
POSTSCRIPT: PHILOSOPHY AND PSYCHOLOGY

It is a commonplace that many fields of endeavor we today regard as distinct sciences began aeons ago as branches of philosophical inquiry. There are various theories about the stages through which a discipline passes en route to becoming an independent science emancipated from the claims of philosophy. For their part, philosophers, since at least the time of Descartes (though the doctrine goes back to Plato and before), have been fond of the notion that the tree of knowledge is rooted in philosophical principles. These comprise the foundations for any systematic attempt to acquire and organize knowledge.

This view comforts philosophers and makes them feel needed and important. But it is comforting as well to those who regard themselves as hard-nosed scientists and who see philosophy as an idle pastime or perhaps a regrettable waste of effort. If philosophical questions concern only the foundations of one's discipline and not its details or substance, then they may be safely ignored. That the world is by and large intelligible, that a good bit of it exists outside our minds, that most of what happens is caused to happen, that the future will in many ways resemble the past, these are assumptions made by everyone engaged in rational inquiry, hence by no one.

The aptness of this view of science and its relation to philosophy is arguable, certainly. I wish only to suggest that it is utterly unsatisfactory as an account of the relation between psychology and philosophy.

As I write these words, experimental psychology has just entered its second century. In 1879, Wundt established at the University of Leipzig what is generally regarded as the first psychological laboratory. This may serve as a reminder, should one be needed, that psychologists have been campaigning under the banner of the experimental sciences for at least several generations. It is somewhat surprising, then, to discover amidst mountains of empirical observations, sophisticated computing machine models, and what have you the presence of commitments that can only be described as philosophical. I am not speaking here of the usual *innocuous* commitments—to the intelligibility of the world or the existence of material bodies—but of commitments to what, at any rate, *appear* to be substantive philosophical theses. Aside from the obvious point that it is unlikely that such theses are true, one may feel that there is something prima facie odd about a self-consciously empirical discipline that incorporates philosophical doctrine in this way.

The most obvious and widespread of these commitments, the one that has concerned me most in the present essay, is to one form or another of *representationalism,* the doctrine that creatures are never aware of their surroundings *directly,* but only via internal constructs, cognitive artifacts, "self-directed" mental caricatures of external objects, and events. Representationalism seems nowadays so widely taken for granted and so rarely challenged that it is seldom argued for or defended. One must look to the early chapters of introductory texts or to books written with a popular audience in mind in order to find it discussed openly (see, e.g., Gregory, 1973, pp. 7 ff.; Lindsay and Norman, 1972, p. 1; Vernon, 1962, pp. 11-15). (In psychology as elsewhere, such books are a useful source of information about fundamental, though perhaps embarrassing, assumptions. Once a budding investigator has been indoctrinated in the appropriate "paradigm" and thus provided with a way of looking at a subject matter, it need not be defended further.[1]

1. I am using the expression "paradigm" here as it is used by psychologists (and others) to mean a particular way of looking at and experimentally manipulating a subject matter, not in the strict Kuhnian sense—whatever that sense is (see Kuhn, 1962). Not that the use of the expression by psychologists is any less vague: it is simply less controversial.

The picture will continue to do its job, exert its influence, even when its origins are long forgotten—or repressed.)

Once the notion that we construct the world inside us is bought, the remaining features of the *Zeitgeist* come relatively cheaply. Memory, for example, "must" be a matter of storing and retrieving experiences that have been previously "coded" (i.e., syntactically structured) in the head; thinking involves the "processing" of coded bits and pieces; finding one's way about is accomplished by means of convenient internal road maps. Who has not heard of the interior clocks, compasses, and sextants thought to be guiding the behavior of creatures adept at ordering their lives and negotiating their habitats? The picture that emerges here is of a control room inside the head where instruments are consulted, calculations are carried out, and items filed in labeled bins, rather as these things are done in the familiar everyday world of maps, compasses, adding machines, and filing cabinets.

With such views, of course, there is a constant threat of homunculi, little interior agents whose job it is to root around in filing cabinets, consult watches and compasses, and keep records of important events. Attempts have been made to skirt this issue by imagining, as it were, an *automated* control room inside the head, one populated by soulless androids rather than long-suffering homunculi. The metaphor has changed, but much else has remained unaltered.

The emphasis on method that has come to characterize psychology in this century has made it appear to some historians that "the difference between modern psychology and its intellectual precursors is not so much in the kinds of questions as in the methods used to seek answers" (Schultz, 1969, p. 1). Here the picture is of white-coated, instrument-laden technicians plumbing the secrets of the mind in ways never dreamed of by earlier workers in the field, workers obliged to employ primitive instruments (the familiar armchair being chief among these) and clumsy techniques of observation and measurement.

Such a picture is, one feels, vastly misleading. It has turned out that the *answers* arising from the employment of sophisticated "new and improved" experimental techniques are often remarkably similar to answers advanced by methodologically naive "intellectual precursors." Theories of memory seem to have moved little beyond Plato and Aristotle except that computer discs have replaced wax tablets as models of storage mechanisms (see e.g., Neisser, 1978; Kreutzer, et al., 1975); the notion that perceptual recognition involves the comparison of a percept with a stored archetype will be familiar to readers of Locke; and representationalism itself goes back to the dawn of philosophical speculation. Often cognitive psychologists seem not merely to be asking the same questions as philosophers, but giving the same answers as well. The role of a special empirical method in such cases is obscure.

Some of the trouble here may be due to the oft-lamented fact that psychological investigation emerged gradually and somewhat painfully from what was at first explicitly philosophical inquiry. The subject matter of cognitive psychology—the mind, its various faculties and components—has always been of particular interest to philosophers bent on solutions to various epistemological puzzles. The latter have occasionally mistaken conceptual questions about knowledge and belief for empirical ones requiring delicate introspective fieldwork and, in so doing, fostered a tradition of inquiry that seems in no danger of dying out (see e.g., Peters, 1953, pp. 29 ff.).

To the cynical observer, the history of modern psychology might appear somewhat as follows. Psychological investigation was once upon a time simply a species of philosophical speculation. Certain investigators, impressed by the success of experimental techniques in the natural sciences (and depressed by the corresponding lack of progress in philosophy), began to separate themselves from their philosophical brethren and, in this way, to isolate their thinking from ongoing philosophical argument and controversy. An island of investigation apart from the mainland sprung up. On this island enormous strides were made in experimental technique and method. Philosophical development, however, was curtailed. Today's islanders exhibit a curious blend of twentieth-century methodological sophistication toted in nineteenth-century philosophical luggage. This, to be sure, is an exaggerated picture—though perhaps not *much* exaggerated. Often the originators of a particular psychological approach were quite explicit in setting their philosophical cards on the table. Perhaps it is this feature of early psychological tracts that nowadays gives them their quaint flavor. We have, one feels, at last got beyond such intellectual fashions. In this way investigators have tended to be less and less sensitive to the philosophical dimension of the theoretical framework they have inherited, regarding it perhaps as nothing more than a curiosity. It is thus carried along unacknowledged, hence unexamined, but nonetheless influential for being out of sight.[2]

It is not my intention to suggest here that philosophers henceforth be employed as underlaborers, clearing away the conceptual underbrush so that cognitive psychologists can get on with their work secure in the knowledge that they are on firm philosophical ground. I doubt, for one thing, that there is enough firm philosophical ground to go around. Anyway, no science worth its salt seeks or needs a philosophical imprimatur. I am suggesting, rather, that psychologists might conceivably profit by coming to recognize which of their commitments are due not to a clear perception of the nature of things, but to gratuitous philosophical prejudices that serve no purpose save that of forcing one's thoughts into certain narrow channels and sparing one the intellectual labor involved in coming to see things differently.

Much of the responsibility for this predicament must be placed at the door of Descartes and his philosophical partisans.

2. The influence, as well, of particularly striking technological and scientific advances on psychological conceptions seems undeniable. Hume regarded his associationistic doctrine as a natural extension of Newtonian principles to the mental realm. Freud and his contemporaries drew inspiration from the laws of thermodynamics. Nowadays, psychologists find the computational idiom an attractive one for the framing of talk about psychological states and processes.

But empiricists and followers of Kant are hardly blameless in the matter. All have contributed their bit to the picture of psychological states and processes that has emerged since the seventeenth century. Nowadays, of course, we like to think of ourselves as beyond dualism. As Wittgenstein pointed out, however, the problem with dualism is not so much that it requires belief in an immaterial substance, but that its accounts of mental goings-on are, in the end, entirely mysterious (see e.g., Wittgenstein, 1958). And it does not make such accounts any less mysterious to suppose that they describe occurrences in brains rather than in minds. One does not convert an occult property into a respectable one simply by relocating it somewhere in space—or in a box in a cognitive flow-chart.

At first blush, the burgeoning field of artificial intelligence might be thought to provide promise of a way out of such theoretical culs de sac. After all, computing machines provide a powerful means of modeling and, at times, simulating psychological occurrences. More importantly, in programming such devices, one is obliged to say precisely how things *work,* something one need not bother with so long as one is allowed, at crucial points in an explanation, to fall back on an assortment of ad hoc properties (as in the case, for example, of the alleged "self-directedness" of certain mental states). But the computing machine vogue has brought with it all manner of aberrations of its own. There is a tendency, remarked on by Hubert Dreyfus (see Dreyfus, 1979), to imagine that computational accounts of simple occurrences can be generalized smoothly and without difficulty to more complex ones (see also Heil, 1981). As a result, solutions to relatively meager and narrowly circumscribed problems tend to be regarded as preliminary solutions to other, far less tractable puzzles.

Worse, perhaps, is the tendency previously noted to assume that biological entities must go about their business in roughly the way in which a cleverly programmed computing machine would. The catch is that there are so often other, far simpler and more economical ways of getting things done. The speedometer in one's automobile, the governor on a steam engine, and the polar planimeter all achieve computationally heady results in disappointingly pedestrian ways (see Runeson, 1977*a*). It is difficult to believe that Nature, in devising intelligent and resourceful creatures, has not taken similar shortcuts. The study of artificial intelligence, of course, does not preclude the investigation of such things, but it tends, at least, in the other direction.

If all is a shambles, then, what *should* cognitive psychology do to get its house in order? In the first place, it is surely not true that all is a shambles. Much more is known today about many more things than was known when Wundt established his laboratory in Leipzig. What seems to be missing amid all the masses of data, however, is any sort of general agreement on how it fits together. In reading through cognitive psychological literature on virtually any experimental topic, one feels comforted so long as one sticks to details. Once broader, more general claims begin to be advanced, however, one's confidence wanes. The overall viewpoint seems, more often than not, to be determined not by observation and experiment but by some source offstage.

It is my conviction that this source is none other than *philosophia,* the same contaminant that Wundt imagined he was leaving behind in 1879. What is to be done? I have rejected already the notion that philosophers trained in such things might be employed by psychologists as underlaborers. Beside the fact that this is an enormously unlikely prospect, it is, I think, both unnecessary and potentially disastrous. Philosophers have too many of their own axes to grind to be very useful to others: beware of philosophers bearing theoretical gifts. What is needed, in any case, is not a more up-to-date batch of philosophical commitments to replace the present, tarnished ones, but something far less grand: the simple recognition of existing commitments for what they are.

Wittgenstein preached that philosophical ideas exercise their influence over us largely unconsciously. They function as pictures with the power to make us see things in certain narrow ways, to incline us to ask certain sorts of question and to expect certain kinds of answer. On this view, philosophers spend much time developing and arguing for theories designed to solve problems that are, in the main, artifacts arising from a disparity between the pictorially imposed conviction that things *must* be a certain way and the everyday observation that they are very often not that way at all. Wittgenstein's contention was that the way out of this self-imposed condition lay not in the development of better, more refined philosophical theories, but in the recognition and appreciation of the way of thinking—what I have called the picture—that leads us to see things as we do. As with a neurosis, the first step in exorcising the influence of something that works on one beneath the threshold of consciousness is to make oneself aware of it.

Wittgenstein seemed convinced that once this was accomplished, familiar philosophical puzzles would simply wither away. Whether this is so is debatable, surely, but whatever the merits of the Wittgensteinian program, it seems clear that our recognition of hidden assumptions that have affected our thinking in countless ways cannot but be beneficial. If these assumptions are discovered to be sound, then so much the better. If, as is more likely, they are found wanting, then we shall be free to look elsewhere for inspiration.

The philosopher's task in all this, as I see it, is simply that of exposing as much of what is below the surface as possible. This requires a familiarity not only with traditions of philosophical inquiry, but also with ongoing work in psychology—and now, "cognitive science." There is, as there always has been, some risk to the philosopher of being dazzled by all that is impressive in psychology and losing, as a result, his critical edge. Psychologists make *empirical* claims and cite *evidence* to back up these claims. It is easy to overlook the fact that a theory may be founded in part on questionable reasoning or dubious assumptions if it issues from the laboratory. In this way one may be led to believe that cognitive theorists have established one or another marvelous truth when, in reality, the alleged truth may be founded on philosophical assumptions that are, for a variety of reasons, unacceptable.

Despite the dangers to all concerned, however, I suspect that the philosophical examination of the foundations of psychological theorizing is by and large a good thing. The subject matter of cognitive psychology is too interesting and too important to be ignored.

Bibliography

Armstrong, D. M. (1973) *Belief, Truth and Knowledge*. London: Cambridge University Press.

Austin, J. L. (1962) *Sense and Sensibilia*. London: Oxford University Press.

Averill, E. (1982) The primary-secondary quality distinction. *Philosophical Review 91:* 343-362.

Ayer, A. J. (1940) *The Foundations of Empirical Knowledge*. London: Macmillan.

Bem, D. J. (1972) Self-perception theory. In *Advances in Experimental Social Psychology*. Vol. 6. Ed. L. Berkowitz. New York: Academic Press.

Bennett, J. (1964) *Rationality*. London: Routledge and Kegan Paul.

Boring, E. G. (1942) *Sensation and Perception in the History of Experimental Psychology*. New York: Appleton-Century.

Brentano, F. (1874/1960) The distinction between mental and physical phenomena. Trans. D. B. Terrell. In *Realism and the Background of Phenomenology*. Ed. R. M. Chisholm. Glencoe, Ill.: The Free Press.

Close, D. (1976) What is non-epistemic seeing? *Mind 85*: 161-170.

Close, D. (1980) More on non-epistemic seeing. *Mind 89*: 99-105.

Collins, A. W. (1979) Could our beliefs be representations in our brains? *Journal of Philosophy 76:* 225-243.

Davidson, D. (1970) Mental events. *In Experience and Theory*. Ed. L. Foster and J. W. Swenson. Amherst, Mass.: University of Massachusetts Press. (Reprinted in Davidson, 1980.)

Davidson, D. (1971) *Philosophy as psychology*. Symposium paper read at the University of Kent and reprinted in *Philosophy of Psychology*. Ed. S. C. Brown. London and New York: Macmillan Press and Barnes and Noble, 1974. (Reprinted in Davidson, 1980.)

Davidson, D. (1973a) On the very idea of a conceptual scheme. *Proceedings and Addresses of the American Philosophical Association* 67: 5-20.

Davidson, D. (1973*b*) Radical interpretation. *Dialectica 27*: 313-328.

Davidson, D. (1974) Belief and the basis of meaning. *Synthese 27*: 309-323.

Davidson, D. (1975) Thought and talk. In *Mind and Language*. Ed. S. D. Guttenplan. London: Oxford University Press.

Davidson, D. (1980) *Essays on Actions and Events*. Oxford: Oxford University Press.

Dennett, D. (1978) *Brainstorms*. Montgomery, Vermont: Bradford Books.

Dretske, F. I. (1969) *Seeing and Knowing*. London: Routledge and Kegan Paul.

Dretske, F. I. (1981) *Knowledge and the Flow of Information*. Cambridge, Mass.: Bradford Books/MIT Press.

Dreyfus, H. (1979) *What Computers Can't Do* (2d ed.). New York: Harper and Row.

Dreyfus, H. (1982) *Husserl, Intentionality and Cognitive Science*. Cambridge, Mass.: Bradford Books/MIT Press.

Erdelyi, M. H., and Goldberg, B. (1979) Let's not sweep repression under the rug. In *Functional Disorders of Memory*. Ed. J. F. Kihlstrom and F. J. Evans. Hillsdale, N.J.: L. J. Erlbaum Associates.

Fingarette, H. (1969) *Self-Deception*. London: Routledge and Kegan Paul.

Fodor, J. (1975) *The Language of Thought*. New York: T. Y. Crowell.

Fodor, J. (1980) Methodological solipsism as a research strategy in cognitive psychology. *Behavioral and Brain Sciences 3:* 63-73. (Reprinted in Fodor, 1981.)

Fodor, J. (1981) *RePresentations*. Brighton, Sussex: Harvester Press.

Fowler, H. W. (1965) *A Dictionary of Modern English Usage* (2d. ed.). Ed. E. Gowers. London: Oxford University Press.

Freud, S. (1956) *Collected Papers*. Vol. 23. Ed. J. Strachey. London: Hogarth Press.

Von Frisch, K. (1971) *Bees: Their Vision, Chemical Senses and Language* (2d ed.). Ithaca, N.Y.: Cornell University Press.

Gibson, J. J. (1966) *The Senses Considered As Perceptual Systems*. Boston: Houghton Mifflin.

Gibson, J. J. (1979) *The Ecological Approach to Visual Perception*. Boston: Houghton Mifflin.

Goldman, A. (1970) *A Theory of Human Action*. Princeton: Princeton University Press.

Goldman, A. (1977) Perceptual objects. *Synthese 35*: 257-284.

Greene, J. (1972) *Psycholinguistics*. Harmondsworth: Penguin Books.

Gregory, R. L. (1973) *Eye and Brain* (2d ed.). New York: McGraw Hill.

Grice, H. P. (1962) Some remarks about the senses. In *Analytical Philosophy* (First Series). Ed. R. J. Butler. Oxford: Basil Blackwell.

Griffin, D. R. (1976) *The Question of Animal Awareness*. New York: The Rockefeller University Press.

Guarniero, G. (1974) Experience of tactile vision. *Perception 3*: 101-104.

Gunderson, K. (1971) *Mentality and Machines*. Garden City, N.Y.: Doubleday and Co.

Hamlyn, D. W. (1977) The concept of information in Gibson's theory of perception. *Journal for the Theory of Social Behavior 7:* 5-16.

Hamlyn, D. W. (1978) *Experience and the Growth of Understanding*. London and Boston: Routledge and Kegan Paul.

Hanson, N. R. (1958) *Patterns of Discovery*. London: Cambridge University Press.

Hare, R. M. (1952) *The Language of Morals*. London: Oxford University Press.

Haugeland, J. (1981) *Mind Design*. Cambridge, Mass.: Bradford Books/MIT Press.

Heil, J. (1981) Does cognitive psychology rest on a mistake? *Mind 90*: 321-342.

Heil, J. (1982) Speechless brutes. *Philosophy and Phenomenological Research 42:* 400-406.

Ittleson, W. H. (1952) *The Ames Demonstrations in Perception*. Princeton: Princeton University Press.

James, W. (1890) *Principles of Psychology* (Vol. 1). New York: Henry Holt.

Kierkegaard, S. (1846/1941) *Concluding Unscientific Postscript*. Trans. D. Swenson. Ed. W. Lowrie. Princeton: Princeton University Press.

Kim, J. (1978) Supervenience and nomological incommensurables. *American Philosophical Quarterly 15*: 149-156.

Kim, J. (1979) Causality, identity and supervenience. In *Midwest*

Studies in Philosophy (Vol. 4). Ed. P. French, T. Uehling, and H. Wettstein. Minneapolis: University of Minnesota Press.

Kim, J. (1982) Psychophysical supervenience. *Philosophical Studies 41*: 51-70.

Kreutzer, M. A., Leonard, C., and Flavell, J. (1975) An interview study of children's knowledge about memory. *Monographs of the society of research in child development 40*, no. 159.

Kuhn, T. (1962) *The Structure of Scientific Revolutions*. Chicago: University of Chicago Press.

Lenneberg, E. H. (1966) The natural history of language. In *The Genesis of Language*. Ed. F. Smith and G. A. Miller. Cambridge, Mass.: MIT Press.

Lindsay, P. H. and Norman, D. A. (1972) *Human Information Processing*. New York: Academic Press.

Mackie, J. L. (1980) *The Cement of the Universe*. Oxford: Oxford University Press.

McLendon, H. J. (1955) The uses of similarity of structure in contemporary philosophy. *Mind 64*: 79-95.

Marcel, A. (1982) Cortical blindness and blind sight: a problem of visual function or consciousness? (Unpublished paper presented at the Department of Psychology, University of California, Berkeley, 7 May, 1982.)

Mehta, V. (1982) Personal history. *The New Yorker*, Nov. 15, 1982: 51-155.

Metzger, W. (1930) Optische in Ganzfeld II. *Psychologische Forschung 13:* 6-29.

Michotte, A. (1946/1963) *The Perception of Causality*. Trans. T. R. Miles and E. Miles. New York: Basic Books.

Morgan, C. L. (1894) *An Introduction to Comparative Psychology*. London: Walter Scott.

Morgan, M. J. (1977) *Molyneux's Question*. London: Cambridge University Press.

Müller, J. (1838) On the specific energies of nerves. In *A Sourcebook in the History of Psychology*. Ed. R. J. Herrnstein and E. G. Boring. Cambridge, Mass.: Harvard University Press, 1965.

Nagel, T. (1974) What is it like to be a bat? *Philosophical Review 83*: 435-450.

Natsoulas, T. (1978) Residual subjectivity. *American Psychologist 33*: 269-283.

Neisser, U. (1976) *Cognition and Reality.* San Francisco: W. H. Freeman.

Neisser, U. (1977) Gibson's ecological optics: consequences of a different stimulus description. *Journal for the Theory of Social Behavior 7:* 17-28.

Neisser, U. (1978) Memory: what are the important questions? (Address delivered to the International Congress on the Practical Aspects of Memory, Cardiff, Wales, 4 September 1978.)

Palmer, S. (1978) Fundamental aspects of cognitive representation. In *Cognition and Categorization* Ed. E. Rosch and B. Lloyd. Hillsdale, N.J.: L. J. Erlbaum Associates.

Pappas, G. S. (1976) Seeing$_e$ and seeing$_n$. *Mind 85:* 171-188.

Peacock, C. (1979) *Holistic Explanation.* London and New York: Oxford University Press.

Peters, R. S. (1953) *Brett's History of Psychology.* London: George Allen and Unwin.

Pfungsst, O. (1911/1965) *Clever Hans.* Trans. C. L. Rahn. Ed. R. Rosenthal. New York: Holt, Rinehart and Winston.

Pitcher, G. (1971) *A Theory of Perception.* Princeton: Princeton University Press.

Porter, S. (1881) Is thought possible without language? *The Princeton Review 57:* 104-128.

Price, H. H. (1932) *Perception.* London: Methuen.

Price, H. H. (1946) Thinking and representation. *Proceedings of the British Academy 32:* 1-40.

Putnam, H. (1981) *Reason, Truth and History.* Cambridge: Cambridge University Press.

Pylyshyn, Z. (1980) Computation and cognition. *Behavioral and Brain Sciences 3:* 111-132.

Quine, W. V. (1960) *Word and Object.* Cambridge, Mass.: MIT Press.

Reed, E. S. and Jones, R. K. (1978) Gibson's theory of perception: a case of hasty epistemologizing? *Philosophy of Science 45:* 519-530.

Reid, T. (1764/1970) *An Enquiry Into the Human Mind, On the Principles of Common Sense.* Ed. T. Duggan. Chicago: University of Chicago Press.

Rosch, E. (1977) Human categorization. In *Advances in Cross-Cultural Psychology* (Vol. 1). Ed. N. Warren. London: Academic Press.

Rosch, E. (1978) Principles of categorization. *In Cognition and Categorization.* Ed. E. Rosch and B. Lloyd. Hillsdale, N. J.: L. J. Erlbaum Associates.

Roxbee Cox, J. W. (1970) Distinguishing the senses. *Mind 79*: 530-550.

Runeson, S. (1977*a*) On the possibility of "smart" perceptual mechanisms. *Scandanavian Journal of Psychology 18*: 172-179.

Runeson, S. (1977*b*) "On Visual Perception of Dynamic Events." Doctoral dissertation, University of Uppsala.

Schiffman, H. R. (1976) *Sensation and Perception.* New York: John Wiley.

Schultz, D. P. (1969) *A History of Modern Psychology.* New York: Academic Press.

Searle, J. (1980) Minds, brains and programs. *Behavioral and Brain Sciences 3*: 417-424. (Reprinted in Haugeland, 1981.)

Shannon, C. E. and Weaver, W. (1949) *The Mathematical Theory of Communication.* Urbana: University of Illinois Press.

Sibley, F. N. (1971) Analysing seeing. In *Perception.* Ed. F. N. Sibley. London: Methuen.

Smith, B. (Forthcoming) *The Computational Metaphor.* Cambridge, Mass.: Bradford Books/MIT Press.

Stich, S. (1978) Autonomous psychology and the belief-desire thesis. *The Monist 61*: 573-591.

Vermazen, B. (1982) General beliefs and the principle of charity. *Philosophical Studies 42:* 111-118.

Vernon, M. D. (1962) *The Psychology of Perception.* Harmondsworth: Penguin Books.

Weiskrantz, L. (1977) Trying to bridge the neuropsychological gap between monkey and man. *British Journal of Psychology 68*: 431-435.

White, B. W., Saunders, F. A., Scadden, L., Bach-y-Rita, P., and Collins, C. C. (1970) Seeing with the skin. *Perception and Psychophysics 7*: 23-27.

Wilkerson, T. E. (1974) *Minds, Brains and People.* London: Oxford University Press.

Wittgenstein, L. (1921/1961) *Tractatus Logico-Philosophicus.* Trans. D. F. Pears and B. F. McGuinness. London: Routledge and Kegan Paul.

Wittgenstein, L. (1953) *Philosophical Investigations.* Trans. G. E. M. Anscombe. New York: Macmillan.

Wittgenstein, L. (1958) *The Blue and Brown Books.* Oxford: Basil Blackwell.

INDEX

Animals: belief of, 188–191, 196, 210, 214; perception of, 213; senses of, 18–23, 119; thought of, 212–214
Anthropomorphism, 155, 209, 212
Armstrong, D.M., 176–177, 178–192, 197, 201–203, 206
Attending (attention), 71, 104, 133
Attitude, and mental content, 177
Audition. *See* Hearing
Autonomy: psychological, 163–170, 172; representational, 168
Awareness, 64, 75, 81, 106-107, 217

Ballard, Melville, 193, 201–205
Belief: acquisition of, 4, 12, 17, 34, 61, 65, 72–74, 84, 86, 91, 93, 102–108, 122, 216, 219; attribution of, 156, 158, 160–161, 191, 195–196, 207, 211; background, 70, 89, 98, 127; characterization of, 83–84, 143, 213; as cognitive state, 2, 34, 61, 74; as computational feature, 144; concept of, 214–215; content of, 81–83, 155–156, 169, 179, 219; derivative, 73n; expression of, 172–173, 190–193, 196–198, 200, 201–210, 215, 219; first-, second-, and third-order, 102–108, 118; and ideas, 181; idle, 196–198; and information, 60, 61; interdependence of, 143; and language, 177, 188–193; 205–215; nonconscious, 104–107, 121; and nonhuman species, 188–191, 196, 210, 214; object of, 82–83; vs. perceptual object, 58; as perceptual state, 13, 63, 65, 80, 91, 106, 118, 178;

significance of, 81, 85–86, 121, 178; and thought, 177, 178; truth or falsity of, 156, 168, 214; and visual experience, 70
Belief-complex, 36
Belief-state, 155, 172, 179–182, 198
Blindness, 13–18, 19, 74–76, 78–81

Categories. *See* Classes
Causal relations, 36–41, 122–126
Chemoreception. *See* Smell; Taste
Classes, 148–149, 152, 186–187
Cognition: and computation, 139–144, 148; and linguistic rules, 116; models of, 117; vs. perception, 133–134n; and sensation, 63
Cognitive state: belief as, 34, 139, 178, 216; vs. noncognitive, 33; perception as, 1–2, 33, 45; as representational, 139; and senses, 22
Color, 21, 22
Computational states, 139–144, 171, 219
Concept, 47, 57, 64, 94, 97–102; application, 42–43, 44, 92, 101, 103; and belief, 85–86, 189, 214–215; defined, 43, 98, 118; as dispositional, 182; empiricist view of, 99–100; and idea, 182–186; and language, 102; and perception, 86, 117–118; and relativism, 92–94
Conceptualization, 35, 44, 85, 92
Consciousness, 118
Construct, 33, 108–112, 222
Content: of belief, 82–83, 155–156, 169, 179, 219; perceptual, 45–46; representational, 154–155
Conventionalism, 110, 113, 115, 117

239

Designer:	UC Press Staff
Compositor:	Computer Typesetting Services, Inc.
Printer:	Vail-Ballou
Binder:	Vail-Ballou
Text:	11/13 Baskerville
Display:	Baskerville